REPERCUSSIONS

A Celebration of African-American Music

Edited by
Geoffrey Haydon
and Dennis Marks

Based on REPERCUSSIONS
A Celebration of African-American Music
A Third Eye Production
for RM Arts and Channel Four

Century Publishing
London

Copyright © RM Arts Fernseh und
Film GmbH 1985

Text ©
(*introduction*) Geoffrey Haydon
(*chapter one*) Sidia Jatta
(*chapter two*) Doug Seroff
(*chapter three*) Ian Whitcomb
(*chapter four*) Charles Fox
(*chapter five*) John Miller Chernoff
(*chapter six*) Kenneth Bilby
(*chapter seven*) John Miller Chernoff
(*afterword*) Dennis Marks

First published in Great Britain in 1985
by Century Publishing Co. Ltd,
Portland House,
12–13 Greek Street,
London W1V 5LE

ISBN 0 7126 0492 8

Typeset by Servis Filmsetting Ltd, Manchester
Printed in Great Britain in 1985 by R. J. Acford
Chichester, Sussex

Credits

REPERCUSSIONS The Book

Editors
Geoffrey Haydon
Dennis Marks

Designer
Behram Kapadia

Contributors
Sidia Jatta
Doug Seroff
Ian Whitcomb
Charles Fox
John Miller Chernoff
Kenneth Bilby

Book Co-ordinator for Third Eye
Productions: Winnie Wishart

Book Co-ordinator for
RM Arts: Sally Fairhead

**REPERCUSSIONS
The Television Series**

A Third Eye Production
for RM Arts and Channel Four
Distributed Worldwide by
Arts International

Devised and directed by
Geoffrey Haydon and
Dennis Marks

Producer
Penny Corke

Production Supervisor
Mandy Ruben

Consultants
Sidia Jatta
Doug Seroff
Ian Whitcomb
Charles Fox
John Miller Chernoff
Kenneth Bilby
Tony Russell
Lucy Duran

Production Team
Winnie Wishart
Janice Richardson
Ronaldo Vasconcellos

Film Editors
Ben Morris
Charles Rees
Don Fairservice
David Hope
Helen Cook

Dubbing Mixer
Andy Nelson

Sound Recordists
Michael Lax
Albert Bailey
Colin Nicolson
John Lundsten
Malcolm Hirst

Photography
Michael Coulter
Roger Deakins
Mike Fox
Christopher Cox
John Davey

Graphic Designer
Colin Cheesman

Acknowledgements

RM Arts and the publishers would like to thank the following organisations and individuals for permission to use their photographs: © Third Eye Productions, front and back cover and pp. 15, 17, 20, 24, 26, 28, 39, 49, 55, 74(L), 74(R), 79, 99, 102, 104, 114, 123, 130, 134, 137, 139, 142; © John Miller Chernoff, pp. 109, 113, 117, 119, 120, 124, 157, 162, 165, 170, 174(L), 174(R), 176, 184; © Rarepic Collection, frontispiece, 68, 93, 182; © Jazz Music Books, pp. 71, 84(R), 91(L); © Lucy Duran, p. 22; © Fisk University Library Special Collections, pp. 31, 35; © Cheryl T. Evans, p. 36; © Robert Pruter, p. 37; © Mrs Essie Battle, p. 42/3; © Geoff Haydon Collection, courtesy of Big Mama Thornton, p. 67, p. 72 (courtesy of Joe Liggins); © Frank Driggs Collection, pp. 84(L), 85, © Max Jones, pp. 89, 91(R); © Dennis Morris, p. 145; © Chris Horler, p. 147; © Jon Blackmore, pp. 148, 153(L); © Channel Four, p. 153(R); © Jak Kilby, p. 154; © Arts International (Susie Johns), p. 180.

Contents

Introduction

BY GEOFFREY HAYDON

'The Mandinka conception of the terms "music" and "musician" is profoundly different from the European one' SIDIA JATTA

'In Africa, music serves a crucial integrative function and musicians perform a complex social role' JOHN MILLER CHERNOFF

'European music resembles a cathedral, very decidedly a structure, while African music moves like a river, open ended' CHARLES FOX

On 30 June 1972 I dined at the White House (the London hotel) with Professor Alex Haley from America. Next day he was to give a lecture to an international gathering of scholars, assembled to study the ancient Manding civilisation of West Africa. Professor Haley had already delivered this lecture to Black Studies departments in the USA. It concerned his five-year pursuit of his exact ancestry, which had led him finally to a Mandinka village in the Gambia, West Africa. An expansion of the lecture, a book provisionally entitled *Before this Anger*, was due to be published soon. I was preparing a film of cultural exploration in West Africa and North America, based on the book *Savannah Syncopators* by the blues scholar Paul Oliver. This pioneering work sprang from a journey north from the coast of Ghana to the sub-Saharan savannah region: a vast scrubland which runs across West Africa from Senegal and the Gambia in the west to Lake Chad in the east. There Paul Oliver heard stringed instrumental music distinctly different from anything on the tropical coast, but uncannily familiar to a man steeped in the blues. Previous historians of jazz and blues had searched for African antecedents in the tropical rain forests along the old Gold and Slave coasts, noted for their heavy drum orchestras. Connections had been strained and implausible. Paul Oliver opened a line of enquiry into the savannah terrain of such ethnic groups as the Mandinkas.

Alex Haley's claim to Mandinka origin was news indeed. He had already authored the *Autobiography of Malcolm X*. Recollections of dinner with genial Professor Haley include his tip about the Gambian shortage of air conditioning, his admiration for Winston Churchill, and his brilliant display of American credit cards which, he warned, would cut no ice in the Gambia.

Next day's lecture to the Manding conference at London University was an emotional affair: a triumph of rhetoric in the face of some discreet academic head-shaking. When he reached the climax of his impassioned tale, Professor Haley brought forward musicians from the Gambia who repeated in song his story of the capture by slavers of his great-great-grandfather, Kunta Kinteh.

Back in America, Alex Haley launched his book, now called *Roots*. It became an immediate bestseller and spawned a smash-hit TV serial. The BBC film of cultural exploration was shelved. Instead, I made *The Friendly Invasion*: a trilogy of films tracing the Americanisation of English popular music. . .

In 1981 Dennis Marks showed me a tentative outline for a series of films on Afro-American music based on the writings of Christopher Small, which seemed to him a logical successor to *The Friendly Invasion*. I pointed to files covered in nine years of dust. We took our case to Jeremy Isaacs at Channel Four and met unqualified enthusiasm. Funds were made available for the project to be developed.

First call was to London University. Dr Tony King, lecturer in African Music Studies at the time of the Manding Conference, had moved to the National Sound Archive. There I met Lucy Duran, a specialist in Mandinka music. Inspired by Dr King's groundwork, Lucy Duran had spent three months in the Gambia studying with the senior kooraa player, Aamadu Bansang Jeebaate. Under her guidance, I immersed myself in the music, and through her I met Sidia Jatta, a linguistics expert from the Gambia who was working at London University on a uniform orthography for African languages. As recreation, he was learning to play the kooraa.

Mandinka music was still as good a starting point as it had been back in 1972. And now that the heady excitement of *Roots* had died down, there was less pressure to find blatant links with the New World. It would be insulting and absurd to value such a rich tradition only because of its ancestral relationship to more familiar musics.

The policy of the series was established. The primary aim of each film would be to do justice to its immediate subject. Once filming started, cross-referencing would stay behind on the office drawing board. As with the films, so with the chapters of this book. Each author was invited to describe his special subject, without concern for context. The connections are there to be felt, but they are not spelled out. *Repercussions* is not offered as a detective story.

Three films would be made in the United States under the broad banners of 'Gospel', 'Blues' and 'Jazz'. The trick lay in choosing resonating specifics. Fruitful advice came from Tony Russell, an authority on American folk music whose book *Blacks, Whites and Blues* was published in the same series as Paul Oliver's *Savannah Syncopators* (both books, unfortunately, are now out of print). Through his grapevine of specialist magazines, Tony knew of pioneering research by Doug Seroff on Gospel quartet singing in the Southern States, and he was able to recommend someone who would know the details. Bob Laughton, a telephone engineer in Sidcup, Kent, is Britain's leading Gospel music authority. I made the pilgrimage to a house comprehensively crammed with Gospel recordings. The pristine quality of the quartet style rediscovered by Doug Seroff was highlighted and the Seroff whereabouts in the States was disclosed.

Since musicians had first beaten out the blues path from the Mississippi Delta to Memphis and on up to Chicago, it had been endlessly trampled by folklorists and filmmakers. Other paths were considered. Raw country blues were the most likely to deliver patent Africanisms. But this was 1982, not '72, and the search for "Africanisms" was demeaning the blues form, just as the search for blues roots in Africa was insulting the traditional musics there. Less reputable scholars than Paul Oliver had jumped on the bandwagon. The best track led elsewhere. Excited letters had arrived from Ian Whitcomb describing the rhythm and blues scene in Los Angeles. Could this blues tributary be the right one for our series? Tony Russell confirmed the historical importance of L.A. rhythm and blues. He produced ample recorded evidence of the impact of this style on twentieth-century popular music.

To pinpoint a specific subject within 'jazz', I conferred with Charles Fox. A set of radio broadcasts by Charles had prompted my film *The Three Faces of Jazz*. The "three faces" had been "folk", "showbiz", and "art". The logic of the *Repercussions* series dictated that "art" should be the subject of the jazz episode. Ideally it should be commanded by a major artist with a strong sense of history and a creatively active present. All arrows pointed to Max Roach. When this musical giant was approached, he was most encouraging.

The remaining three film subjects were fixed in principle. They would range from the traditional drum culture of Ghana, through the Caribbean melting pot to the vibrancy of modern African popular music. Charles Fox, with his reviewer's brief to roam all African–American cultural happenings, had been well placed to monitor developments since 1972. He supplied a list of records and books, including *African Rhythm and African Sensibility* by the American academic John Miller Chernoff, who ended up as Dennis Marks' collaborator in Africa. Two other books on the list were by John Storm Roberts: *Black Music of Two Worlds* and *The Latin Tinge*. John Storm Roberts gave Dennis his launch pad, although it was folklorist Kenneth Bilby who became prime consultant to the Caribbean film.

When the UK homework was done, Dennis and I flew off to check theory against reality. Findings in Ghana and the Caribbean are described in Dennis's afterword. Here is a synopsis of discovery in the Gambia and the USA.

Communications with Doug Seroff established the Easter Sunday pro-gramme in Bessemer, Alabama, as an ideal opportunity to check out the local quartets. I time-tabled a trip accordingly, stopping off in Atlanta, Georgia, on Good Friday for a huge Gospel Convention. Lectures were in progress on "Gospel Music's impact on the music market", "How to select the right Producer for your Product" and "The Travis Winkey concept of fashion: how to improve your total presentation". A famous Gospel male in a tight pink jump suit thanked the Lord for the opportunity to sing His praises in Las Vegas cabaret. On Easter Sunday, Doug Seroff conducted me to the modest auditorium in Bessemer, Alabama, where the only concession to showbiz was a bunch of pink Easter Bunny balloons. Bessemer offered beautiful singing in the grimmest of industrial landscapes. The history of this music is recounted in Doug Seroff's chapter.

In the Gambia, West Africa, Sidia Jatta's name turned out to be a passport to any Mandinka musician; and I had a letter from him to his elder brother, the chief of Sutukoba village in the Upper River Division. I was graciously thanked for troubling to find my way to such a remote spot. Musicians who look to the Jatta family for patronage include the Kanute family. I reached the Kanute compound late one evening. News spread that I had been sent by Sidia. Kanute family members appeared from everywhere. Three brothers took up their instruments and their eleven wives grouped behind them. In the gathering darkness, they burst into a praise song for Sidia Jatta. The beauty of the music and the vocal power of the wives was overwhelming. On leaving the Gambia, I was asked by a Mandinka immigration official if I intended to return and make a film like *Roots*. The Gambian government had acquired a copy of *Roots* for its mobile cinema. It had not been well received. "We don't want to see any more dressed-up Americans pretending to be Mandinkas. It was a ridiculous pantomime," the official told me in excellent English.

In New York, Max Roach insisted I should abandon my hotel and stay in his apartment. It was strange to breakfast with a musician I had idolised since childhood. Max premiered his double quartet – jazz quartet plus classical string quartet – at the Lincoln Centre. Then he acted as tour guide. He reflected on what it is to be an American as we roamed the parklands of the Pepsi Cola company, littered with expensive European statuary. And again at the Audubon Ballroom in Harlem, where his friend Malcolm X was assassinated. We went to an outdoor charity concert in Stamford, Connecticut, where Max was a celebrity performer. Suddenly, a sharply dressed young man was ushered to the concert platform by bodyguards. There was a mini-riot, as squealing girls tried to rush the stage. "$10 for a kiss from Lemar Burton", shouted the charity organiser. Who on earth was Lemar Burton? "Oh, he's a big name," Max explained. "He does cabaret and Broadway shows. He became a star as young Kunta Kinteh in that series *Roots*. You remember?"

The visit to Ian Whitcomb in Los Angeles was another memory jogger. We first worked there together in 1973 on the *Friendly Invasion* series. The quest for the best in Los Angeles rhythm and blues is chronicled in Ian's chapter.

With the field research behind us, all that remained was to film the series! Dennis Marks headed for the Caribbean in December 1982. I started filming in the Gambia in January 1983, by which time Sidia Jatta was back there and invaluable as guide and interpreter.

Film-makers are sometimes envied the globe-trotting glamour of their lives. This envy is commonly rebuffed with accounts of grinding toil and hardship, but it is undeniably an honour to meet the greatest music makers of many cultures on their home ground and to become their personal friends. This enormous privilege carries the responsiblity of delivering the most faithful possible account of the glories of the music.

Films, and therefore chapters, 2, 3 and 4 represent a continuum bedrocked in the church music of black America. As Max Roach put it, "The church is an integral part of any black community in the United States and the fountainhead, the music school, if you will, of some of the greatest artists that America has produced." Our rhythm and blues musicians regularly testified to their church origins. Bluesman Lowell Fulson had this to say: "There are some blues songs you can't tell from a spiritual. When you're doing it you're not looking at it as a blues or a spiritual. It's just the way you're interpreting the story that you have within your soul."

The threads running to and fro between Africa and the New World are endlessly complex. The first film closes with the Kanute family performing a piece from the Mandinka repertoire called "Alaa laa Ke", which means "God wills it". The second film opens with the Sterling Jubilee Singers of Bessemer, Alabama: elderly gentlemen offering up "The Lord's Prayer" in deepest vocal harmony. The music has suffered a sea change into something rich and strange.

Towards the end of his chapter, Sidia Jatta affirms that "if there is anything rooted in human society which transcends the barriers of race and culture it is the language of music". A leaflet commemorating the fifty-fourth anniversary of the Sterling Jubilee Singers takes as its text a quotation from Longfellow: "Music is the universal language of mankind". This generality is especially appropriate to the African–American music of our series, which is characterised above all by its endless power of metamorphosis in response to life's shifting circumstances.

CHAPTER 1

Born Musicians
Traditional music from the Gambia

BY SIDIA JATTA

This essay differs from most other works that deal with African music in general and Gambian music in particular. Such works are generally written by specialists, namely musicologists and/or ethnomusicologists.[1] They are often intended for a small caste of ivory-tower academics and therefore remain largely inaccessible to the lay public. I am writing neither as a musician nor as a musicologist, but simply as one who has been experiencing the music from childhood, and rather than discussing it from a purely technical point of view, my aim here is to talk about it in relation to the multiple social contexts in which it is played. That means dealing with the nature and organisation of the society within which the musicians operate, in order to give an insight into the music they produce. Traditional music, or folk music as others would call it, particularly of the type under consideration here, is greatly determined by the culture, society and social organisation in which it is rooted and from which it takes its nourishment.

It is not uncommon to find music from the Gambia being treated under the heading "Gambian music". This term is misleading: it often includes music which cannot be categorised as specifically Gambian.

Tiny as it is (population half a million), the Gambia is composed of many ethnic groups: Mandinka, Fula, Wolof, Soninke, Jola, Serer. Each of these has its own distinct language, music, and forms of entertainment, and these ethnic groups are by no means exclusive to the Gambia. Ethnic groupings and post-colonial frontiers do not conveniently coincide. Mandinkas and Fulas are found in Senegal, Guinea-Bissau, Mali and Guinea. Once this is understood, it becomes clear that the term "Gambian music" is not helpful.

However, there is a certain unity which underlines this diversity of people and cultures in the Gambia. Mandinkas, for example, who form by far the largest ethnic group in the country, mingle freely with the Fulas (the second most populous group). In the provinces – particularly in the Upper River Division, where I come from – Mandinkas and Fulas often inhabit the same village. They are familiar with each other's cultures and often speak each other's language. Intermarriage between Mandinkas and Fulas is quite common. For instance, my mother is a Fula and my father Mandinka. This chapter, like the film which gave rise to it, is concerned primarily with Mandinka music. Fula music is also included, but only when it comes within the Mandinka orbit.

Keba Kanute (right) and Morro Suusoo playing kooraas at the Kanute home

All our musical examples were filmed in the Gambia, but they represent a reality and an historical continuum that goes far beyond the country's boundaries. I shall henceforth use the term Mandinka to refer to all those people who trace their origin to historical Manding, found somewhere in the present-day republic of Mali.

There are, of course, regional variations, characterised not only by stylistic devices used in playing the various pieces but also by systems of tuning. However, these stylistic variations cut across countries as well as regions. Added to this is the potential of each individual player to stamp each piece he plays with his own style.

Mandinka pieces and styles of playing are fundamentally common to both the baloo (xylophone), which is held to be the first Mandinka instrument used by professional musicians, and to the kooraa, the 21-string harp-lute. Because of its versatility and brilliance and because it is unique to the Mandinka people, the kooraa is regarded by some Westerners as a trademark of Mandinka music as a whole. It is certainly the instrument which has received the most attention from visiting "ethnomusicologists".

It could be said that there are four different schools of kooraa playing, named here after the players who are their founders and chief promoters. They are the Sidiiki Jeebaate, Batuuru Seeku Kuyaate, Laalo Keebaa Daraame and the Yenyeŋo* schools. The first two of these originate in Tiliboo (the East: Mali), and the last two come from Tilijii (the West: Gambia, Senegal, and Guinea-Bissau). All four schools have their adherents in the Gambia.

The difference between the first two schools lies fundamentally in their systems of tuning. The differences between these and the last two schools lie

---

* Throughout this chapter I have used the official orthography of Gambian languages, as adopted at the Curriculum Development Centre in Banjul in 1979. The letter ŋ represents the sound "ng" as in such English words as "king".

in both their tuning systems and the pieces they play. The fourth school (Yenyeŋo) is the one which differs most from all the others: its adherents use twenty-two strings instead of the normal twenty-one; they draw from a repertoire which is strictly of recent creation; and, finally, the music they produce is akin to a sort of pop music. Their instruments are sometimes electrically amplified. In brief, the Yenyeŋo school of kooraa music is to traditional kooraa music what pop music is to European classical music.

I have so far used the terms "musician" and "player" for want of better ones. Neither the widely used French term "griot", nor the English word "bard", sometimes used by English scholars, is adequate to designate the type of musician under consideration. These European nouns do not embrace all that is meant and implied by the Mandinka word *jali*. For reasons of clarity and precision, therefore, I shall from now on use the term *jali*. Similarly, I shall use the Mandinka word *jaliyaa*, which is derived from *jali*, for want of a precise equivalent in English. The Mandinka conception of the terms "music" and "musician" is profoundly different from the European one. In Europe, the art of music is taught to any gifted person who wishes to make music his profession. In Mandinka society a *jali* is not simply a *jali* by virtue of his profession, but also, and more importantly, by virtue of inheritance. Thus anybody born of *jali* parentage is called a *jali* whether or not he/she exercises the profession. I shall come back later to a more detailed explanation of the word *jaliyaa*.

*   *   *

Mandinka society has, to put it simply, a tripartite social structure. At the top of the social hierarchy is the class of nobles/freemen (*foroolu*). It will be readily appreciated by an outsider that this class is in a position of privilege. Less easy to grasp is the fact that this class traditionally carries profound obligations to those below it in the social system.

Next comes the class of *ñamaaloolu*, the artisans. This class includes blacksmiths, leatherworkers and *jalis*. Finally, there are the slaves (*joŋolu*). These slaves were captives or are descendants of captives, which is why they bear the patronyms of their masters. In theory this group does not exist any longer, for since independence the constitution has prohibited the ownership of slaves. In practice, however, it continues to exist even though the so-called slaves no longer work for those who are now nothing more than their nominal masters. There are cases where slaves have ransomed themselves, but they are still not considered as belonging to the class of freemen.

Blacksmiths (*numoolu*) and leatherworkers (*karankeolu*) are artisans. Both produce articles of utilitarian value. A blacksmith works on iron, transforming it into such tools as knives and axes. He also works on silver and gold which he makes into all types of jewellery needed by women. The wives of blacksmiths engage in making pottery such as jars and some cooking utensils. Similarly, a leatherworker transforms hide into leather which he uses to make shoes, bridles, saddles, leather mats and so on. Traditionally, plaiting of women's hair is a speciality of leatherworkers' wives. In addition, the

leatherworkers' wives specialise in tattooing girls' lower lips and upper gums. This job is done by wives of blacksmiths too.

Another task performed by a blacksmith or a leatherworker is the circumcision of boys. Traditionally, this operation is surrounded by much ceremonial, including music and dancing. When I was a child I was taken with other boys from my village to a remote camp in the bush. After the operation, we were kept in the camp for three months, undergoing a variety of initiation rites. Since the introduction of compulsory schooling, the period of confinement in the circumcision camp has been drastically reduced. For example, the circumcision dispersal ceremony which we filmed in the village of Maaneekundaa followed a confinement of only three weeks. In the capital, Banjul, it is not uncommon for the operation to be performed in a hospital.

Just as it is traditional for boys to be circumcised by blacksmiths or leatherworkers, girls are excised by either the wife of a blacksmith or the wife of a leatherworker. The way in which husbands and wives in the artisan classes complement each others' functions is an important part of the Mandinka social structure. I shall come back to this phenomenon when I deal in more detail with *jaliyaa*.

The *jali* class is composed of two subgroups. On the one hand there are the *jalis* proper, born musicians who inherit the profession from their fathers; and on the other there are the *finas* (poet-praisesingers) who do not play any musical instrument. In the *jali* social hierarchy, *finas* occupy the lower echelon, and those above them are their patrons. So although *finas* are *jalis* in their own right, *jalis* proper are to them as nobles-patrons are to *jalis*.

Circumcised boys perform ritual dispersal dance

A *jali's* function goes far beyond the sphere of playing music and singing songs for entertainment. I discussed the matter with Mawdo Suusoo, an excellent baloo player who comes from a village not far from my own and who has only recently moved to the capital, Banjul. He confirmed that a *jali* not only plays music and sings beautiful songs for the listening pleasure of others, he also mediates between disputants to bring about peace and happiness. *Jalis* are marriage brokers; they serve as intermediaries between suitors and the parents of the girls concerned.

Like blacksmiths and leatherworkers, who are artisans in the true sense of the term, it could be said metaphorically that *jalis* are artisans specialising in the spoken word. During ceremonies, such as weddings and the naming of new babies where presents are given accompanied by speeches, they serve as links between a speaker and his audience. The speaker speaks low and the *jali* not only transmits to the audience what he says, he develops and embellishes it in conformity with the occasion. Because of their expressive power with the spoken word, *jalis* are said to have the ability to popularise as well as depopularise personalities. For this reason they are feared by all *foroolu* (the "noblemen" or "freeborn citizens" who do not belong to the class of "casted" people). Little wonder that *jalis* have become important personalities who are to be reckoned with in contemporary African politics. They are employed to promote the popularity of political leaders and, in some cases, to build cults around them.

All three socio-professional groups (blacksmiths, leatherworkers and *jalis*) enjoy one privilege denied to the *foroolu*: they are able to infringe the customs of society, to break taboos and ignore social restraints without fear of reprisal. For example, a *jali* could insult someone's mother or run naked down the street without serious consequences. But I, as a freeborn citizen, could not.

On the other hand, members of these artisan groups are traditionally expected to marry within their own group: a *jali* has to marry into a *jali* family, just as blacksmiths and leatherworkers should marry into families which are blacksmith and leatherworker respectively. The *foroolu* are also endogamous, but not as strictly as the three groups above. Male members of the class of so-called freemen sometimes marry girls from *jali* families, though the reverse is not true. The explanation for this uni-directional marriage arrangement is simple: when a male member of the class of *foroolu* marries a *jali*, the latter is considered to have moved up the social ladder; whereas when a female member of the same class marries into a *jali* family, it is seen as social debasement for the former.

It is important to note that this exogamous practice is a phenomenon of urban rather than rural areas, where traditional and customary practices remain relatively intact. Parents, of course, still often oppose exogamous marriages, but if the parties involved are determined to marry, in spite of parental opposition, they can legally do so. For those readers not aware of the fact, I should point out that Mandinka society (like all the others in the Gambia) is polygamous and overwhelmingly Islamic.

*   *   *

The term *jaliyaa* is derived from *jali*; it is an abstract noun which I find difficult to render in English. The European term "art" is somewhat removed from human life, and consequently it would be inappropriate to translate *jaliyaa* as the "art of musicians". From the Mandinka point of view, *jaliyaa* goes far beyond the limits of musical performance. It includes, for instance, such things as running errands for the patron, hosting his important visitors, as well as serving as an intermediary between suitors and the patron in the marriage arrangements of the latter's daughters. For want of an adequate equivalent in English I would say that *jaliyaa* denotes all the functions performed by a *jali*.

Before I delve into the question of *jaliyaa* and its practice, I wish to dispel the notion promoted by some European "authorities" that a *jali* has one and only one patron. Nothing could be further from the truth! Traditionally, a *jali* has what I would call a primary patron and secondary patrons. In general, a *jali* is more attached to the primary patron and owes more allegiance to him than to secondary ones. When he visits a village where he has both primary and secondary patrons, it is always with the former that he stays, and if his party includes a lot of people such as his students, he lodges them with his secondary patrons. There are basically two explanations for this practice: to lighten the primary patron's burden; and to facilitate the creation of a network of patrons for the *jali*'s sons and students, for in some cases secondary patrons become, eventually, primary patrons to the sons and students when they in turn become independent practitioners in the profession.

It is worth noting here that a primary patron's son does not necessarily become a primary patron to his *jali*'s son. My father was a primary patron to a *jali* whose son does not consider me to be his primary patron. Human relationships, particularly between a *jali* and a patron, are too complex to be brought about in hereditary fashion. The *jalis* to whom I consider myself to be a patron of one sort or the other are not my father's *jali*'s sons, nor were they his students. As the Mandinka saying goes: "*Jannin i be à fola n faa la muru baa à fo n faŋo la murubaa*": "It is better to pride oneself on the fruits of one's own efforts than on those of one's father."[2]

This does not mean that I have absolutely no connection with my father's *jali*'s son. The fact is, by virtue of being uncasted, I am a potential patron to every *jali* and consequently open to being begged by them. My father's *jali*'s son is not an exception to that, which is not to be equated with my being a primary patron to him. Having said that, I will now turn to the discussion of *jaliyaa* and its practice.

Traditionally, a *jali* travels with his family visiting his patrons. The dry season is the ideal time for their seasonal tours. The family travels on foot with men carrying their musical instruments and the wives their clothing in baskets carried on their heads. Depending on how many patrons, primary and secondary, they have in a given village, and how long such patrons would desire them to stay, the family spends two to three days in each village they visit. In exceptional cases the visit could last as long as a week or more.

Although they are hosted by one primary patron who bears the brunt of responsibility for their boarding and feeding during the period of their stay, once in a village, *jalis* are considered to be there for the entire village community. For that reason their performances are not private. When they perform for the primary patron in his home, other villagers could and do come to listen uninvited. In fact, the larger the audience is swelled by people coming to listen from outside the patron's immediate family circle, the better for him and his *jalis*; for in that way the *jalis* are likely to be offered more, to supplement whatever the patron ultimately gives them. When a *jali* is visiting a village where he has both a primary and a secondary patron, he usually solicits the consent of the former before performing for the latter, and can only do so after he has performed for the primary patron. Usually it is at the end of his stay that a primary patron offers his *jali* what he intends to give him, supplemented by gifts and donations from his wives, brothers and other close relatives, as well as from his friends.

Aamadu Jeebaate, a kooraa virtuoso and one of the most senior *jalis* in the Gambia, recalled for me another practice common in the past: that of two or more *jali* families combining to go on their seasonal tours together. He cited the case of his father to illustrate the point. Although such a group was composed of families, the head of each of which was a senior independent practitioner in his own right, there was always one who by virtue of his seniority in age as well as in the profession was chosen to head the overall group. Aamadu Jeebaate's father was such a person: he always travelled during the dry season with this type of a group composed of families headed by him. His function in such a capacity was to see to the welfare of the group as well as to its management.

Night performance for a patron by Mandinka jalis: baloo and kooraa players with their singing wives

When they visited a village where both he and the other family heads in the group had primary patrons, each would be hosted by the latter and the other members of the group would be lodged with secondary patrons. The first collective performance of the group in such a village was for the primary patron of the most senior *jali* among them, in this case the overall head of the group. Performances for the rest of the primary patrons were also given in order of seniority, that is, seniority of the remaining senior *jalis*. It was only after this that the junior members of the group could perform, either individually or collectively, for the secondary patrons with whom they were lodged.

At the end of their stay in the village each primary patron and secondary patron would give them whatever they could afford. The overall head of the group was the custodian of whatever was given to them during the entire tour. And when the tour came to an end it was he who gave to each member of the tour group, male and female alike, whatever he deemed fit from the amount of money, clothing and other gifts received. Nobody ever challenged his decision as to how much he gave to each person.

Contrary to what some Europeans believe, *jalis* are not paid for their performance. That is why in Mandinka we say: *Ka jaloo so* (to give to a *jali*), not *Ka jaloo joo* (to pay a *jali*). Similarly, it is gross misinformation to say that each time a *jali* sings a person's praise and praises his deeds, that person is obliged to give him something. Just as patrons give money and clothing to *jalis* without the latter having to sing their praise songs, *jalis* also sing praise songs without their patrons having to give them money each time.

*   *   *

The traditional practice of *jaliyaa* that I have described above contrasts fundamentally with its current state. The change is due primarily to a mass exodus of *jalis* from rural areas to the capital and its neighbourhoods, where most of them are now settled. Most *jali* homes in the rural areas are now virtually deserted. The only people, if any at all, one occasionally finds there are the old, whose attachment to their villages remains profoundly intact and who refuse to move away to urban areas where their sons have built themselves new homes. The concentration in the urban areas of *jalis* has altered the traditional patron-*jali* relationship; the system of patronage is now open, loose and lacking attachment. Traditionally, for example, the privilege of being a patron to *jalis* was accorded only to those who were uncasted. Now, however, anyone who is lucky enough to become rich, uncasted or casted, can become a patron to *jalis*.

The seasonal tours have not totally ceased, but they have taken a different form. *Jalis* do still travel, and in fact cover much greater distances. But instead of travelling as a family on foot and staying with a patron for from three days to a week or more, the current state of *jaliyaa* practice consists of three or four male *jalis* combining to hire a taxi on a daily basis with a view to going around visiting patrons and any other person who has money but is not necessarily their patron. When their arrival in a village coincides with nightfall, they will

Aamadu Bansang Jeebaate

stay with a patron overnight. Otherwise, the longest they will generally stay is between thirty minutes and one hour. The reason for this is simple: since the car they use is hired on a daily basis, the more patrons they visit within a day, the more money they are likely to make.

Straying even further from tradition are those *jalis* who manage to find the money to travel all the way to Europe. Some traditional patrons from Senegal, Mali and the Gambia have now taken up jobs in Paris, for example, and the *jalis* come to seek them out. They know that once they arrive the patrons will feel obliged to take care of them.

Another phenomenon which distinguishes the present practice of *jaliyaa* from its traditional practice is the emergence of musical troupes. I discussed this phenomenon with several *jalis* of my acquaintance. Aamadu Kanute, the head of the Kanute family, an extended family of *jalis* living on the outskirts of Basse (the administrative capital of the Upper River Division), made it clear that the recently formed Upper River Division Troupe, which is registered with the Gambian government, contains some excellent musicians, including members of his own family. But "troupe music" cannot be compared with traditional *jaliyaa*. "For instance," said Aamadu Kanute, "the European idea of having to rehearse before a performance never existed in *jaliyaa*. A true *jali* is sufficiently trained to perform in all traditional situations without prior rehearsal." I put it to Aamadu Kanute that the emergence of troupes was resulting in the distortion of playing styles. He agreed emphatically, pointing out that the government officials responsible for promoting troupes often had no background in *jaliyaa*.

Aamadu Jeebaate, the senior kooraa *jali* I mentioned earlier, was once a member of the Gambian National Troupe. He had this to say: "The best analogy to a musical troupe is a troop of soldiers under the control of a commander. Troupes such as the Gambian National Troupe are managed and controlled by Western-educated persons and the *jalis* are given no say. Whenever they give a concert, the money received belongs to the government. The *jalis* get nothing other than their monthly salaries. This is quite contrary to everything we *jalis* know from inheritance. I was a member of the national troupe for a very short period. We went to Farafeñe to give a concert. We performed there for a night then returned to the capital. And as soon as we returned I gave them back their uniform and withdrew from the troupe. I told them that the whole thing was alien to me and that I was not a soldier to be regimented in that fashion."

Mawdo Suusoo, the baloo player from a village near my own, has recently become a member of the Gambian National Troupe, based in the capital Banjul. He has regrets about leaving the provinces, but made the following observations: "When I toured in my own district, in traditional fashion, for a period of a month, visiting my patrons, I made more than I earn in a month with the troupe; in fact, what I now earn in a month might well have been given to me by a patron in one day.

I have certainly been frustrated by the troupe, where it is a question of regular role playing (often in tourist hotels). But the troupe assures me of a certain fixed income at the end of every month, however small that income. One cannot go to beg one's patrons every month!"

I expressed to Mawdo my fear that the steady exodus of *jalis* from rural areas to urban centres was seriously weakening *jaliyaa*. He agreed there was a danger, but went on as follows: "The explanation for this exodus is the presence in Banjul of so many of our patrons – including yourself – who have been to school and are now working here. For instance, I come here in the knowledge that you are here and that another of my patrons, the M.P. Seeni Singateh, is also here. You have left your villages behind. We come here for fear that your being here without *jalis* might lead you to forget about our traditional ways."

*   *   *

The Mandinka repertoire consists of some pieces which date back to the twelfth century, the time of the ancient Mali Empire under the reign of Sunjata, the most famous of the Manding emperors. One such piece is Sunjata, so called because it was composed for the emperor. Not all the pieces in the repertoire bear personal names as their titles, but most of them are named after the personalities for whom they were originally composed. Some examples of these are: FodeKabaa, Kelefaa, Saane, Saamoori, Alfaa Yaayaa, Mammadu Maasina, Satan Madi, Sirifu Siidi and Jula Jekere, all of which bear the names of historic figures.

The repertoire also contains contemporary pieces. These are either new compositions or modified and developed versions of old ones. As far as I know, at least two new versions of the Sunjata piece have been developed: one by the Sidiiki school and one by the Bantuuru school. Jula Jekere was, according to Aamadu Jeebaate, derived from an older piece called Janjumbaa. The latter piece is said to have been composed for persons bearing the patronym Suusoo, much in the same way that *jalis* bearing the patronym Kuyaate claim that Lambaŋo was originally composed for their wives.

Lambaŋo is traditionally played by *jalis* for their own entertainment. The husbands play for their wives to dance – *jaliyaa* for *jalis*: music for musicians.

The new school of kooraa playing, which I referred to as Yenyeŋo, is quite prolific in new compositions. However, although its adherents compose new pieces, particularly songs, the drawback with this school is that the rhythm used remains relatively the same. This new style of kooraa playing, with its strong pop-music flavour, has gained popularity in the Gambia and Senegal. Generally, people dance to the music as they do to that of the local pop bands. The style is strictly an invention of the younger generation.

Old versions of the songs still continue to be sung, but, more often than not, by the older generation of female *jalis*. New versions have also been developed to accompany new ways of playing the pieces. For example, the two new instrumental versions of the Sunjata piece have corresponding new versions of the epic song. Furthermore, there is the practice of changing the words of a song and substituting new ones to conform to the occasion. When the Sunjata piece is played for a patron, for instance, the singers replace Sunjata's praise-names with those of the patron in question. Thus, although the same pieces are played for different patrons, the song content varies.

*   *   *

The most common Mandinka musical instruments are as follows: baloo (xylophone with 19 to 21 keys); kontiŋo (5-string lute); boloŋo (3-string harp-lute); kooraa (21-string harp-lute); dunduŋo (big double-ended drum played to accompany the kooraa); tamoo (a small double-ended drum with strings running from one end to the other); tantaŋo (a drum with a skin at one end only).

Aamadu Kanute, Aamadu Jeebaate and Mawdo Suusoo all declared that the baloo is the oldest Mandinka musical instrument. Oral tradition dates it

Members of the Kanute family at home: the husbands will play for their wives to dance back to the twelfth century, before the rise to power of Sunjata, when Manding was still under the tutelage of Sumawuru, the Suusu emperor. The second oldest Mandinka musical instrument is the kontiŋo, which is a five-string lute played somewhat like the guitar. According to Aamadu Jeebaate both the baloo and the kontiŋo originated in Tiliboo (the East), that is to say in Manding. The origin of the kooraa, the 21-string harp-lute, is a controversial issue among oral historians. There are some who claim that it originated from Saanementereŋ, near the village of Burufut in the Gambia; others trace its origin to Kaabu, in the present republic of Guinea-Bissau. Aamadu Jeebaate supports the latter claim. Whatever the truth of the matter, the fact remains that the kooraa is a much later invention than either the baloo or the kontiŋo.

The boloŋo is an instrument surrounded by mystery and superstition. It is believed that it is constructed in the cemetery and is connected with supernatural forces. It is said to have been used in the olden days to accompany warrior kings to battle. In Aamadu Jeebaate's view, a boloŋo player is not a *jali*, because he does not inherit his profession. He likens a boloŋo player to the drummers (the tantaŋo players) who simply entertain young girls and boys at the village *bantaba* (meeting place). This analogy is right in my view, because as a child I saw boloŋo players entertaining young people in my village – a practice rarely found in the Gambia nowadays.

The boloŋo player we filmed in the remote village of Missira is the first I have seen since my childhood, still entertaining at the *bantaba* in exactly the same way. His pieces are very similar in character to those played by the drummers, and likewise provoke the girls to dance. The boloŋo is perhaps best described as a percussive stringed instrument, since the player thumps the base of the instrument with his fists as well as plucking the strings. The player we filmed had once been invited to join the official Upper River Division Troupe. He declined because of his great popularity at home, where he is in demand to enliven every kind of village ceremony.

*   *   *

When people talk about *jaliyaa* they always do so in terms of the *jali*, that is to say the one who plays the instrument. To the question: "Would a good instrumentalist, for example one like you, be complete without a singer?" Mawdo Suusoo answered: "A gold that has not been gold-plated is limited in beauty. And however good a gold may be, if it is not gold-plated it would look inferior to a bad one which is gold-plated." What Mawdo Suusoo is saying here in metaphorical terms is simply that a good instrumentalist does not feel complete unless he has at least one wife who is a good vocalist. A characteristic mark of an instrumental virtuoso is the singing power of his wife. Just as there are instrumental virtuosi, there is also what in Mandinka is called ŋaaraa, a female singer who is not only good at singing, but also has tremendous expressive power in narrating family genealogies and epics. It is very rare to find a good instrumentalist who is also a good singer. In general, therefore, a good instrumentalist looks for a wife from a family noted for its vocal ability.

The training of female *jalis* and their role in the body of *jaliyaa* is no less important than that of the men, and the women are trained in much the same way as their male counterparts. Generally, it is the mother who bears the brunt of training the daughter in their profession, if the latter happens to be either a good singer or perhaps a potential ŋaaraa. It is important to note that a good singer is not synonomous with ŋaaraa, for there are good singers who are not necessarily ŋaaraa. In cases where the mother is neither ŋaaraa nor a good singer, the training of the daughter is usually assigned to an aunt or some other close relative.

The most propitious time for training the daughter is when the family is on its seasonal tours. During these tours the family gives more performances than it does at home: every stay in a village involves nightly performances for one patron or another. At home, performances are much less frequent. Moreover, when they perform at home *jalis* generally do so for their own entertainment and consequently do not include certain elements which are involved when they perform to a patron. For instance, performing for a patron is an occasion for them to indulge in singing or inventing praise songs for him, as well as narrating his family genealogy.

The training of the daughter is not accomplished by the mother single-handedly. Fathers also contribute to the education of their daughters. Male *jalis* are often more versed in narrating epics and family genealogies than their wives, and it is in historical narrative that most fathers are best able to help their daughters. There are also cases where a daughter is sent to complete her education in a family other than her own. This is generally when the mother

Mawdo Suusoo (baloo) and his singing wife, Fune Kuyaate

recognises the superiority of somebody else's knowledge in some area of their profession.

With the exception of a cylindrical piece of iron, on which they beat an accompaniment to the music and their song, women do not play any musical instrument. Thus, in the profession of *jaliyaa*, the vocal function is performed primarily by female *jalis* and the instrumental function is performed by male *jalis* – a division of labour which brings a feeling of completeness.

*   *   *

There was a time, not long ago, when the belief was commonly held in Europe and elsewhere outside Africa that the only musical instrument black Africa could boast of was the drum; that music for dance was consequently the only one known to black Africans. This belief gave birth to the further fallacy that every African, male and female, was a dancer. It was said, for example, that "When the moon shines the whole of Africa dances".

Such beliefs and statements about sub-Sahara Africa are products of colonial prejudice. To justify itself, colonialism had to impose its own culture and negate the existence of indigenous ones. "People without culture" is a contradiction in terms. It is common sense that where there are people there must be some form of culture, for "culture" is the total of daily existential experience.

All is not drumming in Africa south of the Sahara, though there are still many people in Europe who believe the contrary. The drum is neither the only musical instrument in black Africa, nor the most important. Black Africa has a variety of stringed instruments, some of which rank among the most complex and melodious found in any culture. For instance, the kooraa, the 21-string Mandinka instrument, produces a richness of melody comparable to that of any stringed instrument found anywhere. Partisans of colonial prejudice who wrote about Africa claimed and argued that the kooraa was either a borrowing or literally copied from the Arabs, and they not only likened its melody to that of Arab music, they also said that it was strictly Arab. Implicit in this fallacy is the notion that black Africans are neither technically nor intellectually capable of producing an instrument of such melodic value. Thus the origin of the kooraa was attributed to a culture the writers considered superior to that of the Africans south of the Sahara. But the unshakeable fact is that the kooraa is neither a copy of nor a borrowing from any Arab instrument. The kooraa is a development by refinement from an older Manding instrument known as the kuraŋo, which is said to have had less than twenty-one strings. Improvements are still being made to the kooraa. The new kooraa school of Yenyeŋo mostly uses twenty-two strings instead of twenty-one.

An important change which is shaking the very roots of social tradition has to do with members of the so-called "freemen class" desiring to play the kooraa. I am one such keen lover of kooraa music and this love has led me to learn to play the instrument. However, I am torn between my ardent desire to play the kooraa and the opposition of my parents to my playing it – for they

see it as a social debasement for me. Although I have not yet come to terms with playing the instrument in the presence of my mother, I shall continue to learn to play, because I believe that music belongs to whoever loves it.

Other musical instruments appearing in the film which are non-Mandinka, but no less important, are the ñaañeeru (the fiddle, or Riti-Riti as my colleagues call it), and the moolo. The former is a one-string instrument played like a violin, and the latter, also a one-string instrument, is played somewhat like the guitar. Both are Fula instruments, found not only in the Gambia but also in Senegal and Guinea-Bissau.

Like the Mandinka boloŋo, mystery surrounds the moolo. The instrument is a night instrument *par excellence*. Superstition has it that when played late at night it invokes supernatural forces. The person who plays it is said to be imbued with supernatural powers, particularly when he is playing the instrument late at night. He is said to have the ability to tell a person's future. Not many people are courageous enough to be around a moolo player when he is playing the instrument late at night. A moolo player often narrates stories which he punctuates with songs. These stories are quite often educative and have deep moral values.

The first question Geoffrey Haydon asked me at the start of our work in Basse in 1983 was: "What form should the presentation of such a film take to make it understood and appreciated by the Western audience?" My answer is as follows: if there is a language whose phonology and syntax are common to all humans on planet earth, if there is anything rooted in human society which transcends the barriers of race and culture, it is the language of music. And if there is any way by which we might bring about peace and understanding among the diverse peoples of the world it will surely be through music. It is thanks to music that those such as Bob Marley and the

Fula musicians playing "Riti-Riti" (fiddles) and tama (small drum)

Rolling Stones have in a way succeeded in uniting the young people of this world.

At his concert performances in London and Bristol in 1981, I saw people moved to tears by the Gambian virtuoso, Aamadu Jeebaate, with his kooraa music. Thus I am sure that even though the words of the songs are in Mandinka or Fula, this does not hamper an appreciation of the music.

This chapter has been written to throw some light on the multiple social contexts in which the music is produced. It is not intended to explain or interpret a music film, which is self-explanatory and self-interpretive.

NOTES
1. I am sceptical of the use that is made of the term "ethnomusicologist". It seems to me that the term is applied to designate only those people who specialise in the study of music from the so-called Third World countries, particularly Africa; whereas the term musicologist is used to designate those specialising in the study of some European music. This is a spurious distinction in my view, tinted with ethnocentrism.
2. Literally: before saying my father's big knife, say my own big knife.

CHAPTER 2

On the Battlefield

Gospel quartets in Jefferson County, Alabama

BY DOUG SEROFF

In the midst of chaos and strife, all-embracing *harmony* is re-identified as the elixir of creation! Harmony in music, elevated as it was by black songsters, expresses a clarity of perception, a spirit of resolution, and a devotion to God that lifted souls above demoralising circumstances.

The oral tradition of spiritual singing in the South has been spoken of as the only literature of slavery in America and the jewels that the slave brought out of his bondage. These are the "sorrow songs" of the slave's furtive worship, anonymously conceived under unknown circumstances. There is an ineffable, poignant quality of sanctity and reverence in much of this music, which imparts to it a capacity to "heal the wounded spirit". This was art as worship, and its bountiful fruits, its unparalleled durability, suggest it was pleasing in God's sight.

When the Southern slaves were emancipated at the end of the American Civil War more than 4 million blacks had to somehow become part of a ravaged, embittered society. Slaves had been kept illiterate in accordance with the law. In 1866 Fisk University was founded in Nashville, Tennessee, one of seven "chartered institutions" established in the South by the American Missionary Association of New York for the purpose of educating the former slaves.

Adam K. Spence, principal of Fisk School, wrote in 1890: "At noon-time and before and after school hours during the years of 1870 and '71 it was a common thing to see a company of a dozen or so gathered around a piano at which sat Miss Ella Sheppard, afterwards pianist of the Jubilee Singers . . . Out of this little circle grew the Jubilee Singers."[1]

The Fisk Jubilee Singers left Nashville on 6 October 1871, called into existence by the needs of the University. Fisk was facing imminent closure due to lack of funds when George L. White, treasurer and music instructor of the infant university, asked permission to take a company of singers on an extended fund-raising tour through the North. Mr White had no formal music education, but he had a superb ear for harmony and an instinct for training voices. At first White's students were reluctant to expose the sacred songs of generations in servitude, but after a time he gained their confidence. George L. White and his recently emancipated students were about to embark on an inspired mission, one that would instigate an American cultural revolution. Between 1871 and 1878 the Jubilee Singers contributed $150,000

to Fisk's treasury, enough money to build Jubilee Hall, the first permanent structure erected for the purpose of black education in the United States. Nothing similar had ever been attempted before. Theologian Henry Ward Beecher said of the accomplishments of the Fisk Jubilee Singers: "I think there never was such a phenomenon as the building of Fisk University. We talk about castles in the air. That is the only castle that ever I knew built by singing from foundation to top."[2]

On 11 April 1873 the Fisk company sailed from Boston harbour on their first tour of Great Britain. The public thronged the halls. British audiences were enormously interested in hearing spirituals performed by ex-slaves, and were sympathetic to fund-raising efforts on behalf of Fisk University. This was the initial exposure of the British people to a new and strange music. British critics described the music as "possessing a fervour, a wildness of melody, a quaintness of expression, and even an occasional grotesqueness, unlike anything we have ever heard before". *The Manchester Examiner* observed: "These are veritable negroes!" and a Brighton newspaper added: "The burnt cork negroes if they do not henceforward hide their diminished wigs, will surely take the hint."[3]

The Fisk Jubilee Singers were the first to publicly render such songs as "Steal Away to Jesus", "The Gospel Train", "Swing Low Sweet Chariot", "Go Down Moses" and many others which have enjoyed more than a century of currency and persist in the repertoires of gospel singers to the present day. In offering "The Lord's Prayer" as prelude to the film *On the Battlefield* the Sterling Jubilees of Bessemer conjure up spirits of the Fisk Jubilee Singers, whose rendering of "The Lord's Prayer" was characterised in the *Berliner Musikzeitung* in 1878 as: ". . . wholely intoned, without time nor palpable melody but on the other hand with what wealth of shading, what accuracy of declamation!"[4]

There is little evidence to substantiate the theory, long popular among folklorists, that the group from Fisk essentially altered the music they sang.

The Jubilee Singers

Whatever refinements the original Fisk Jubilee Singers brought to the slave spiritual were the results of laborious hours of practice and the extraordinary vocal skills of the individual members. Those who would summarily dismiss the epochal work of the Fisk troupe ignore the fact that black religious harmony singing, whether in choir, chorus or quartet, observes technical formalities based on sound musical criteria. An *ideal* born with the Fisk Jubilee Singers became a model that would guide black religious singing groups for another fifty years or longer.

Black entertainers of the era, forever tethered to the pejorative designation of "minstrels", took the field en masse following the successes of the Fisk company. As early as October 1872, George L. White had written to Fisk President Cravath concerning a company "styling themselves the Canaan Jubilee Singers . . . they advertise that they are giving concerts in the interests of 'the colored brethren'."[5] White had reason to be alarmed at this unexpected genesis; he had coined the term "Jubilee Singers" himself, less than a year before, in giving a name to the Fisk Jubilee Singers. There was considerable deception in the Canaan Jubilee Singers' advertising, which suggested they were in fact the (Fisk) Jubilee Singers.

When the Fisk Jubilee Singers visited Boston, Massachusetts, in 1879, after an absence of several years abroad, the press reported: "It was some time before the public could be convinced that the Singers were really the old favorites from Fisk University. So many bogus companies had used their name and palmed themselves off as the 'Original Jubilee Singers'."[6]

The road was perilous and often cruel for the first generation of itinerant jubilee minstrels, who did not have a great university to justify their existence and attract patrons. Black troupes were routinely denied lodgings and restaurant service, and were discriminated against on public conveyances. The majority of the public had a kind of novelty interest in jubilee music. Along with those whose attendance betokened interest in the singing, these concerts attracted a troublesome, disruptive element of young white hooligans. Somehow this miserable life appealed to struggling black entertainers more than the alternative back at home.

All nineteenth-century jubilee singers performed a mixed repertoire of sacred and secular tunes. The secular pieces provided an opportunity for the stars of the troupe to step forward. The prima donna sang romantic soprano solos; dramatic bass solos were another popular feature of the entertainment. Male quartets performed medleys of "patriotic" or "Southern" tunes. Solos and duets were often accompanied by piano or organ. As a rule, the spirituals or "jubilee songs" were rendered *a cappella* (that is, without any instrumental accompaniment) and sung in choruses of from six to twelve voices.

The Fisk Jubilee Singers' programme was about seventy-five per cent spirituals and the rest secular. The ratio of jubilee to secular songs and the degree of evangelism varied according to the natural inclination of the group. The Fisk group was "on the battlefield, working for the Lord". In addition to their work as university builders and representatives of an emancipated Black America, they also saw their mission as Christian and evangelical.

While in Britain, the Fisk Jubilees assisted evangelists Messrs Moody and Sankey. Ella Sheppard related: "Once we surprised them. We arrived late and had to go into the small fifth gallery. During a pause following an earnest appeal to sinners we softly sang, 'There Are Angels Hovering Round to carry the tidings home.' The effect was wonderful and most impressive. Some people said they really thought for a moment that the music came from an angelic band. Mr Moody looked as though he would not have been more surprised had his Lord appeared."[7]

Simplicity and adaptability may account for the great attraction of the quartet form. By 1890 male quartets had replaced the larger choruses as the popularly favoured group for both the jubilee and secular songs. A talented, properly trained quartet could fill an auditorium with sound, and did so for many years without the benefit of amplification. Four-part vocal harmony could accommodate many types of music. White barbershop harmony singing became very popular at the end of the nineteenth century.

In June 1890 bass singer F.J. Loudin's Fisk Jubilee Singers completed a triumphant world tour, which included four years touring in Australia, New Zealand and Asia. Loudin told a reporter: "The first thing a good singer has to learn when he joins the company is that his voice has to blend with the others, and the singers become extremely sensitive to the least absence of harmony. The object aimed at is to make the voices blend into one grand whole – one beautiful volume. We practice almost every day – every day when possible."[8] The sound that Professor Loudin described has been referred to as "organophonic harmony", in which a singular *presence* is created out of the wholeness and balance of the singing.

Jubilee quartets of the 1890s were a breeding ground for the finest black musicians of the coming era. Ernest Hogan and Noble Sissle both started their careers in successful jubilee minstrel quartets; Louis Armstrong and Jelly Roll Morton spoke of youthful experiences singing with quartets in New Orleans; W.C. Handy sang with a quartet in Florence, Alabama; the legendary black concert tenor Roland Hayes participated in this immensely popular amusement.

As researcher Lynn Abbott has noted: "James Weldon Johnson and educator Laurence C. Jones (of Piney Woods School, Miss.) both offer the generality that 'any four colored boys are a quartet'. The statement is likely meant as a testimony to the *pervasiveness* of quartet singing, the Black national pastime of the early 1900s."[9]

Along with the jubilee minstrels, a parallel religious singing tradition developed in the Southern black universities. The movement reached a summit of activity during the early part of this century, when most black colleges and many normal and industrial schools had a travelling jubilee group singing in the interest of the institution.

Life in a university jubilee quartet had its vicissitudes. A tour made in 1903 by the Utica Institute Jubilee Singers of Mississippi ended tragically when a teacher/escort died as a result of exposure, suffered during a night spent sleeping on the cold ground, when the group was unable to secure shelter in a

New Hampshire town. A later generation of Utica Jubilee Singers was brought to New York City in 1927 and became the first black quartet to secure a sustaining weekly radio broadcast on N.B.C.; originating from WJZ studio in New York. *The New York Telegram* radio columnist said of their broadcast: "Here were negro spirituals given in the way in which they were intended to be, with all the sonorous beauty of phrasing, all the depth of feeling and all the barbaric pagan beauty that the negro brings to white men's religion."[10]

During the late nineteenth century contradictory attitudes concerning the singing of spirituals had developed at Fisk and also in the wider black academic and intellectual community. Educated blacks saw themselves rising above and away from the humiliating conditions of their former servitude; many viewed the spirituals as compromising vestiges of slavery. Concurrently, popular racist opinion had miscast all jubilee minstrelsy as a nostalgic revival of "old times down South", a notion which alienated progressive blacks.

In 1899, after two decades of inactivity, the Fisk Jubilee Singers, sponsored and endorsed by the university, were resurrected under the inspired directorship of Professor John Wesley Work II. Professor Work was an outspoken champion of the cause of jubilee music. In March 1898 he wrote in the Fisk literary journal: "It has been goading to hear the slight remarks made about Jubilee Music . . . What the best critics have pronounced 'excellent', and the world has approved and wept over, let *us* not despise."[11]

As director of the Jubilee Singers, Professor Work attempted to reconcile the forward-looking attitude of his contemporaries with the spiritual tradition. Under Professor Work the Jubilee Singers exemplified "a generation of culture". While a student at Fisk in the early 1890s, Work obtained a thorough training in vocal music under Miss Jennie A. Robinson. Miss Robinson, a white woman, became head of the music department at Fisk in 1887. During her lengthy tenure all Fisk students were required to take voice culture class, and to have at least rudimentary knowledge of sight reading.

The main work of Fisk University had always been the education of black teachers. By the First World War, Fisk graduates held teaching and administrative positions at black schools and colleges all over the South. Black teachers stressed the singing of spirituals in schools, and passed along training and aesthetic precepts learned at Fisk, and at Tuskegee Institute in Alabama, to the children of the black working class.

Although jubilee minstrels and university singers were the visible manifestation and popular disseminators of the spiritual during this period, one can speak with confidence of the continuity of the oral tradition within the community. As the Victorian age drew to a close, and the industrial revolution asserted itself in the Southern states, conditions were ripe for a renaissance in religious singing within the black working class.

Jefferson County, Alabama, encompasses the adjacent cities of Birmingham, Fairfield, and Bessemer, and their rural suburbs. A distinctive, community-based quartet style emerged there, which answered the needs

Professor John Wesley Work, *c.* 1910

and conformed to the tastes of an increasingly urban twentieth-century black population.

The development of the coal and iron industry led to a great influx of blacks from rural south Alabama and Georgia into Jefferson County. Between 1890 and 1920 Birmingham's black population increased from 30,000 to 130,000. Sprawling settlements of industrial workers and their families broadened out from the coal and ore mines and the steel mills. Community life within the mining camps, company quarters and other segregated black settlements around Bessemer was unusually rich in fellowship.

Mass immigration brought together a variety of regional experience in the singing of traditional spirituals. Quartets were organised in the churches

R.C. Foster, Bessemer, 1980
Right: Charles Bridges in his
Chicago apartment, 1979

(predominantly but not exclusively Baptist), and in the schools and places of work. Denied access to other forms of popular entertainment and diversion, quartet singing became a general pastime for Jefferson County's black youth.

The area's elder quartet veterans generally agree that Mr R.C. Foster organised and trained Bessemer's first significant black quartet, the Foster Singers, when he migrated to Bessemer in 1915. Mr Foster told me: "I was in school under a young man graduated from Tuskegee Institute, who learned to sing there, and he taught me quartet music: Professor Vernon W. Barnett. He was a black man, and he came out to teach a little small school; that was the Charity High Industrial School in Lowndes County, Alabama. A certain portion of the day we had practice. We called it voice culture.

"All the voices were trained to sing evenly, not one higher than the others. You could hear the four voices, but they were so *even* that if you were sitting out there you couldn't hardly tell who was singing what. And it come down just like one solid voice and it sounded just like a brass band! Barnett taught us how to get those parts out there distinctly and leave each man staying on his part. If he's singing baritone he stayed on the baritone level. That's the way they learned it at Tuskegee.

"We didn't holler out loud, we sang quietly. And the harmony was even, and it was balanced in a way where it was just like music itself. You couldn't hardly find a quartet around here now that could sing four-part harmony through a song, but they put it on the gospel level, you know. They like the folks to holler back at 'em. But I sang where anybody would enjoy it."[12]

As Bessemer's lone exponent of the university style the Foster Singers played a transitional role in the county's musical development. By Mr Foster's time the university jubilee style had become rigidly classicised. Innovation and embellishment were welcomed only within prescribed limits. Simplicity was judged to be the essential refinement.

Mr Foster adds: "Now Charlie Bridges, he was the author of the gospel singing. Charlie Bridges used to have a wonderful voice . . . Gospel singing, and it was nice; I didn't have a thing against that. But it was different."

Rather than reviling or rejecting the university style, the new generation of gospel quartets incorporated it as one distinct component of an expanded repertoire. "Slow-meter" spirituals, given in the subdued, even-harmony method of the university jubilee singers, are still part of the performance repertoire of many Bessemer quartets. In the local vernacular, this type of song arrangement is classified as "music" singing, redolent of R.C. Foster's comments concerning the essence of balanced harmony, and indicative of the sense of continuity rooted in the consciousness of these musicians.

The concerns of aesthetes are seldom the concerns of coal miners and mill workers. This new music was more the outgrowth of a lifting of prior restraints than the result of any grand design. The true achievement of community-based quartet masters like Charles Bridges was the ability to apply the *method* and sound musical precepts of the voice culture class to a new kind of song arrangement, not constrained by outmoded prejudgments. The gospel style admitted contrapuntal and rhythmic elements accentuated in jazz, barbershop harmony and other popular secular music of the day. The specific application and proper administration of these new artistic freedoms must be duly credited to a coterie of inspired local quartet trainers.

Some scholars have tried to lay all the credit for the development of the gospel sound at the feet of venerable songwriters such as Thomas A. Dorsey. While this claim may be justified as it applies to black choral singing and the religious soloists of the era, no songwriter could have fathered gospel quartet music; that distinctive sound is a function of *song arrangement* and performance practice. As interpreted by the Golden Gate Quartet, *gospel* compositions "Precious Lord" and "Bedside Of A Neighbour" become *rhythmic spirituals*, stylistically quite a different thing. Conversely, in the hands of community quartets, nineteenth-century spirituals "Old Ship of Zion", "Inching Along" and "Nobody Knows The Trouble I've Seen" were readily accessible to gospel arrangement.

Charles Bridges, most eminent of quartet trainers, had no formal music training, but he received special instruction in vocal music while a student at Parker High School in Birmingham. As a young man, Bridges' lusty, lionesque lead voice and superior skills as song arranger and instructor attracted the attention of a rapidly mushrooming circle of area quartet devotees. The Birmingham Jubilee Singers were formed in 1925, when Charles Bridges joined forces with Ed Sherrill, who is consistently spoken of as the "heaviest" (deepest voiced) bass singer that has ever sung in Jefferson County. Their majestic, deep-pitched harmonies set Bridges' rich and rounded lead upon Ed Sherrill's powerful bass underpinning. Much of what is great and distinctive about the Jefferson County quartet style was synthesised in the work of the Birmingham Jubilee Singers.

Recordings made by the Birmingham Jubilee Singers for the Columbia Record Company between 1926 and 1930 were widely distributed and exerted a direct influence on young quartets across the U.S. These recordings help to illuminate the nature of the changes which mark the advent of the gospel era. The Birmingham Jubilee Singers aspired to please and excite their peers by exploring the possibilities of a variety of vocal tactics and devices, which were a distinct point of departure from the established classic jubilee style. A calculated emphasis on the lessons of the voice culture class – attack and release, time, harmony and articulation, *et al* – survived the transition intact. A somewhat looser, richer fabric of harmony predominates, as voices formerly used simply to fill out chords are given greater latitude. Wailing interjections by the tenor or baritone create a layered effect in the harmony. The high tenor employs an eccentric falsetto designed to add a keenness to the blending of the voices and breadth to the harmony. Restrained, "slow-meter" cadences had been the staple of the older spiritual style. The introduction of syncopation and up-tempo "fast-time" arrangements, propelled by agitated, hyperactive bass singing, was a telling factor in the popularisation of the new gospel form. Finally, the passive, sweet singing delivery of the jubilee leader is supplanted by a pressing, entreating lead style that would become the hallmark of the gospel sound.

In Jefferson County, Charles Bridges' harmony technique, style of lead singing, and above all his quartet training methods became accepted standards of excellence.

*   *   *

At eighty-three, Tom Lacy is still musically active as baritone and senior member of the Sterling Jubilees of Bessemer. He has been singing with gospel quartets in Bessemer since 1925 and is an astute observer of quartet singing activity there. Mr Lacy recalls: "Every house you go, somebody was in a quartet. Bessemer was full of 'em! Back in the old days, when I was coming up, I used to eavesdrop at the houses when Charlie Bridges and different ones

Tom Lacy of the Sterling Jubilees

used to practice them quartets. I'd get around the window. They sounded like somebody was blowing a harp or something! They'd run us away from there sometimes . . . I learned time, harmony and articulation and different things through trainers who used to train me. Man, back in them days Charlie Bridges was good!

"Now Charlie would start right on that lead fella. He'd get the lead part straightened out and then he'd commence to looking at you. First thing he's going to get that tenor straight. And next he'd get on that baritone. Directly he'd get on that bass. If you going to train, you got to know them four voices and you got to can sing some of it. When a tenor was wrong you got to show him *where* he's wrong. You must can sing tenor, you must know baritone, you must know bass. If you can't sing that bass to show that bass, you just can't train him. You can't tell me how to do nothing unless you can do it yourself, know how it's done."

The practice of employing a trainer for the purpose of coaching a young quartet was neither universal nor indispensable. In the Tidewater district of Virginia a parallel regional quartet movement of significance was taking shape, but in Virginia a strong sense of individual innovation fuelled the musical development, and trainers played no significant role.

Taking an outside trainer was a serious matter. It meant a quartet was to some extent sacrificing the right to determine and create its own style in favour of the guidance of an established master trainer. Usually the trainer would be invited to the quartet's practice session and would work with them in that setting. Often the training was rendered without remuneration; where a fee was charged, it was nominal. Sometimes a trainer would work with a quartet for only a few evenings, but often they would maintain a long association. Occasionally, after a group had attained a certain level of proficiency, the trainer would actually join them, as singer/director.

Working with a newly organised quartet, a trainer would "give the singers their voices". As Tom Lacy, who has trained several quartets over the years, explains: "Say four come, and they want to start a quartet. They come to me, and they don't know nothing. Well, I'll give them a little song to sing, and then I would pick out the voices. Which I think would make a tenor, which a baritone . . . Everybody wants to sing tenor he ain't a tenor. He must have the equipment. He must be able. Then you have them sing a little song, have them pray a little prayer. You got to learn them where they'll be quiet and listen at you in every way. When you can listen, then you're able to hear something that might do some good."[13]

Jefferson County was the hub of a far-reaching training culture. Most of the area quartets took trainers, and it was through these community-based trainers that a distinctive regional quartet style took form and was ultimately disseminated abroad. More than any other single factor, trainers account for the pre-eminence of the Jefferson County quartet movement.

Charlie Alf "Son" Dunham was an outstanding instructor of area quartets, a unique songster whose lifelong occupation was that of itinerant quartet trainer. The Dunham Jubilee Singers travelled extensively and made a number of commercial sound recordings, including one session with Bessie Smith in 1930. For a time, this group sang under contract with the Penn Central Railroad on special excursions and at company functions. Dunham had an arrangement with the Paramount movie theatre chain; his quartet would appear after the picture show as a "vaudeville". The group also sang in churches and school auditoriums on barnstorming tours. The Dunham Jubilee Singers carried the new gospel banner into Mobile, Alabama, with marked effect. According to Mr James Allen, who was a member of the Dunham Jubilee Singers at the time: "The Mobile Big Four had been one of the best quartets around. We met 'em in Mobile, so shucks, we just tore that place up! You see they were singing that long-meter stuff. We come in with that fast-time stuff – it wasn't *going* down that-a-ways, see. Dunham brought that fast-time stuff in; that's what we had. They had this here long-meter stuff, and them good old chords though, they was right in there. But we come in there with that short-time stuff, and that just socked them folks, just standing up, jumping up and just shouting, just tearing things up!"[14] Mr Allen's account has been independently verified by several elder members of Mobile's gospel community.

Nowhere was the Bessemer quartet ethos absorbed more thoroughly or with greater enthusiasm than in New Orleans. Former Bessemer resident Gilbert Porterfield touched off what has been described by one veteran singer as a "quartet fever" in New Orleans. Mr Porterfield was tenor voice for the Bessemer Red Rose, a storied combination; and prior to leaving Jefferson County he had been training quartets in the mining settlement of Winona, on the southern outskirts of Bessemer. In 1932 the Red Rose visited New Orleans on a singing tour. When the rest of the quartet returned to Alabama, Mr Porterfield and Sandy Newell, the Red Rose manager, decided to stay on and make New Orleans their home. Porterfield became trainer and longstanding adviser to the Duncan Brothers Quartet. William Duncan of the Duncan Brothers has attested: "Mr Porterfield came through New Orleans with his group, and we begun singing after he started giving us the cue to their different style. He gave us a new kind of harmony . . . I began singing plenty falsetto . . . and we got more of a *blend*."[15]

In his excellent monograph, "The Soproco Spiritual Singers: A New Orleans Quartet Family Tree", Mr Lynn Abbott has documented the pronounced impact of Gilbert Porterfield and the "Alabama style" on the emerging local quartet form. He wrote: "Gilbert Porterfield and Sandy Newell remained in New Orleans to establish themselves as disciples of the Birmingham quartet 'training culture'. As such, their influence was immediate and profound, especially in the case of Gilbert Porterfield, whose name would become synonymous with first-rate quartet singing in the New Orleans gospel community."[16]

Chicago's gospel choral movement was conceived in April 1932 under the guidance of Professor T.A. Dorsey. The first national conclave of Gospel Choruses of America was held in Pilgrim Baptist Church in August of the following year. An analogous movement among Chicago's quartets was ushered in by the arrival of Norman R. McQueen from Bessemer in 1927.

McQueen had the benefit of ten years' experience as second tenor for Bessemer's oldest quartet, the Foster Singers. Shortly after he arrived in Chicago, Norman McQueen organised and trained the Alabama and Georgia Quartet, which was the city's first important community-based quartet group. He is repeatedly referred to in the pages of the *Chicago Defender* as "Chicago's quartet expert". A church news column in the *Defender* (13 February 1932) recounts: "Norman McQueen, formerly of Bessemer, Alabama, the founder of Alabama & Georgia Quartet, the organiser of quartets on the West Side, the cause of female quartets in Chicago, the founder of the Progressive Quartet Association, is now teaching fifteen quartets who will appear in recital at Community Center."

Norman McQueen organised the Chicago Progressive Quartet Association in March 1931 and was that organisation's first president. In little more than a year the Association membership had grown to include more than seventy-five local quartets, virtually all of whom had the benefit of McQueen's training and experience. He was particularly active in establishing and training female quartets, who enjoyed a period of great popularity during the 1930s. It was through the pioneering efforts of Norman McQueen that "live" quartet broadcasting commenced in Chicago in 1930, on Jack L. Cooper's "all-coloured hour" programme.

While the maxims of Jefferson County's gospel quartet academy were carried across the Deep South and Midwest, the movement was being advanced and elaborated back home in Bessemer. In 1926 the Famous Blue Jay Singers were organised in the Bessemer suburb of Brighton by pioneer bass singer C.D. Parnell. Parnell built his new group around a thirteen-year-old dynamo named Silas Steele.

Silas Steele created pandemonium wherever the Blue Jays sang. He paced the platform, a conspicuous breach of jubilee convention. He expressed his lead as fervent supplication, and his delivery was punctuated with histrionic

gestures. The Blue Jays were impeccable harmony artists, and Steele possessed a marvellous, pliant voice, but it was in the employment of fervid theatrics, previously the domain of the sermonisers, that the Blue Jays distinguished themselves with the public, and Steele fathered a new era in performance practice. He was the first "emotional" gospel lead singer.

The Famous Blue Jays were perhaps the first gospel quartet to travel and sing as a full-time undertaking; as the 1930s drew on, numerous others followed. Distinctive regional quartet singing styles had begun to develop in black population centres across the U.S.

Texas was the site of a feverish proliferation of gospel quartet activity, exhilarated by the arrival from Bessemer of the Famous Blue Jay Singers and their heir apparent, the awesome Kings of Harmony. The Blue Jays established their new base of operations in Dallas in the mid-1930s, where they secured a groundbreaking radio broadcast on KTBC. On a tour through Birmingham the Blue Jays convinced Charles Bridges to join them as a second lead voice and to act as arranger for the quartet.

The Kings of Harmony, first known as the BYPU Specials (Baptist Young People's Training Unit), were organised in Starlight Baptist Church, in the Winona mining district of south Bessemer. 'Kings of Harmony' was as much a characterisation as it was a name. The Kings began touring in the mid-1930s and followed the Blue Jays into Texas, where they settled temporarily in Houston. Houston quartet elder James Singleterry told researcher Ray Funk: "The Kings of Harmony took Texas by storms and jumps . . . They used to come on the radio every Thursday morning at 2.15 a.m. You could walk up and down the street, I guarantee you could hear the Kings of Harmony. It's incredible. People would set their alarms to get up."[17]

Texas gospel quartet had a distinctive cast and a proud, individualistic heritage. The Soul Stirrers, organised in Houston, ventured out as professional gospel singers during the late 1930s. They were enormously influential and innovative practitioners of the gospel style. Their brilliant tenor leader

Above left: The Blue Jay Singers and (centre) The Kings of Harmony, both from Birmingham, Alabama.

Rebert H. Harris concedes no musical influences but "God's little birds". Other Texas veterans more readily acknowledge the impact of the two visiting quartets from Jefferson County, who ruled the ether during this incipient interval.

The onset of the golden age of gospel quartet singing could be fixed at the convergence of the Blue Jays, Kings of Harmony and Soul Stirrers in Texas in about 1938/9. One notable outcome of this clustering was the initial appearance of the "switch lead", which resulted in the expansion of the typical gospel quartet from four men to five. As the term implies, two lead singers are used in a single song, alternating verses or passing phrases back and forth like a baton. This technique redoubled intensity in quartet performance, and intensity was the operative word in gospel music.

With many quartets travelling and vying for public attention, gospel programmes were becoming impassioned battlegrounds. Indeed, the phrase "Battle of Song" was regularly employed in promoting programmes. Groups became extremely sensitive to their audiences' moods and responses, and performance styles were geared toward evoking maximum audience reaction. There are numerous stories of quartets "turning out the house"; that is, inciting such an epidemic of spiritual catharsis that while the majority of the patrons left the hall after the group's performance, exhausted and thoroughly satiated, the remaining groups sang to an emptied auditorium!

In many parts of the South, programmes of spiritual singing had traditionally attracted audiences that were in some measure racially mixed, though seating was invariably segregated, the choicest seats being reserved for "our white friends". But the gospel mode proved far less palatable for whites and finally resulted in racial exclusivity. Mr James Davis, who has sung with the renowned Dixie Hummingbirds since the 1930s, reminisced: "We'd take that same song and sing it real sweet and smooth for the whites, then get to *our* place and let our hair down. I remember one night we were in Tampa, Florida, and we had twenty-five or thirty whites there that night. We

Right: The Soul Stirrers, *c.* 1944 (l to r) James H. Medlock, R.B. Robinson, Rebert H. Harris, S.R. Crain, J.J. Farley and T.L. Bruster

started off with a Negro spiritual, 'Nobody Knows The Trouble I've Seen', and 'Swing Low'. And we did a couple funny numbers, they ate that up. Said, 'Well, we might as well go for it now . . . better get down.' We wound up sure enough, and people got to running and hollering and shouting. But you could see those white folks getting up [to leave]!''[18]

While the emotionally passionate gospel quartet style coming out of Birmingham and Houston swept the Deep South and Midwest, the "rhythmic spiritual" or latter day "jubilee" quartet style, ushered in by the Golden Gate Quartet of Norfolk, Virginia, had been inspiring legions of followers along the East Coast. The meteoric rise of the Golden Gates during the late 1930s vividly demonstrated the wider accessibility of the rhythmic spiritual, which had broad appeal across racial lines. The late Bill Johnson, musical director of the Golden Gate Quartet, defined this brand of jubilee singing as: "Any music that had a beat and had a joyful sound to it. It was a joyous sort of thing, a thing you patted your foot by. It wasn't a thing that made you want to cry, like 'My mama's dead and gone', like your 'hard rocks' [gospel groups] used to do. It was all light really, entertaining . . . We used to get together in Eddie Griffin's barbershop. At that time we weren't singing the type of stuff that we sang later. We were singing the run-of-the-mill things, like the old Fisk songs. The slow-beat songs . . . We were singing in every church that let a quartet sing in it. And particularly, the main churches that got to me were the Holiness Churches, because they sang with a beat. And whenever I got around to training the group I'd give our things a beat, upbeat it you know . . . I think with this quartet what we tried to create was what I used to call 'vocal percussion'. It was just like a drum, but it had notes to it, it had lyrics to it, you see. And you had different beats, you had different accents. Like a bunch of guys beating a tom-tom somewhere. It had to be done sharply and together, along with the harmony. We sang simple chords, the simple triad. We were trying to sing chords that sounded good to the ear."[19]

The Golden Gate Quartet became the most widely imitated and most commercially successful of all twentieth-century religious quartets. Like the jubilee singing of an earlier period, the latter day jubilee style proved to be a music anyone could enjoy. By 1946 there were hundreds of jubilee quartets active along the East Coast. All of these groups patterned after the Golden Gates to some degree.

The variety and abundance of great quartets active during the mid- and late-1940s represent an artistic zenith in the movement. During the golden age, versatility became imperative. A quartet had to be proficient in artful harmony songs, emotional, hard-hitting gospel numbers, and inspiring jubilee tunes in order to "get over" in the brutally competitive gospel programmes of the day.

A major transformation in the nature of gospel quartet music occurred during the 1940s. A scattered network of community-based folk artists emerged as a powerful force in the national entertainment world. Vast armies of black quartets traversed the country, singing in churches and public auditoriums. Many quartets made commercial phonograph recordings for the numerous independent record companies which appeared immediately following the Second World War. With the proliferation of far-reaching 50,000-watt stations in the 1940s, and the increased opportunities for obtaining commercially sponsored spots, radio became a keystone of gospel music promotion. A significant number of gospel quartets were able to use radio work as a launching pad to successful careers.

Many capable quartets and individual singers rejected the option of itinerancy, and some of these fared quite well. The non-professional, working-class quartet of the golden age often was of a grand stamp. The Ensley Jubilee Singers had the talent and the opportunity to become full-time touring musicians, but were content to stay in Jefferson County and retain steady employment in the steel mills. Though their travelling was limited to weekends and they did not have an opportunity to make commercial phonograph records, their local reputation, nourished by a popular weekly radio broadcast, was such that the group did well by staying at home.

There has always been a large and avid gospel audience and an energetic promotional network in Birmingham. "Major programmes", which brought such luminaries as the Fairfield Four, Soul Stirrers and Pilgrim Travelers into Jefferson County, usually took place in Birmingham City Auditorium and were promoted by one of the city's "big three" gospel radio announcers/promoters, William Blevins, William Polk and Richmond Davis. These men directed a well-oiled, profitable enterprise, in which the Ensley Jubilee Singers played a major part. They were cast in the role of well-loved local champions, against whom all invading visitors must prove themselves. As such, their presence was necessary to ensure a successful promotion, placing the group in an advantageous bargaining position. The Ensley Jubilee Singers have remained musically active, though the extent of their activity has diminished in recent years. They have made some concessions to modern musical trends, which include the addition of electric guitar and electric bass accompaniment.

*   *   *

The golden age of gospel quartet ended more than twenty-five years ago. The intervening period has witnessed the transformation of traditional quartet singing into precipitate anachronism. What was universally understood a generation ago has become obscure in the present. Black vocal quartets play no significant role in "contemporary" gospel music.

The organophonic chord is rapidly becoming a "lost chord"; at present it is a wistful retention. If one were to go out in search of that perfect chord, history clearly designates Jefferson County as a proper starting point. While it is no longer the case that a quartet can be found on every block in Bessemer, the region remains a singular haven of *a cappella* quartet activity. Several of the oldest gospel quartets in the nation reside in Bessemer and each carries a substantial following of devotees. This strong community base has allowed quartets to survive long decades of disregard from the gospel music establishment.

Neither the Sterling Jubilees nor the Four Eagle Gospel Singers have ever enjoyed a national reputation. They have always been what the "major groups" condescendingly refer to as "little local groups". On an occasional weekend they might travel as far as the neighbouring states of Mississippi, Tennessee, or Georgia, but never so far that they could not return to Bessemer and their full-time employment on Monday morning. Only recently, as folklorists have descended on Bessemer and focused attention on them as unique representatives of a rapidly disappearing folk form, has the wider world become aware of the existence of these groups. A "Quartet Reunion" staged at the Birmingham City Auditorium in October 1980 brought some outside exposure, and led to a featured appearance by the Sterlings and Four Eagles at the Smithsonian Institution's "Black American Quartet Tradition Weekend" in November 1981. Both groups have been commercially recorded during the past few years. For their own part, the quartets are only doing what they have always done. All credit to their Creator for the unforeseen recognition that has been allotted them so late in the day.

The Sterling Jubilees are the oldest quartet presently active in Jefferson County. They were organised in 1929 from employees of U.S. Pipe and Foundry, more commonly known as the Bessemer Pipe Shop. The Sterlings have had a historical relationship with the Steel Workers' Union. For many years they sang under the name CIO Singers (Congress of Industrial Organizations). Though Tom Lacy did not join the Sterling Jubilees/CIO Singers until the 1950s, he was present when the Sterlings held their first meeting in 1929. He recalls: "Charlie Bridges come out to the house and got me that night, and me and him walked all the way down into the Pipe Shop quarter. They used to have a quarter . . . living in company houses. We met them boys, and I helped Charlie out with them. The CIO Singers was organised right there in Willie Irving's house. They called him 'Crab', but his name was Willie Irving."

Henry Holston has been with the Sterlings longer than any other member of the present aggregation. Mr Holston retired from his full-time employment at the Pipe Shop with nearly forty years' tenure. The late George Bester, considered the patriarch of the Sterling Jubilees, overheard Holston singing in the Pipe Shop bathhouse in the late 1940s and recruited him into the Sterlings. Mr Holston, an energetic, engaging gentleman in his seventies, combines natural and falsetto tenor with a facility born of a lifetime of gospel quartet singing experience.

The source of much of the authority radiated by the Sterling Jubilees is their baritone, Tom Lacy; a soul with an exceptionally high centre of spiritual gravity. Mr Lacy was born in Pinehurst, Georgia, in the year 1900 and came to Bessemer in 1924. He became an active participant in a bustling quartet theatre, cleaving to the heart of the blossoming movement. He sought and received extensive training from the area's most distinguished quartet masters. For sixty years without interruption Tom Lacy has maintained membership in area gospel quartets. This quiet, unassuming man has gained rare qualities of wisdom and understanding.

Mr Lacy and Mr Holston are the core of the Sterlings' harmony. The

closeness of the blend achieved by these two gospel warhorses is truly uncanny. I have stood directly in front of the two men and been unable aurally to separate their voices. Lacy's baritone is so thoroughly engrained – the space between tenor and bass spanned so extensively – that it is usually impossible to pick out his baritone part. This is the mark of a consummate harmony artiste. Lacy becomes distinguishable only in giving out the characteristic interjected moan, and at those moments, echoes of unfathomable remembrance are made manifest.

The Sterlings have a fine and capable bass singer in Sam Lewis to add "bottom" to the background. These three men form a harmony backdrop that keeps faith with Jefferson County's deep harmony tradition.

The Sterlings have a surfeit of lead vocalists, each with his particular capabilities and specialities. Sam Johnson, Eunise Cook, Dock Terry and John Alexander divide the lead duties. Eunise Cook can double at tenor when needed; and Sam Johnson sometimes sings the "fifth lead", a harmony device popularised in the 1940s in which a falsetto tenor doubles the baritone part, adding fullness and brightness to the blend. Manager John Alexander is perhaps the group's busiest leader. He can fill in at baritone and also sings "false" tenor.

In recent years a kind of philosophical power struggle has taken place between the group's old guard and the younger members. Discord among the membership is an inescapable reality of quartet interaction. Ingenious mechanisms for resolution and reconciliation are built into the structure of the weekly practice session. The Sterlings' fifty-four years of durability attest

CIO Singers, *c.* 1944. Back row (l to r): Cleveland Smith, Bill Williams, Tiger Thomas, George Bester. Front row: Rosco MacDonald, R.C. Noble and Willie Moore to the efficacy of these mechanisms. The very setting of the Sterlings' practice, in little Lily Grove Baptist Church, which has acquired the local sobriquet "Holy Ghost Headquarters", is calculated to lend a reverential, diligently maintained feeling of Christian brotherhood to the meetings. A round of prayer and "testifying" precedes every practice session.

Most quartets elect officers, with clearly defined duties. The president conducts the business meeting with a surprisingly formal parliamentary discipline. Most groups have bylaws, and assess small fines for violations of compact. When the Sterling Jubilees elected new officers this year their internal contentions were mediated through democratic process, for the most part in favour of the "junior" faction. Yet Mr Lacy is not left without resources. He jocularly explains: "We've not got a director or a trainer. We all works more together. When we get the song and I know it ain't right, I won't get my part. Y'all get that. Let someone else sing baritone. I know it ain't right, see."[13]

An aggressive, energetic personality, John Alexander has effectively taken the Sterlings in tow. His original home is in Greene County, Alabama, and he came north to Bessemer in 1942, singing with several local quartets before he joined the Sterlings in 1956. When George Bester died, John Alexander was made the manager of the Sterling Jubilees. Recently Mr Alexander has been successfully promoting programmes prominently featuring unaccompanied singing, providing performance opportunities for the area's many traditional gospel artists. Popular venues for such programmes include the 500-seat Bessemer City Auditorium and the CIO Union Hall in downtown Bessemer, as well as a network of local churches with favourable regard towards the groups or the singing. The success of these programmes is heartening.

Joe Watson, lead singer and spokesman for the Four Eagle Gospel Singers of Bessemer reflects: "I've seen the time, back here thirty years ago, when most all the local groups carried a big crowd. But now it's different. You have to come up with a lot of advertisement and just put a lot in to get a crowd."[20]

As Joe Watson tells it, quartet singing first came to him as a legacy from his uncle, John Watson. "I remember when I was a little boy, around ten or twelve years old, he was living right across the street from where we lived over there in Winona, up on the mountain around the ore mine. I used to go to his house when they was having rehearsal. I used to sit around there and look at them sing. That impressed me." Watson vividly recalls watching the legendary Gilbert Porterfield train his uncle's group, the Silvertone Singers. "That was the man. Porterfield was the trainer of all these groups up there."

Joe Watson learned the song "On The Battlefield" from Silas Steele of the Blue Jays: " 'On The Battlefield, Working For The Lord'; I've been singing that song for forty-some years. I brought that song to the group. That come from the Blue Jay Singers."[20]

The Four Eagle Gospel Singers celebrate their forty-fourth anniversary in November 1984. They maintain a friendly but earnest rivalry with the Sterling Jubilees. The Eagles have a considerable local following, owing in part to their long-lived Sunday morning radio broadcast. Their membership is younger than the Sterlings', and their style of singing less hoary. The Eagles are not so heavy (deep-pitched) in their blend, nor do they attempt the awesome blasts of ecstatic, unified harmony which are the Sterlings' hallmark. Their chords are smoother and their tones lighter. The sparer sound of the Eagles often seems less strange, more accessible to the unconversant listener.

Elorgia Coleman's strong, accurate tenor is the nucleus of the Eagles' harmonic background. The gentle, soft-spoken Coleman is also manager of the Four Eagles. Freeman Farris, the group's bass singer and elder statesman, has lost some of his volume with age, but he is a crafty bass singer with a great deal of quartet know-how. Mr Farris received his training from L.Z. Manley, brilliant leader of the Heavenly Gospel Singers. Charles Bridges has singled out L.Z. Manley as the finest singer he ever trained. Manley overheard Farris singing in the company bathhouse at Fairfield Street Mill where both men were employed in the early 1930s. He subsequently trained Farris's quartet, the Four Blue Eagles, a forerunner of the present Four Eagles. Freeman Farris's forte are the subtle "pumping" runs, which add colour and swing to the Eagles' melodies. He learned how to pump from Porterfield Lewis, basser of the Heavenly Gospel Singers, who is generally credited with popularising this bass technique. Instead of singing the chord, the bass singer affects a sort of vocal imitation of a string bass; the rhythmic "boom, boom, boom . . ." which has become almost a trademark of the genre.

The Eagles have a battery of three lead vocalists: Joe Watson, John Lawrence and Dell Coleman. Joe Watson specialises in leading the "music" numbers, the Eagles' term for the slow-meter harmony songs, like their radio theme "I Have A Mind To Live A Christian". The more forceful gospel leads

The Four Eagles Gospel Singers on air at WENN Radio during their regular Sunday morning live broadcast, with presenter George Stewart in the foreground

are usually handled by the ebullient John Lawrence, who is especially popular with the Eagles' younger followers. Mr Lawrence "sells" his songs with heartfelt evangelistic fervour. His role with the Eagles is analogous to the role Eunise Cook fills with the Sterling Jubilees.

The Four Eagles suffered a setback in 1982, when their baritone voice, Mr L.T. Smoot, the last remaining "original" Eagle, sustained an incapacitating cerebral haemorrhage and was forced to retire from the singing. Rather than find a replacement, the group put their extra lead singers to work as "utility" baritones. When John Lawrence sings lead, Joe Watson baritones, and vice versa. Now that Mr Smoot has begun to regain his strength, he is slowly reassuming his place with the group.

Neither the Sterlings nor the Eagles represent the apex of quartet artistry. Exemplary expression is not commensurate with the vestigial state of the art form. The Sterlings and Eagles are arguably the finest of the present-day quartet survivals. They are the inheritors of the richest of all regional quartet traditions; their commitment to the harmony aesthetic has moderated the irresistible urge to appease the tastes of a younger audience; and they carry a healthy respect for deep harmony, the organophonic chord, into their performance.

The Sterlings and Eagles are not the only *a cappella* quartets active in Jefferson County. On any given weekend the Delta-Aires, Shelby County Big Four, Southernaires, and others can be heard in local black churches and auditoriums. These groups render four-part vocal harmony, with a bass singer, and without instrumentation. Like the Sterlings and Eagles, their membership consists of ageing veteran musicians. Many have spent their entire adult lives singing in gospel groups. The song declares, "I'm on the battlefield, and I'm working for the Lord. I promised him that I would serve him till I die."

The fine points of this music, 100 years of accumulated wisdom, expertise and refinement, have been most effectively transmitted through the work of master trainers, and it is particularly dispiriting that octogenarian maestros such as Charles Bridges and Tom Lacy cannot pass their precious knowledge along to a new generation of quartet singers.

How rewarding, then, to come upon the Birmingham Sunlites, gifted young singers determined to continue in the time-honoured four-part *a cappella* tradition, eager to take training, and properly awestruck by the harmonic accomplishments of the Sterling Jubilees and Four Eagles. The Sunlites have emerged from the Church of Christ, a predominantly white Southern Baptist denomination, by no means noted in the past for its production of black gospel quartets. No musical instruments are permitted in the Church of Christ service, consequently *a cappella* singing has been allowed to proliferate.

The Sunlites are the Taylor brothers – musical director, leader and tenor James Taylor; bass singer and business manager Barry; baritone Steve – plus tenor, leader Wayne Williams and high tenor Eddie Washington.

The Sunlites developed within the confines of their own denomination, unaware of the rich, living heritage of *a cappella* quartet singing within their reach. They were surprisingly unacquainted with the traditional spiritual repertoire. When asked what spirituals they sang, the answer was they did not sing any. Their entire repertoire consisted of their own original gospel compositions, some of which are quite excellent, and random gospel quartet numbers gleaned from a scattered few recordings of the Soul Stirrers, Sensational Nightingales and other groups of the 1950s and 1960s.

The filming of *On the Battlefield* provided an excellent opportunity to bring the Birmingham Sunlites into close contact with the Sterling Jubilees. The idea of a training session was brought before the groups and both agreed to give it a trial. Their initial meeting was a revelation. The older singers were impressed by the raw singing talent and original song arrangements of the Sunlites. The Sunlites were astounded by the richness and weirdness of the Sterlings' chords. They were introduced to a whole "new way" of singing their parts, a different approach to harmony singing which they drank in with keen enthusiasm.

In the course of several training sessions which have taken place since the first meeting, the Sunlites have been taught something more than just a handful of specific songs; they have begun to learn the traditional "formula" by which groups such as the Sterlings construct deep harmony arrangements. The Sunlites do not see this instruction as a means of supplanting their already impressive original style, but of augmenting that style and achieving versatility. The Sterlings, struggling against age with a fierce determination to prolong their marathon history, see latent meaningfulness in the breaking forth of the Sunlites.

Despite an illustrious history, gospel quartet singing faces an uncertain future. Yet the form is so fundamental, its characteristics of simplicity and adaptability so timeless in their invitation, that an eventual re-emergence of *a cappella* quartet singing seems almost inevitable.

There has been an increased level of awareness and a modest revival of interest in the gospel quartet tradition during the past few years. Only time will tell whether *On the Battlefield* represents the journey's end of a vanishing tradition or a benchmark in its restoration. However that may be, the film remains a chronicle of the abiding love of a humble circle of community musicians, who lift their heavy voices to God. Tom Lacy told me: "The angels in Heaven had a quartet. They sang."

NOTES

1. Adam K. Spence, "The Origin of the Jubilee Singers", *The Fisk Herald*, October 1890.

2. Henry Ward Beecher, text of speech made in London, England, 16 October 1887, before Freedmen's Aid Society. Reprinted in *The Fisk Herald*, March 1888.

3. Clippings from "The George L. White Scrapbooks", Fisk University Library Special Collections: *Daily News* (February 1874); *The Manchester Examiner* (January 1874); Brighton newspaper (24 March 1874).

4. *Ibid.*, *Berliner Musikzeitung* (November 1877), reprinted and translated in *Tonic Fa Sol La Reporter* (date unknown).

5. Letter in American Missionary Association Archive, Amistad Research Center, Dillard University.

6. "Is It True Music?", *Boston Daily Traveller*, 15 January 1880.

7. Ella Sheppard Moore, "Historical Sketch of the Jubilee Singers", *The Fisk University News*, vol.II, no.5 (October 1911), p.52.

8. "Interview with Mr F.J. Loudin", Melbourne (Australia) *Daily Telegraph*, 31 July 1886.

9. Lynn Abbott, "The Soproco Spiritual Singers: A New Orleans Quartet Family Tree" (1983), pp.4–6, monograph published by Jean Lafitte National Historical Park, New Orleans.

10. *New York Telegram*, 21 November 1927, from the private collection of Mr and Mrs Marshall Cole.

11. John W. Work II, "Jubilee Music", *The Fisk Herald*, March 1898, pp.5–6.

12. Personal interviews with R.C. Foster, 24 July 1980, 23 October 1981.

13. Personal interviews with Tom Lacy, October 1978, 5 February 1979, 19 August 1979, 23 October 1981, 1 August 1983, 28 November 1983, 9 and 19 January 1984.

14. Personal interview with James Allen, February 1979.

15. Personal interview with William Duncan, conducted by Lynn Abbott, 17 February 1983.

16. Abbott, *op. cit.*, p.22

17. Personal interview with James Singleterry, conducted by Ray Funk, 16 January 1982.

18. Personal interview with James Davis, conducted by Lynn Abbott, 27 February 1984.

19. Personal interview with Bill Johnson, 23 and 25 January 1980.

20. Personal interview with Joe Watson, 22 April 1984.

BIBLIOGRAPHY

The author wishes to acknowledge the freely shared researches of Lynn Abbott and Ray Funk.

ABBOTT, Lynn. "The Soproco Spiritual Singers: A New Orleans Quartet Family Tree", monograph published by Jean Lafitte National Historical Park, 1983.

DIXON, R.M.W. and GODRICH, J. *Blues and Gospel Records 1902–1943.* Storyville Publications, 1982.

FUNK, Ray. Bibliography of quartet references in *The Chicago Defender*, 1983 (unpublished).

HEILBUT, Tony. *The Gospel Sound: Good News and Bad Times.* Simon and Schuster, 1971.

LAUGHTON, Robert and HAYES, Cedric. "Post-War Gospel Records Discography" (unpublished manuscript).

MARSH, J.B.T. *The Story of the Jubilee Singers and Their Songs.* Houghton, Osgood and Company, 1880, reproduced A.M.S. Press.

McCALLUM, Brenda. "Birmingham Boys – Jubilee Gospel Quartets from Jefferson County, Alabama", Alabama Traditions 101, 12-inch L.P. liner note booklet, 1982.

SEROFF, Doug. "Bibliography of Fisk Jubilee Singers Materials in Fisk University Library Special Collections", 1983–4 (unpublished).

—— "Birmingham Quartet Anthology", Clanka Lanka 144, 001/002, 12-inch L.P. liner note booklet, 1980.

—— "Birmingham Quartet Scrapbook: A Quartet Reunion in Jefferson County". Publication funded by National Endowment for the Arts, 1980.

—— "Black American Quartet Traditions". Publication of Smithsonian Performing Arts, Programme in Black American Culture, 1981.

—— "The Continuity of the Black Gospel Quartet Tradition". Unpublished paper read at Conference on Sacred Music in the Black Church, at Sunday School Publishing Board, Nashville, Tennessee, 9 December 1982.

RECORDINGS

All Of My Appointed Time, Stash ST-144 (U.S.A.). A 1978 reissue of gospel quartets and soloists, originally recorded primarily during the 1936–1951 period. Annotated by Tony Heilbut.

The Best Of The Dixie Hummingbirds, Peacock/MCA 28021 (U.S.A.).

The Best Of The Sensational Nightingales, Peacock/MCA 28020 (U.S.A.).

Birmingham Boys, Brenda McCallum (congress catalogue 81/750547) Alabama Stereo Traditions 101.

Birmingham Quartet Anthology, Clanka Lanka 144,001/002 (Sweden). A 2-L.P. set, with booklet notes, prepared by Doug Seroff. Includes thirty-two historic recordings of Jefferson County, Alabama, gospel quartets, originally recorded 1926–1953. Artists include the Birmingham Jubilee Singers, Famous Blue Jay Singers, C.I.O. Singers, others. Nominated for Grammy Award as 'Best Historical Album' of 1981. Manufacturer: Mr R&B Records, Pl. 8300, 643 00 Vingaker, Sweden.

Bless My Bones, P-Vine Special PLP-9051 (Japan). A 1982 release, featuring rare radio transcriptions originally recorded during the 1950s at WDIA radio station in Memphis, Tennessee. Booklet notes by Doug Seroff. Manufacturer: Blues Interactions, Sun-East Bldg. 402, 24–9 Higashi 3-chome, Shibuya-ku, Tokyo 150, Japan.

The Fairfield Four – One Religion, Nashboro 7232 (U.S.A.).

Fifty Years: The Four Eagles, WENN Radio, Birmingham, Alabama, SRS 1293.

Get Right With God, Krazy Kat KK 7417 (England). A 1983 reissue of gospel quartets and soloists, originally recorded from 1947–1953.

The Golden Gate Quartet, RCA CL 42111 (Germany). A 2-L.P. set, released in 1977, which makes available thirty-five classic recordings of this seminal jubilee quartet, originally recorded for Bluebird 1937–1939.

The Gospel Soul Of Sam Cooke With The Soul Stirrers, vol. 1, Speciality SPS 2116 (U.S.A.).

Happy In The Service Of The Lord, High Water 1002 (U.S.A.) Traditional gospel quartets from Memphis, Tennessee, recorded in 1983. Artists include the Pattersonaires and Harps of Melody. Booklet notes are included. Manufacturer: High Water Records, Memphis, TN 38152.

The Spirit of Memphis Quartet – Greatest Hits, Starday 5020 (U.S.A.).

Swan Silvertones – Greatest Hits, Starday 5022 (U.S.A.).

CHAPTER 3

Legends of Rhythm and Blues

BY IAN WHITCOMB

Judge Geo. A. Carpenter: "What is this new thing called Blues? And what is this new Rhythm?"

Alcide "Yellow" Nunez: "Nuttin' new about 'em, jedge. They's part of our life for donkey's years. Jest lately we expose 'em to you public and you all hot and bothered. Some complain, but others dance. We always play 'em natural — like the flow of a stream, the lope of a buzzard, the roll and rock of well-oiled wheels on steady rails. We jest layin' easy on the back o' the beat. But you jump ahead o' that beat and twist and jerk like a Ford flivver in a tantrum. Go with it, jedge, go with it! It's the world's music now!!"

Judge: "I must say, sir, I am none the wiser."

"Yellow" Nunez: "Agreed, jedge — but you're much better informed!"

(From the "Livery Stable Blues" copyright case as reported in the Chicago *Daily News*, 23 October 1917.)

Rufus ("Walkin' the Dog") Thomas: "Blues will always be there. Of all the other music in the world, watch it — it'll tail out and change. But you'll always be able to hear twelve-bar blues. Always. It's the backbone of American music — blues and country, 'cause country and western and blues are right there together, just that close, and gospel. Everything else comes from that."

(As reported by Peter Guralnick in *Lost Highway*, David R. Godine, Boston 1979.)

Johnny Otis: "We started rhythm and blues right here in the Forties in smoky old Los Angeles. A hybrid mixture of Big Band jazz and bebop, of small group good-time swing, of country blues, and basic boogie-woogie. We amplified it up, we squashed it down for modern dancing, we added a honking sax and a whopping great side-drum back beat. Behold! It swept the world as R&B and became the foundation of Rock 'n' Roll! But it started here in L.A."

(Transcribed from *The Johnny Otis Show* on KPFK FM Radio, L.A., April 1983.)

It was Geoff, film director and friend, who voiced it first: "Where are the slums?" I'd been pondering along similar lines and so I added: "Where the suffering?" We didn't mean to sound flippant – but it wasn't Blues Country according to the gospel of book and myth and liner note.

We had been driving through the black neighbourhoods of Los Angeles, deep into preparations for filming *The Legends of Rhythm and Blues*, and we were having a good time, a sunny carnival time. As a British Angelino (since 1965) I felt proud of L.A.: the air was crisp and springy, the streets were clean and orderly, the houses big and old but well-maintained. Many were built in the Spanish Mission style of the 1920s, some were Ancient Greek-pillared, a few Tudored with black beams and planks. Deep green swards, unfenced in the democratic manner, swept down to tidy sidewalks lined with tall, venerable palm trees. Neat, brushed schoolchildren hurried on their way to the schoolhouse round the corner, businessmen in natty three-piece suits greeted each other as they clambered into gargantuan cars, an elderly man on the lines of Uncle Remus was gently revving up his lawnmower to manicure his sward to the level of perfection surrounding him.

We turned into South Wilton Place and pulled up at 1230. Then we got out and soaked in the sweet situation. Lloyd Glenn's house was enormous and

Lloyd Glenn on stage at the Variety Arts Centre, downtown Los Angeles

green and sprawling; a cavernous carport nestled against the north side wall and a fleet of cars lazed around inside; a mixed chorus of exotic birds sang up a storm; luxuriant plants and bushes sat fatly and comfortably in the freshly-minted warmth. It was indeed a sylvan scene in urbania – and then we heard drifting across the grass from the closed-curtained windows of the Glenn home the plaintive and carefully-picked and beautiful notes of a piano playing "How Long Blues". It was delicious. And it was typical of our experiences during the filming of this segment.

One might well conclude from this blissful picture that R&B is a music made in a world of roses and rainbows, that it celebrates the joy of life and constantly and syncopatingly sends a directive to the body to get up and dance and have a good time and a nice day.

The horrific story of the black experience in America has been accompanied by a musical soundtrack of vital and mostly uplifting music. Sometimes, true, full of yelps and complaint (of blues all round the bed), but most days sunlit with dance music powered by the ever-rolling trundle-train of boogie-woogie! And this treasure is amazingly moving to behold when you read of the race sold into slavery, shipped as cattle to the colonies, whipped and chained by Simon Legrees, lynched into strange fruit, barbecued and dismembered, and all this not only in the bad old South but in the North too. Even out here in sunny California, in Los Angeles, a town noted as "good for niggers", we read in the *Los Angeles News* for 2 March 1867: "The soul of the Negro is as black and putrid as his body. Should such a creature vote? He has no more capacity for reason than his native hyena or crocodile."

Barging into the "progressive" twentieth century came this death ship of prejudice and segregation, and even today its wake of poverty and hopelessness still churns and spreads. So it's not surprising that few young blacks have any interest in their American roots, in the gospel chants, worksongs, ragtime, country blues and boogie, big band swing, and L.A.-bred R&B that formed the strand that led to the current butt-waggling, boom-bass astringency of "soul music". That old black music was forged in dark times, so forget it and get with the here and now! Those old black sambos, living in the soft surroundings that Geoff and I were witnessing, were just fossils! And maybe we, the documentary film-makers, were mere mouldy figs, digging up a music that was dead, and that was the reason we dug it: because it's now harmless – full of delight and quaintness but lacking the fearful social conditions that inflamed it in the first place and made it powerful, urgent and immediate for blacks of the forties; and later (as a catsup pop flavour) for young whites of the fifties.

Well and good. Such soul-searching is necessary if only to clear away the dead wood of such arguments. The stark fact remained: we liked this forties R&B as good music. Stripped of its lurid history and contemporary conditions – of stories concerning a leeching entertainment industry, of royalties unpaid and a million breached promises – the music of Joe Liggins, Charles Brown, Big Jay McNeely, Lowell Fulson, and Big Mama Thornton (the "legends" of our film) remains fresh and wondrous – and valid as pure music.

This pure music was pouring out towards us still as we stood on that South Wilton Place lawn and listened to the piano of Lloyd Glenn, Texas-bred so many years ago. And yet, pure music aside, there was a plangency that bespoke tales, myths, legends and facts, and I felt a need to find them, assemble them and tell how this past connects with the world we live in now.

*   *   *

In the beginning was Africa, but what exactly the unwilling black immigrants brought with them musically to America is not clear. We have to rely on the written word and note, and how can these capture the wild celebration of the passing moment as an echo of eternity?

The blacks were the invisible Americans, fashioning their own way of life out of poverty and oppression, forced socially into their own compound - be it plantation shack or city ghetto. And around them in this vast land, this yet unravished woman, was growing a salad bar of all manner of different races and cultures (known to stay-at-home Europeans as the riff-raff of the world) with their special accents and speech patterns and cookery and ways of walking, talking, dancing. So that by the end of the nineteenth century America was a-buzz with the folklore chatter of peoples untainted by the strictures of High Culture, of Grand Opera and European classical music. So that the land was full of chatter-music that was an extension of the lives of working folk – be that music jig and reel from the British Isles, military march from Germany, polka from Poland, Neapolitan melody from Italy. Infecting all this lively folk salad so that it tossed and turned in ecstasy was the polyrhythmic beat of the ex-African.

By the end of the century there was a name for this weird, exotic, but delicious *beat*: ragtime. But that name had been given to the new rhythm music by an equally new industry: Tin Pan Alley, the New York-based pop music factory that machined off-the-peg pop for all occasions, marketing it to those new city masses who needed instant music for recreation.

Tin Pan Alley could produce dreamy ballad or lively two-step or topical song. Whatever the market demanded. But in the years before industrialisation there had been little division of demand. Blacks and whites (outside of "respectable" society) had enjoyed, and been influenced by, many different ethnic musics. Songs and dances from the British Isles, the culture treasures of the "white trash" descendants of indentured servants, had been absorbed into black music (for example, the harmony of the blues; and elements of the Lancashire clog dance in black "buck and wing" tap-dancing). European popular songs had formed the basic music of the immensely popular "nigger minstrel" shows. And the German march had provided the form for the otherwise black contribution of ragtime.

But with pop music industrialisation came division. Special material for special peoples. In the era of sheet music this was hard to achieve – the written score couldn't trap the feeling, the raw emotions, of true folk music. With the invention of sound recording on cylinder and disc it became possible to trap these wild and wonderful passing moments and market them to the appropriate ethnic groups. By the 1910s the record companies, based – like show business – in New York, realised that it was ragtime that paid the bills; by 1919 they were selling ragtime's child, entitled "jass" (later spelled "jazz"); in 1920 Mamie Smith's "Crazy Blues" on OKeh Records started a craze for blues so sudden that *Metronome* reported, "Every phonograph company has a colored girl recording blues."

And so, by the middle 1920s, American pop had been "streamed". The warehouses stored stacks of records labelled "Race" for the newly-discovered Negro market, "Songs of Hill and Dales" or "Old-Timey Favorites" for the newly-discovered hillbilly market, and "Pole", "German", "Serbo-Croatian", etc., for the rest.

This was the age, in the black market, of the classic blues singers – big women like Bessie Smith, Sippie Wallace, Ma Rainey, and Ida Cox belting out vaudeville blues to studio jazz band accompaniment. But by the thirties the record companies had ventured out into the field itself to seek raw and un-tapped talent, and they returned with all manner of music from jug and kazoo bands to washboard rhythms, lone harmonicats – and the odd genius like Robert Johnson who was here today and gone with the wind tomorrow, pursued by hellhounds as the blues fell like hail around him. But it was the guitar-picking of Blind Lemon Jefferson and the casual crooning of Leroy Carr that had more immediate influence on embryonic blues artists growing up on farm and in ghetto.

Into the cities poured more and more blacks, eager to escape the boredom, drudgery and racism of rural life. They despised all that old down-home corn and cottonfield blues moaning; they wanted music that was more redolent of fast-paced city life – albeit black ghetto life with its own kind of boredom, drudgery and racism. The music they supported was high-speed big band bashing that you could strut your stuff to, jitterbugging in couples or sometimes breaking away to do some solo flash dancing, clad in your shiny derby hat and tight bumhugging jacket. Clothes, fast cars, fast women, jive talk – all these desired objects were reflected in the songs and dances and atmosphere to be experienced at the Savoy Ballroom, New York, when there was a Battle of the Bands between Chick Webb and the Savoy Sultans, and then maybe Cab Calloway would turn up in the very latest drape suit and wide-brimmed fedora and flash some smiles and gold rings to display American success. It was here that Real America – the brash, the loud, the vulgar – was celebrated, here that high-energy music was pulsed and pumped out to enable city blacks to siphon off their frustrations in a sea of righteous sweat. How ironic that the energetic style of Real America was displayed by Jailed America!

At its height, in the late thirties, the Savoy Ballroom housed the hippest dance audience in the world. The big test for any band was to win the approval of those black hepcats. The trick in winning a band-battle was to dream up a set of crazy riffs that built and built throughout a set of blues choruses until they chased away competition and whooshed everybody up in a tornado twister to an azure heaven. This moving staircase had been laid long before in the black brimstone gospel churches of the 19th century.

The black big band rhythm scene was bopping in other cities as well as New York – Chicago, and especially in Kansas City where the traditional Old South met the antsy, ballsy New North. K.C. was a wide-open town under the Boss Pendergast regime and it had bred Bennie Moten, Count Basie, Ben Webster, Coleman Hawkins – and boogie-woogie piano ace Pete Johnson. "Roll 'em Pete, we gonna jump for joy," yelled Joe Turner, bartender and blues shouter at a dive near the notorious red light 12th Street district (setting of the ragtime era's "12th Street Rag"). The K.C. jump blues and boogie trailed no hellhounds or back porch plantation blues moans. The New Negro was through with forelock tugging, back bent shuffling, servitude. "Jump for Joy" was the slogan, and boogie-woogie train trundle was the exact music for those hopeful times.

Boogie's progressive beat reached out and touched the mainstream pop public via John Hammond's 1938 "Spirituals to Swing" concert in New York's famed classical music shrine Carnegie Hall. Here Joe Turner and Pete Johnson were joined by boogie pianists (and taxi drivers) Albert Ammons and Meade Lux Lewis for an eight-to-the-bar orgy that was to set America on a boogie craze that rolled right into the Second World War. White swingers like Freddy Slack and Tommy Dorsey scored instrumental hits with boogie-woogie, while the Andrews Sisters caught the war spirit with "The Boogie-Woogie Bugle Boy From Company C". The new rhythm fed the burgeoning jukebox business and helped revive record sales (which had slumped during the Depression). Local "one-lung" radio stations, unaffiliated with the big New York networks, were starting to feature all-record shows, guided by "disc jockeys", as an economy measure and in response to listener appreciation; and these listeners were requesting more and more of the basic stuff and less and less Broadway/Hollywood show tune sophistication. Less Jerome Kern and Cole Porter, more Bob Wills and Slim & Slam. The latter duo had hit the race record charts with their novel nonsense song, "Flat Foot Floogie (With The Floy Floy)". Magazines and newspapers picked up on this black underground "jive talk" and published articles explaining "basic swinglish". Socially, things were easing up a little for Negroes: more clubs were opening for mixed audiences, some big swing bands (like Benny Goodman's) employed coloured players; and in the coming war Negroes were to have their hopes raised for complete emancipation. There's nothing like a war to effect big social changes.

The new hilarity and hope was best epitomised by the success of Louis Jordan and his Tympany Five. In 1936 Jordan had been playing sax and singing the odd novelty song with Chick Webb's band at the Savoy. Two years later he'd organised a stripped-down swing band, the Tympany Five, and was winning raves from all colours and classes in clubs and lounges. A smart white manager fixed him a contract with Decca and from 1938 till the early fifties Jordan's shuffle-beat fun songs like "Ain't Nobody Here But Us Chickens", "Knock Me A Kiss", and "Caldonia", were to hit high in the trade magazine race charts. The light beat tripped along gaily, the sax tootled, and Jordan narrated high-speed tall tales from the minstrel tradition of Deep Arkansas razorback hog country where he'd grown up. Self-deprecating stories of chicken-stealing, high jinks at the Saturday night fish fry till the "poelees" arrived, and all told hoarsely through big lips and bug eyes. Decca dubbed him the "Modern Bert Williams".

All these elements were to be mixed into the brew that became R&B in L.A., but there was another element that came roaring in from the South-West, particularly from Oklahoma and Texas. Down there, during the thirties, a looser and more fundamental beat music had been developing, free from the restrictions of the East as dictated by mainline show business. From Houston came the Milt Larkins Band, a frenzied aggregation playing arrangements from the ear and not from the written score, featuring the screaming and honking saxes of Illinois Jacquet, Arnett Cobb, and Eddie "Cleanhead" Vinson. To a solid thumping drum on the back beat these saxmen would worry that note till it was theirs to take higher and higher, till they were screeching with a religious fervour that put you in mind of those black gospel preachers hollering up a hot sermon. Illinois Jacquet came West, was picked up by Lionel Hampton, and in 1942 was released on shellac to impress saxmen and horrify cerebral jazz critics with his monotone honking on "Flying Home", truly a seminal record in the history of the honking sax.

This untramelled South-West of the thirties was also breeding the sound of the amplified guitar, soon, like the angry sax, to be an important element in West Coast R&B. It had been the hillbillies who'd first hooked up loudspeakers to their guitars; for example, Bob Dunn of Milton Brown's Brownies had electrified his guitar in the early thirties and was playing that wonderful hybrid of traditional country hoedown, New Orleans jazz, Alley pop, and black blues, that soon became dubbed by the record business as "Western Swing". These Western dance bands were popular on local radio and record and made many appearances in Oklahoma. Cross-fertilisation went to work and young black Charlie Christian was inspired to electrify his guitar, in Oklahoma City in 1937. Christian concentrated on single note picking at high volume to even out the score with the loud swing band brass and was soon elevated to the Benny Goodman outfit where he revolutionised jazz guitar.

Meanwhile, Texan T-Bone Walker went electric and applied the new technology to blues performances. Walker held a fine blues diploma: he was lead boy for Blind Lemon Jefferson in the Dallas streets of 1920; toured in medicine shows with blues queens Ida Cox and Ma Rainey in the early thirties; and later solo guitared with Milt Larkins and Cab Calloway. By this time he was singing, too – in the lazy laid-back style of Leroy Carr. By the late thirties he was established in Los Angeles, playing places like the Little Harlem Club, and in 1942 a new independent label called Capitol recorded him singing and playing an early version of "Stormy Monday Blues". With his lean, astringent guitar lines – punchy phrases, every note urgently stated, blue notes bent and wobbled and made to cry – and his advanced chording and smooth arpeggiated runs, he was to be the prime influence on almost every future R&B guitarist. And on stage he proved himself to be a great showman – slinging his axe between his widespread legs and aiming like a submachine gunner, picking out great licks even when he had the machine slung on his back.

*   *   *

The scene is shifting to the West Coast, to L.A. The basics of R&B had been formed in the East and South-West, and now the new audience was moving from Texas and Oklahoma and Kansas into California. In 1880 there were but 188 blacks in L.A. county; by 1935 there were a few thousand; in 1940 the census reported more than 75,000, but most of these had come from the poorest areas of Mississippi and Alabama. It was only in the Second World War, when the war industries needed more skilled workers, that blacks (and whites) from Texas and Oklahoma were attracted into Los Angeles. The whites, the "Okies", staked out their territory, like Southgate and Bellflower, and the blacks moved into the traditional Watts – once known as "Mud Town", but, for all that, a pleasant leafy spot where doors could be left unlocked without fear of burglary – and into South Central L.A. It was, of course, an exchange of one ghetto for another, but it was less openly brutal than the Jim Crow-land of their origins. The sun shone almost every day, it was hard to actually starve, there were cotton fields in the nearby San Joachim Valley, race hatred was filtered off onto other ethnics like the Mexicans and Japanese. And it was possible to be a successful black businessman: since the teen years there had been black wealth in such businesses as real estate and hog farming – and music. There had been Sunshine Records in Culver City in the twenties, releasing such records as Kid Ory's "Ory's Creole Trombone"; in the thirties Leon and Otis René started Exclusive Records with money from their hits "When It's Sleepy Time Down South" and "When The Swallows Come Back To Capistrano"; and there was Old Man Fulbright, who could pass for white, and had once played banjo for Ma Rainey and Frankie "Half Pint" Jaxon down in bayou country. Now, in his backyard, he'd set up a press to squeeze out records from a mixture of sand, cardboard and a little shellac.

True, it was nickels and dimes stuff compared with the New York major labels and their smart record stores, but a good living in specialty music could set up a home in a nice neighbourhood away from the ghetto in what blacks termed the "green lawn" section. In 1947 Horace Cayron, a black writer, noted that many blacks had "purchased attractive private dwellings in nice quiet neighbourhoods" and that "people up and down Central Avenue seem very happy". By 1950 there were 200,000 blacks in L.A., and by 1965 that number had increased to 650,000 – but only 21,000 lived outside the city's central district and two-thirds lived in Watts. So there was still the geographical segregation and in August 1965 anger at the slowness of the realisation of the American Dream erupted in the Watts riots. The black middle class was quick to condemn this uprising and, in truth, its origins were more economic than social. By the late seventies a calm had settled on Los Angeles as it became the most racially-mixed city in the world, a true "rainbow coalition".

And in 1980 I moved into Altadena, a suburb of L.A., to find myself in a street where middle-class blacks and whites live next door to each other and there is no crime, no tension, no misunderstanding: except, perhaps when my grass has lain uncut for too long; and when I am gently reproved by the black preacher next door for pounding out piano blues a little too loudly. The question is – in this atmosphere of growing affluence in a rainbow coalition, what sort of pop music results? Pretty bland and mindless, I'm afraid. But as a historian of R&B I'm not obliged to deal with the muzak of today. What is evident from a study of the L.A. of the forties is that geographical segregation and relative economic security produced a special kind of black pop music: rhythm and blues. It was a music of fast-moving action, of Saturday night functions, of dancing and drinking and high spirits to a low-down beat. It was good-time music to set the feet tapping and the body pulsing. And when it was spread via radio to the white teen majority, R&B was to be one of the fundamentals of rock 'n' roll. Today it is part of the world's music.

But back to the caged stage: L.A., city of dreams on the edge of the last frontier, cosmopolitan yet divided into racial sections; a new army of black war worker immigrants from the South-West; a new audience free of the old cotton-field moan blues, yet not satisfied with the convoluted bebop jazz of Charlie Parker and Dizzy Gillespie or the huge arrays of business-suited big bands with their sugar-clogged chords. An audience with record players in their stucco ghetto homes, a dance-hungry crowd with clubs, bars and theatres, a world war that promised to sweep away the old inequalities and iniquities. A new market for a new business!

By 1945 the big bands were rapidly becoming economically impossible. Tin Pan Alley's monopoly of pop music had been broken by the radio industry. And *Billboard* was not only running a "Harlem Hit Parade" but also a list of "Most Played Jukebox Race Records". One of the hottest discs in both sections was a ballad recorded in an L.A. garage and released on an obscure label, Gilt Edge of 500 North Western Avenue. "I Wonder", crooned by Private Cecil Gant ("The G.I. Sing-sation") to his own boogie piano, was soon selling 100,000 records a week, and stayed on the Harlem Hit Parade for twenty weeks. This "Sepia Sinatra" had busted the market wide open.

Now, with wartime restrictions on shellac lifted, it was possible for small independent record companies with tiny overheads to corner the new market, a market neglected by the major labels. The black René brothers were joined by the white Mesner brothers with Aladdin, the Bihari brothers with Modern, Mr and Mrs Reiner with Black & White, Art Rupe with Atlas and then Specialty. The label bosses themselves would scour clubs like the Chicken Shack, Club Plantation, Club Alabam, Cobra Club, in search of talent. Art Rupe would even attend gospel services in the hopes of securing a certain back-beat swing coupled with a "churchy feel" that he felt he could score. He found it eventually in a hole-in-the-wall "after hours" dive in Watts where Roy Milton and his Solid Senders were jamming tight blue jump numbers after an evening of grinding out background pop at a white nightclub in Hollywood. "RM Blues", polished but gutsy, became an instant national race hit in 1945. That same year the Renés released "The Honeydripper" by another local combo, Joe Liggins and his Honeydrippers. Both bands were lean in numbers but fat in sound, and very, very, together – most musical. What need for big band bashing or down home solo guitar moping when these stripped action groups could call the right tune for the right era and the right public?

Soon the little L.A. labels had gathered their own house arranger/producers – Jake Porter, Maxwell Davis, Johnny Otis, Lloyd Glenn. Soon their product was being shipped not only to the regular central city record stores, shoe-shine stalls and hamburger stands, but also to hungry jukebox distributors around the country. But it took radio to finally spread the new music to a white audience. In L.A. Hunter Hancock, a white disc jockey, had run a Sunday show aimed at black listeners since back in 1943. By 1949 he had a regular weekly show spinning the new music under advice from a representative of Modern Records. On 25 June of that year *Billboard* dropped the term "Race Records" and started a "Rhythm and Blues" chart. In 1951 a teenager, Dick "Huggy Boy" Hugg got a job spinning R&B records from a radio remote at Dolphin's Record Store, deep in the heart of the Central Avenue black district. There were lots of calls from white teenagers in the San Fernando Valley, a white compound. There were lots of requests for obscure records at the big stores.

This pattern was being repeated in the East where Alan Freed, first in Cleveland and then in New York, on a powerhouse station, was playing R&B while pounding his gloved fist on a telephone book – and shouting about "rock an' roll". Mainstream pop was quick to cover R&B hits like "Sh-Boom" and "Ko-Ko-Mo" with records in the old crooning close harmony style. But Bill Haley's cover of Joe Turner's "Shake, Rattle And Roll" had a sound of its own – a little Louis Jordan, but also a little country and western boogie too. And when Elvis Presley struck with versions of blues songs like "That's Alright" and "Hound Dog" there was no question that here was a special, new sound.

The rock 'n' roll bonanza passed by West Coast R&B without really letting it win any prizes. Johnny Otis (via his group the Three Tons of Joy) made the British charts with his rocked-up version of the twenties oldie "Ma! He's Making Eyes At Me", but apart from that, none of the legends in our film had pop rock hits, although sometimes their songs were honourably recorded by Elvis. But it was West Coast R&B that breathed fire into the instrumental rock 'n' roll of the fifties, just as it was Mississippi country blues and electric Chicago blues that inspired heavy rock groups of the late sixties like Cream and Led Zeppelin.

Our L.A. legends had to wait till the late seventies for a local revival of interest in their contribution to American pop. And by that time many were in semi-retirement: Johnny Otis had become a preacher and politician, Big Jay McNeely (once king of the honking sax players) was a mailman, and Joe Liggins was a piano bar entertainer in a marina complex.

Meanwhile Lloyd Glenn, born in San Antonio, Texas, in 1909 and a key session pianist and A&R man for pioneering R&B labels in the L.A. of the forties (whom Johnny Otis credited with being one of the fathers of rock 'n' roll) – meanwhile Lloyd Glenn had finished playing his mournful version of "How Long Blues", and was peeking at us between green baize curtains from the gloaming of his rambling great Wilton Place home.

Soon bells had been rung, peepholes peered through, bolts and chains released, and introductions made. In no time Geoffrey Haydon and I were sitting on a couch in Lloyd Glenn's lounge as he played us examples of the Texas barrelhouse piano style, the Pine Top Smith boogie-woogie, the Modern Jazz Quartet's baroque voicings, and his own Afro-Cuban shuffle tunes like "Chica Boo". He's a player, a well-rounded musician, not a theorist. He was dapper and immaculately suited. After a while he took us on a tour of his garden, showing us the painted rocks around the fishpond and apologising for the neglect of nature. He tours a lot in France, Germany, Switzerland. They appreciate his music over there. Back home he's a forgotten legend; known to his neighbours as a kindly old dude who often escorts his grand-daughter to the school round the corner, she in her neat pinafore and the dude in a three-piece suit.

It was easy for me, too, to see Lloyd Glenn as a dear old gentleman, a friend rather than a key factor in the story of R&B. Two years before this morning's encounter I had begun my association with the L.A. blues people. My entry had been gained through the guidance of one Steve Brigati, a blues freak who had suddenly appeared at my house from nowhere. He lived for the blues people, finding difficulty with the manners and mores of his own white middle class. He had 78 r.p.m. records of even the most arcane blues artists; he knew the first names of all the Smiths and Browns who'd ever given birth to a blue moan; he had their phone numbers; he knew I'd like them.

I did. But at first I was a wide-eyed fan and a little nervous – for as an ex-member of the British Invasion rockers of the sixties I was aware that the source of many of our pop hits was Afro-American folk music. But within weeks I had graduated, thanks to introductions by Steve Brigati, from announcer of blues acts at local cabarets to piano accompanist to the likes of Big Jay McNeely, Big Joe Turner, and Big Mama Thornton. Within months they had ceased to be "Big" in the sense of being remote and of an alien culture. They had become friends and musical associates. I had begun to see them as individuals, using their music not just as a means of making money but also as a way of self expression purer and more direct than painting, writing, movie-making. At times on stage there seemed to be no line dividing their art from their civilian life. They were pure self-expression, living works of art!

So let me detail a blues odyssey, towards a film celebration and testament, in terms of the individuals encountered. And the very first encounter was gutbucket basic, the most stunning example of how folk art draws no line between conversation and performance. It was at a cabaret club in Pasadena where Steve Brigati had posted me as host of a show starring Big Mama Thornton and Big Joe Turner.

The audience was all ages but all white. This whiteness is typical of today's R&B following. At the cabaret, Turner and Thornton, being no longer ambulatory, did their respective acts from chairs on the stage. During the second set they actually performed from a bench in the auditorium. They had been having an animated chat about rabbits, chickens, and errant lovers who return clandestinely by jumping through kitchen windows. Gradually, like a black baptist preacher-hollerer, the chat became musical, became a blues, and a new song was born. The *ad hoc* white backing band picked up the spirit and were soon grooving under the direction of Big Mama's stick and Big Joe's crutch. It was quite a learning experience.

And then, after they'd turned out their required hits – like "Hound Dog" and "Shake, Rattle And Roll" – Big Mama suddenly about-faced and went into a story about her recent accident and this story was transmogrified into a lachrymose gospel number. Big Joe showed his appreciation by banging his crutch on the floor and by grunting and swooping "yeagh-yeaghs".

It was a pity that Joe Turner was out of town (performing at various East Coast festivals) when we came to make our film. For Turner is the senior citizen of the blues shouting fraternity. Born in Kansas City in 1911, he was a singing waiter and bartender in the city's notorious 12th Street district from 1925 to 1935. To the piano of his friend Pete Johnson he put a raucous and rhythmic voice to boogie-woogie, as we have seen. In 1951 Atlantic Records, New York, signed him, and their clout enabled him to enjoy pop hits with "Chains Of Love" and, later, "Honey Hush". In 1954 he hit with "Shake, Rattle And Roll", but his lusty original was out-raced on the national charts by the Bill Haley cover. Rock 'n' roll success eluded him, as it did other R&B greats, because white teenagers, being conservative, couldn't identify with a black tower of power like Joe Turner, even if he had by then been acclaimed as the "Boss of the Blues" and the father of rock 'n' roll.

By contrast with Big Joe's city origins, Willie Mae Thornton was born and raised in the rural Deep South – in Montgomery County, Alabama, 1926. Real Jim Crow country and very rich in black gospel music. Her father was a minister, her mother sang in church. At fourteen she was touring the South in a black minstrel show called "The Hot Harlem Revue"; in 1948 she moved to Houston, Texas, and was recorded by the local label, Peacock. By that time she had developed a sonorous and authoritative "Empress of the Blues" voice and specialised in songs depicting males as timid mice or dirty rats. She had also won a reputation as a feisty battle-axe who could drink any man under the table and give as good as she got. Joe Liggins worked with her in the Houston area and he remembers the night she discovered her cigarette lighter had been purloined by some backstage lizard. On finding the culprit she literally shook him down – by holding him up by the ankles and rattling the lighter out of his pocket.

In August 1952 Peacock had her recorded in L.A. under the supervision of Johnny Otis. Jerry Leiber and Mike Stoller, neophyte teenage songwriters, had brought Otis the perfect vehicle for Big Mama: "You Ain't Nothin' But A Hound Dog", the randy man as a dog sniffing and snooping round the bitch on heat. The record hit Number One on the R&B charts in March 1955. When Elvis covered it the song lost its point – unless you saw Elvis as the sex object supreme. Yet as a slice of rock shouting with machine-gun drumming, it did have a certain abstract excitement. I bought Presley's version. But when Big Mama sings "Hound Dog" she's slow and easy and also menacing, smiling like a sabre-tooth tiger, her black diamond eyes glinting fiercely. Then, with the band in full roar, she leaves her chair to ambulate off in a swaying promenade that has a certain military regality, and the whole house cheers like loyal subjects.

After the cabaret show in the tiny Pasadena club I sat with Turner and Thornton in an elongated car parked outside and plied them with blues buff questions. But neither could supply me with the dates and facts required. With Big Mama I kept off the subject of royalties and record labels for I knew she'd been screwed too many times in the twilight underworld of "indies" and I had no wish to spoil a marvellous night.

Big Mama may not get writer credit for "Hound Dog" but she did write a classic in "Ball And Chain", which became associated with Janis Joplin via a hit record. But whereas Joplin's performance was always cultivated and laboured, Thornton's is straight from the heart with a punch to the belly. From out of the chaos of messy real life she fashions a beautifully structured and controlled performance that always contains an element of danger: whatever will she do next? It's a cliffhanger.

Lately she had not been well and had taken to performing seated behind a table on which were laid out her harmonicas, her cigarette packets, and a fruit jar containing spiked milk. She sometimes wore a voluminous African robe, sometimes boots and a stetson and always a look of malice aforethought. But I knew her better than that because we struck up a friendship after that Pasadena gig and a little later I became her piano man, playing with her at the Hollywood Bowl and assorted venues, including a flatbed truck in a downtown square. During off-stage moments I entertained her with Alley ballads such as "Mistakes" ("We make mistakes when we worry all over nothing at all") and she responded with comments like "That's the truth!" which infused these old warhorses with a new life and meaning. Circumstances and personality kept her ever close to the ground.

Also from a rural setting is Lowell Fulson, another star of our film. I had known the Fulson name (sometimes spelled "Fulsom") from label credits. His composition "Reconsider Baby" had been well cut by Elvis, while "Everyday I Have The Blues" had become B.B. King's theme. But I didn't know Fulson in person until my guide Steve Brigati led me out to the L.A. suburb of Gardena, the only town where gambling is legal. The venue was a neat but gaudy bar on a Sunday afternoon and Lowell Fulson came onto the postage stamp stage in a bright burgundy suit and frilly shirt. His beard was garden-hedge trimmed

Vintage Big Mama Thornton,
c. 1950

and altogether he looked foxy and French. But his guitar playing was full of lean and biting lines, few and well-chosen, shrill cries into a frosty clear night. His singing was far from a bar or cotton-field shout, though – it was mellow and croony like Leroy Carr. The normal white band backed him and seated in the red plastic booths was a sprinkling of older blacks all dressed up as if for a wedding. It struck me as a very polite atmosphere in which to dig the mean old blues. But I was still learning. And I was soon sitting in with him on piano and learning even more.

Lowell comes from impeccable blues roots. Part Cherokee, he was born in 1921 in Tulsa, Oklahoma, and raised in Indian country. His father played hoedown fiddle and Lowell learned country songs from a man who had once played with Jimmie Rodgers, the first country music star. Lowell was also imbibing the traditional folk blues and listening to records by Blind Lemon Jefferson, a seminal influence on future blues artists and a repository for black culture. By the age of fifteen Lowell was singing and playing guitar at country balls as part of a string band. He was also playing church socials, picnics, fish fries, and even white clubs (where he would play standards like "By The Light Of The Silvery Moon" and latest smashes like "Beer Barrel Polka").

But music couldn't support him and he had to take tedious jobs as a dishwasher, fry cook, hog butcher. He even picked a little cotton – but that was largely to escape the clutches of his then wife who detested the music life. Come on back home, she ordered, but Lowell went even further than those Deep South cotton fields and started rambling around the juke joints of Texas picking up coins by strumming out the country blues on a beat-up old box. When the war came he joined the navy and in the South Pacific he got his hands on an electric guitar and some Louis Jordan and Leroy Carr records. He became electrified and citified and he liked bands with horns and smart suits. After the war he settled in Oakland, Northern California, working by day in the shipyards and by night in clubs and taverns, still free from the wife's clutches. Records he made for a local black-owned label were leased to L.A. companies Swingtime and Big Time but nothing much happened till 1950 when his "Every Day I Have The Blues" became a national R&B hit.

Fulson moved to the Big Orange and Swingtime placed him under the artistic direction of Lloyd Glenn who nursed, rehearsed, and generally licked him into a polished shape so that records like "Blue Shadows" and "Lonesome Christmas" hit big. He was soon on the road cashing in on success, but Lloyd Glenn, pianist, was a stay-at-home family man, and so young Ray Charles, with his hair grey-streaked to resemble the notable Glenn, substituted. Glenn also taught Charles how to drive, it is claimed by Steve Brigati, my blues guide. "Reconsider Baby", Fulson's last smash, was released in 1955 when he was under contract to Checker of Chicago. By that time, however, the swamp wave of rock 'n' roll had submerged R&B. However, Fulson kept working and trying to change with the times. He's always liked big bands with lots of brass and smooth arrangements: he doesn't want to be thought of as an old-time country boy. In the sixties he had songs cut by Otis Redding, Joe Tex, and Leon Russell. In the seventies he recorded a Beatles song, went "heavy" with the Muscle Shoals rhythm section, dabbled in disco, and was lionised in Britain by the superstar rock brigade. He remembers going to George Harrison's house, or was it Jimmy Page's. One of those British dudes.

I got to play piano with Lowell at several badly-organised gigs in Hollywood clubs. We never seemed to have time to rehearse and frequently

Lowell Fulson

local punks sat in on drums, bashing away on that neo-Nazi first beat of the bar. Lowell took all this philosophically, but I tore my hair. Then we were asked to take part in a massive R&B night at the Country Club, a converted supermarket in the lily-white San Fernando Valley. Again there was no organisation – the promoter had recently been into "rock 'n' country" and after this show went into the croissant trade – but I had a chance to witness a "Battle of the Saxes" between exponents of the honking saxophone including Joe Houston, Chuck Higgins, and Big Jay McNeely. The last was easily the winner.

McNeely's act was outlandish, offensive to Western notions of taste, and hypnotic theatre. He began by rushing in from the back of the ex-supermarket braying maniacally, and these brays which became screams and then honks were all we knew on stage until suddenly there leapt into our group a figure in a black jump suit lit only by bulging neon eyeballs set in a ring of fire. And a shiny gold sax, going up and down and whirling round. Then he proceeded to lie on his back, kicking like a big baby crying for candy, and still honking. Very musically, too.

He performed one other number (it took up the rest of the night): "Deacon's Hop", a gospel-jazz-blues fusion piece that went round and round eternally. During this number he left us to go on an odyssey through the Country Club, stopping at tables and chairs and the laps of women to offer some individual sax therapy. He spent a good twenty minutes at the knees of Chuck Landis, the owner of the club.

This extraordinary exhibition of a perambulating "speaking in tongues" was nothing, as I later learned from Big Jay himself. In his younger days he had once spent a whole day repeating the good news of his honk note. It was in San Diego at a dance and Jay had departed for his "walk around" in the usual manner, leaving the band to bang away on a certain chord. The weather being clement and springy he decided to march out into the streets and down towards the ocean. Here he was arrested as a vagrant and carted off, tooting, to the county jail. Later the band received a phone call from the cops demanding removal of this madman. But the band was still playing and so a fan was despatched to bail out the star. Jay went back to his hotel, had a late supper, showered and changed into fresh linen, re-appearing on stage at around dawn to relieve the drummer of his interminable solo by rounding out the dance with a well-chosen sax note.

The man I got to know after the Country Club affair was nothing like the extrovert described above. Unlike Jerry Lee Lewis, Elvis Presley or Janis Joplin, McNeely knows that when the curtain falls he's back to being a private citizen – or he's dead. I wondered whether his sax blasting was a sermon and the club his church. I wondered whether his fevered screaming was "a conscious or unconscious projection of the postwar segregation of black people, an abysmal expression of the separateness of the black ghettos" (as Arnold Shaw wrote in his book *Honkers and Shouters*). I wondered whether Big Jay was in the great tradition of Al Jolson and Show Biz.

But Big Jay is not a man for verbal analysis or explanation. When I eventually got invited to his spruce and tidy little apartment on a clean and quiet side street of Wilshire Boulevard (near Koreatown) I found the saxist to be quiet, thoughtful, and given to long moments of silent staring into space through those billiard-ball eyes.

We talked records that day and I invited Jay to join me as a guest on an album I was making. He arrived at the session on the dot, dressed in the regulation grey shorts and shirt of an L.A. mailman. He'd just finished his daily round. But within minutes he was honking wildly to the backing track. And in subsequent meetings we formed a mutual admiration society, with Jay getting a kick out of my music hall numbers, just as Lowell had enjoyed learning Irish drinking songs and Big Mama had got into Tin Pan Alley material.

It was only through the published record and long investigative chats with Jay that I could piece together something of his background. Cecil McNeely was born in Watts in 1928 when it was a mixed neighbourhood, and orange groves and farms abounded. The few blacks in the county were made invisible as individual human beings and were only encountered as service workers: field hands, Pullman porters, domestics and janitors. After work they disappeared back into their own world in Watts and environs. Big Jay's mother worked at home on quilts and cookery while his father was swabbing the deck on the S.S. *Tango*, a gambling ship moored off the Santa Monica coast. Cecil was free to roam at will in black territory, but one night he strayed into a Long Beach café and was instantly ejected on the grounds of colour. "At least in the South they had signs spelling it out," says Big Jay, smiling sadly.

Early on he decided on a route out of this circumscribed life. He and his brother, in their teens, formed a band. His high school buddies had included such future jazz luminaries as Hampton Hawes and Sonny Criss; he was later to jam in Watts clubs with Charlie Parker. But the dense thickets of modern jazz were not for McNeely. He wanted to entertain, he wanted to make people feel good when he played. He started out in the world of show biz by wanting to make people laugh. As a comic he made an appearance at Johnny Otis's Barrel House club. Within minutes he was gonged off the stage. Next week he returned armed with a saxophone – and blew the place apart. A little later, while playing the Largo Theatre in Watts, he was spotted by Savoy Records talent scout Ralph Bass. They cut the gospel-tinged screamer "Deacon's Hop" and in 1949 it landed on the R&B charts.

Now Cecil became "Big Jay" and a star attraction around the theatres and drive-ins even outside of Watts. He was particularly popular with the large Mexican-American population of East Los Angeles. These "pachukos" in their drape zoot suits were not beloved of the cops and white folks. But white disc jockey Dick "Huggy Boy" Hugg presented Big Jay's crazy action show at the Golden Gate Drive-In, a pachuko hang-out, and all hell was let loose when Huggy and Jay raced around on roller skates, dressed in cast-off costumes from M.G.M.'s *Ben Hur*. They were both arrested for "exciting Mexicans".

After "Deacon's Hop" Big Jay had another hit in "Big Jay's Shuffle", but, like so many of the other honkers, Jay's style re-emerged in the shape of Bill

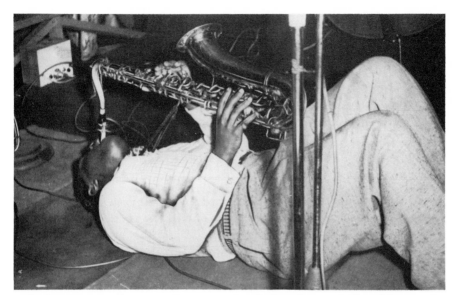

Haley's saxist, Rudy Pompilli. He too honked and squealed and lay on the floor. And we, the fans of rock 'n' roll, marvelled and gasped because we'd never seen Big Jay and we never did, in that era.

But Big Jay bided his time, avoided the drug and booze life of so many beat-music performers, attended Jehovah's Witness meetings, and eventually got a job as a mailman. At weekends he held court at a restaurant in nearby Orange County, a friendly neighbourhood joint patronised by old zoot suiters, blonde nubiles from nearby Disneyland, blue-rinse matrons, petro-chemical workers, coal-black firemen, and more of the rich stew that makes up Southern California.

The restaurant is called the Rim Ram, but when the neon's on the blink it's the Im Am, which lends a mysterious, Middle Eastern air. It was there that Geoffrey Haydon saw Big Jay perform. Geoff had arrived in L.A. the day before, all hot from a reconnaissance trip to Africa where he'd been setting up another film in the series.

Jay did his stuff, kneeling at Geoff's feet as he belched out his beat, and then setting off outside for his customary walk-around, and perhaps walkabout. After an hour's waiting we took our leave and motored off to a piano bar in the Long Beach marina. We had heard that Joe Liggins (of Joe Liggins and the Honeydrippers fame) was entertaining nightly at this distant venue. The marina was an endless concrete and steel sprawl and somewhere inside we found a hideous night-life complex of mixed and dubious design. And deep inside this complex we found Joe Liggins surrounded by pebble-dash stucco, shoved in a corner behind a measly spinet piano, almost hidden by the required oversize brandy snifter (in which a solitary dollar bill lay safe from the air-conditioned gale raging in the bar).

We had enjoyed "Saturday Night Fish Fry" and were sitting out "Happy Birthday To You" when competitive music – noise actually – broke through

Big Jay McNeely

and conquered. In the next room a punk disco evening had begun. It became impossible to hear Liggins and his poor little spinet so we went over and introduced ourselves. Joe, upright and businesslike but beaming benignly, sat with us and gave us his card. Oh yes, he assured us, the Honeydrippers are still very active around town, at Elks Meetings and American Legion Halls and Mexican-American weddings. "The Honeydripper" is still wheeled out, he smiled and sighed. "Roy Milton and I are accused of starting the whole R&B thing", he chuckled. "Willie Jackson's still with me – he laid down those baritone sax boogie patterns. It was the rhythm that kicked off R&B here in the forties – it's still blues, but it's dance blues with an earthy feel in the melody, phrasing and stories."

This is what the black immigrants from the South-West wanted to hear when they settled in Southern California in the war years. But it wasn't by any means the only music that Joe Liggins loved or played. He was born in Guthrie, Oklahoma, in 1915, and raised in what he calls a "church family". There was much singing around home and church but he was the only family member who got music lessons, on the piano. In 1932 the Ligginses moved to San Diego, California, and a few years later Joe was playing piano in local groups and teaching himself to read music fast and to arrange. He was soon playing and arranging for black big bands of the Swing era. He was also developing a taste for classical music.

In 1939 he left home and moved to L.A. He gigged around from big band, to small combo, to party pick-up group. He remembers playing a party with Illinois Jacquet and advising him that he'd get a more impressive bullfrog sound if he switched from alto to tenor. Jacquet did so – and the next thing Joe heard was "Flying Home". In 1942 Joe lashed together a series of riffs featuring his saxist friend Willie Jackson. "We had no name for the thing but

girls loved it; they flocked round my piano – I was a real ladies' man then – and I heard my drummer say, 'He's a sweet man – he's a honeydripper!' Honey*dripper*, mind – not a 'honey dipper'. That's a dirty name."

It wasn't until the band situation in the Second World War forced him into forming a small combo that Joe had a chance to record this "honeydripper" number. With two saxes, bass, drums, guitar, and piano he recorded the number for Leon René's Exclusive label in the spring of 1944. It was Number One on the Harlem Hit Parade in *Billboard* for six months in a row. It established the band sound of R&B. But Joe Liggins and the Honeydrippers, a band full of fine jazzmen like Willie Jackson and the bassist Red Callendar, showed that they had real musicianship on such subsequent recordings as "Sweet Georgia Brown" and "Got A Right To Cry".

A money wrangle caused Joe to leave Exclusive and sign with Art Rupe's Specialty label, where fellow Oklahoman Roy Milton had scored a race smash with "RM Blues", the same year as "The Honeydripper". Rupe liked Liggins the way he liked Milton. They were 110 per cent professional, they ran tight ships, they rehearsed, played in tune, were always at the date on time, and always got the allotted four cuts done to schedule. This, unfortunately, was rare in the blues world. Rupe and Liggins had their excellence rewarded with the hit "Pink Champagne" and Joe went on the road till the time came to settle for L.A. domesticity and the Elks and American Legion dates.

After our interview with Joe we whizzed on back to the Rim Ram club in time to catch Big Jay winding up another marathon "Deacon's Hop". Or was it "Big Jay's Shuffle"? Anyway, everyone was happy and exhausted and flopped out around the red plastic booths.

*   *   *

Margie Evans, the singer/actress/businessperson, had been helping us enormously in our enquiries concerning the whereabouts of local R&B legends. We had seen her first at a jazz club where she'd dazzled us with her classic blues renditions and her Empress of the Blues outfit and hair-do. Meeting with her backstage she impressed us with her business acumen and general air of complete "togetherness". A few days later we visited Margie in her spic and span house. We saw her surrounded by her "work centre" desk with its stacks of books on the music industry and on black history, with its sharpened pencils and active phones. We listened to her animated discourse on the black condition; we saw her on the line sweet-talking tradesmen and blues people. Then we witnessed her singing gospel in church and we heard her magnificent secular recordings with the Johnny Otis Show.

She became our guide: a sort of genial den mother, attending to contract details, copyrights, and the search for missing artists.

One of the most elusive artists had been Charles Brown, a blues crooner in the manner of the "Sepia Sinatras". A year before, led by Steve Brigati, I had seen Brown's club act at a South Seas Island joint in the heart of Watts. In a murky gloom dotted with papier-mâché palm trees Brown had delivered a classy show at the grand piano. His playing was impeccable, his singing a

mellifluous murmur, and he was dressed up in stiff white shirt and spotless tuxedo. Afterwards he sat on a threadbare couch and talked of his high regard for George Gershwin and Richard "Warsaw Concerto" Addinsell. Then I lost track of him: he'd been seen at this racetrack or that; residing with a certain lady, and then with another; he had no home; he was in New York.

It was the New York location that stuck me. I phoned and phoned but could never seem to reach him at his hotel or nightclub. And then Margie came into the picture and put her sweet lips to the phone and cooed Charles Brown into talking to us. Some of his elusiveness may have been due to much double-dealing by promoters in his past.

Charles Brown had had a melancholy life, full of awful visions and auguries of suffering and death. Born in 1920 he was soon an orphan; his grandparents raised him in Texas. His grandmother was the director of a Baptist choir, the only female director in Texas. She was a strong woman, and young Charles saw many visions of her after she died; she was always warning him of pitfalls ahead but she wouldn't be specific. Charles was prone to having childhood friends die young, like the six-year-old Octavia Green whom he'd groomed at a Tom Thumb mock wedding. They toddled down the aisle to a record of Gene Austin crooning "Tomorrow"; next morning Octavia was dead.

Charles liked that Gene Austin song. He learned it and later, when he was a star, he recorded it. He also liked pumping out Fats Waller piano rolls on his grand-daddy's player piano. He soon started playing piano himself, for himself. He liked to walk and drift on his own, whirling up visions of good and evil. He started dreaming up songs like "Alone And Lost In The Night", modelling his singing on Gene Austin and then later on Ivory Joe Hunter.

Margie Evans and (right) Charles Brown

Meanwhile he graduated from college with a B.A. in science and was awarded the Department of Science headship at the George Washington Carver High School in Texas. He cheered up here, partly due to the job and partly because he discovered the records of Louis Jordan. He adored "Knock Me A Kiss".

When the war came he served as a government chemist at an Arkansas arsenal. But asthma, encouraged by extreme melancholy, ended his war work. He headed for L.A. The streets were alive with scurrying people, everybody working hard, and relaxing in the active night life. Brown at once felt much better. He lived on Sugar Hill, a smart black neighbourhood, as a lodger of a Reverend. One day a fortune-teller predicted immediate success; at the time Brown was an elevator operator. But next thing he'd won first prize at the Lincoln Theatre talent night by playing "Warsaw Concerto" and a bit of boogie-woogie.

Ivy Anderson, a Duke Ellington vocalist, was impressed and gave him a job at her Chicken Shack Club playing slow tunes and light classics. This was classy and he met Bobby Short and Nat "King" Cole and Ivory Joe Hunter and Lowell Fulson. Private Cecil Gant was very sweet to him, too. These crooner acts told Brown that swank white clubs would go for his playing. He joined Johnny Moore's Three Blazers, a group modelled on the Nat Cole Trio, and they got a gig at The Talk Of The Town in Beverly Hills. Ritzy stuff, but the manager insisted on a vocalist. So Brown obliged and sounded husky, moony, and croony, full of self-pity, and this fitted right in with the postwar blue mood. At the Swing Club on Hollywood Boulevard a burly singer called Frankie Laine became an ardent student of Brown's. Later they got to record together.

At the Copa Club at dawn the gypsy's words became even truer: the Mesner brothers of Aladdin Records, led by scout Sammy Goldberg (known as the "Black Jew") came rat-tatting at the window and they soon had a contract ready. "Driftin' Blues", a Brown composition, came out and eventually sold a million. In 1948 Brown split from the Blazers after a quarrel, but went on recording his troubles. As a solo artist he had "Black Night", "Hard Times", "Racetrack Blues", and "Jilted Blues". He worked with producers like Maxwell Davis and the fledglings Leiber and Stoller. But rock 'n' roll success evaded him. He tried for it: he recorded in New Orleans with Fats Domino band members, rocking up oldies like "It's A Sin To Tell A Lie"; he was teamed with boogie ace Amos Milburn in the hopes of a hot duet for the teen charts. Nothing clicked. A few years later, oddly enough, he had a decent seller with a Christmas number on King called "Please Come Home For Christmas". The follow-up did OK but there was no earth-shaking for this artist who seemed to have all it needed to be a star. However, Brown maintained a reasonable standard of living by playing the clubs, increasingly in the New York area. The racetracks knew him and he had his doting ladies.

*   *   *

We needed an authority figure for our film, somebody who'd played a part in the development of R&B and could be articulate about it on camera. We had recently heard Johnny Otis, the "Godfather" of R&B, on the car radio, hosting his show on the minority station KPFK. He brought plenty of spare ribs and pig's feet to the show, plus a few blues veterans, some cooking records – and a husky articulateness. He was wont to state categorically that R&B started right here in L.A.

We had to track him down. We rang his church, we rang the political figures he'd recently been working for, we finally discovered he'd gone back on the road again. He had taken his show up to Lake Tahoe, a gambling resort on the California/Nevada border. This was good news for R&B (of the original variety) but it turned out that Otis's show wasn't playing a main showroom (those are reserved for the likes of Mack Davis, John Denver, or Frank Sinatra Jnr) but a small lounge, where people carry on conversations while the act is performing.

Geoff and I flew up to Lake Tahoe and tracked Johnny Otis down at his lodgings. From statements and photographs I knew that Otis, born of Greek immigrant parents under the name of Veliotes, was of white pigmentation. But Otis himself has always claimed to be black. Fair enough – if being black is taken as a state of mind, a society, a culture.

Perhaps to make his racial preferences as clear as a Fox's glacier mint, Johnny Otis was cooking up a mess of pig trotters, bull's beads, and collard greens in a greasy old pot on his motel kitchenette stove when we arrived to interview him. While the soul food banquet simmered, Otis sat us down on one of his beds and answered all questions of blacks, blues and history. We knew we *had* to have him set the historical scene in the film.

He was born in Vallejo, Northern California, in 1921. But he was raised in nearby Berkeley, in an integrated neighbourhood. As a child he grew to love the style of black life – the speech patterns, melodies, and rhythms; the cooking, the way of walking and relaxing; the music. He decided, in his teens, to be black.

In the early forties he got to play drums and vibes with local black bands like Count Otis Matthews. Then he did a stint with various territory bands in Nebraska; in Kansas City he joined the Kansas City Rockets and he came with them when they moved to L.A., settling as house band at the Club Alabam on Central Avenue.

In 1946 he formed an eighteen-piece big band after scoring a hit on Exclusive with "Harlem Nocturne". But next year with the big band business sliding into rapid decline, he took a tip from the success of cut-down outfits like Roy Milton and Joe Liggins and formed himself a little band with that hard-driving dance sound. He had all the ingredients, down to the electric guitar twang-bite and the snare-drum afterbeat *crack*. Always enterprising, he opened his own club, the Barrel House, across from the Watts Towers, in 1948. "Midnight In The Barrel House" sold well on Excelsior.

Thursday nights were talent nights at the club and Otis discovered many future record acts here; but he also frequented Watts theatres – where he discovered a teenage girl who was to become Little Esther and, under Otis's supervision, have a series of hits for Modern Records. As a producer Otis moved from label to label – it was tough getting your royalties – and on Savoy he recorded the Robins (a Barrel House find) who later split into the Coasters under the direction of those smart kids Leiber and Stoller. With the latter he recorded Big Mama Thornton on "Hound Dog". Then, in 1958, the Johnny Otis Show signed with Capitol Records and had a Top Ten rock 'n' roll hit with "Willie And The Hand Jive".

Out on the road in the fifties the Johnny Otis Rhythm and Blues Caravan toured the States with packages that contained such acts as Big Mama Thornton, Hank Ballard (who later cut the original version of "The Twist"), and Jackie Wilson (later to be Michael Jackson's favourite singer). He also found time to run a radio show and a T.V. show in the L.A. area. He seemed to have a tentacle everywhere in the field of R&B. But in the sixties, with Beatlemania, even Otis's bustling scene ground down to almost a halt. He forsook music temporarily to become involved in civil rights and politics. He wrote a book about the Watts riots of 1965. He became the Reverend Otis in the seventies. By the eighties, with the American show biz steamroller slowing down and a revival of interest among whites in black root music, Otis returned to recording, to radio, and to appearances.

*   *   *

So we now had our cast set for the filming of *Legends of Rhythm and Blues*. Next the Scottish film crew arrived and off we all went to shoot background material not normally seen in pictures set around Hollywoodland: of leafy green and tranquil neighbourhoods like Lloyd Glenn's; of a street full of wig shoppes; of Popeye's Fried Chicken sign slowly rotating high in the downtown sky in front of an ornate Roman Catholic cathedral.

Meanwhile the press had not been idle. We had fed them releases about our upcoming, and *free*, extravaganza of R&B legends to be held at the Variety Arts Theatre in downtown L.A. They responded with articles speaking of "Forty Years of Rhythm and Blues In One Writhing Night", "Englishman Gets To the Roots of L.A. R&B", and (mistakenly) "Boppin' For the BBC". Still, the spirit was right and we were told we could expect hundreds of fans.

On the big day, Saturday, 28 May 1983, the film crew and an army of technicians were hard at work from crack of dawn setting up their hardware down at the theatre – under the generalship of director Geoff Haydon.

At noon I was standing in South Wilton Place, near the Lloyd Glenn home. Margie Evans would be down in a minute to collect Lloyd and me. Somewhere in her great car would be Lowell Fulson. Then off we'd go to the Variety Arts.

In the clear, clean air of this lovely neighbourhood I took time out to reflect on how our recent experiences had shattered myths of black life: when we had originally told Angelino natives about our plans to visit black neighbourhoods, these natives, white and white-collared, were aghast, warning us of the dangers of stopping at intersections *down there*, let alone rolling down car windows or – heaven forbid! – getting out of the car.

This advice was all rubbish. We had enjoyed nothing but grand hospitality in the middle of notorious Watts, and at one cocktail bar there a demure young black eagle approached our attractive lady producer to ask whether he might discuss the pleasures of Stratford-upon-Avon, etc.

Besides delightful neighbourhoods and chance acquaintances, there were the memories of the blues people themselves, living legends who had become friends of ours. Memories of Lowell Fulson's rambling house on the hill near the oil derricks, where the master had regaled us with tales of playing "Piggly Wiggly Blues" in broken-down juke joints in 1930s Oklahoma; the house where he'd wondered to me just how his composition "Reconsider Baby" had turned out when recorded by Elvis in the late 1950s, and I'd replied that it was a pretty good record and played him a cassette I had of it and Lowell smiled benignly and took a drag at the gold holder that housed the black cigarette. Memories of Joe Liggins's tidy, tight bungalow in Watts, dominated by the hulking Hammond organ and the presence of this highly-skilled musician whose memory for facts and dates was excellent, and who, in his dapper sartorial state (complete with slippers) and with his love of Debussy and Beethoven, seemed a far blue shout from his sexy boast as "The Honeydripper". Memories of Big Mama Thornton entertaining a clutch of her friends with wine and song in her afternoon club – the interior of an experienced near-vintage Fleetwood sedan, parked forever outside her house. Memories of Big Jay McNeely's spotless bachelor apartment with its unguents and ointments and books relating to Jehovah's Witnesses; with its tankful of brilliantly-lit fish darting about pointlessly, and the nearby music stand stacked with Bach, and the well-polished flute.

Where were the myths now? Gone – but the music, vibrant and always immediate, we were about to celebrate. And, of course, Margie Evans was right on time, with Lowell Fulson safely ensconced in the back of her car. The three of us walked up to the Lloyd Glenn home. The two bluesmen hadn't seen each other for years. After they'd done a spot of joshing we were off to the theatre and the show. Big Jay arrived in his Volkswagen; the Joe Liggins band was already there, as was Mama Thornton (comfy in her dressing-room with a T.V. set and her fruit jar of that milk mixture).

We had expected an audience of hundreds. We got a crowd of thousands; the queue went round the block and then some. The fans were a perfect representation of Jesse Jackson's "Rainbow Coalition". I spotted the producers of an Elvis special, a tap-dancer from Josephine Baker's last show, a clutch of grey-clothed and cockney-voiced blues buffs from Britain. When the theatre contained 1,500 fans we had to close the doors – but it took our three hired cops to keep them closed, and later they had to call for help. But it was all in the name of fine music, a music that lifts you off your seat and makes you want to dance or holler or slip back into the American past. Whichever way you react to it there should be little doubt that the R&B that originated in L.A. in the 1940s can now take its rightful place in the canon of America's classical music.

The injustices of society had created a ghetto culture that had, in turn, created a beautiful and joyous sound of both escape and reality. We had tried to re-assemble those ingredients and document them on film. But were we

Big Mama Thornton
at home, May 1983

being too cut-and-dried in our historicism? All I know is that after the concert, in the upstairs W.C. Fields bar, I saw Big Mama Thornton* requesting "Underneath The Arches", Big Jay McNeely enquiring about classic ragtime, and Lowell Fulson singing Dublin drinking songs to anyone who would listen. I didn't stay for the "Hokey Cokey".

*Sadly, Willie Mae "Big Mama" Thornton died in Los Angeles on 25 July 1984, at the age of fifty-seven.

BIBLIOGRAPHY
SHAW, Arnold. *Honkers and Shouters: the Golden Years of Rhythm and Blues.* Collier.

RECORDINGS
Ball and Chain. Arhoolie Records 1039. Includes late 1960s recording by Big Mama Thornton.
Charles Brown. Route 66, Kix-17 – a Swedish label. Re-issues of Charles Brown tracks recorded between 1945 and 1953.
Honkers and Screamers. Savoy Records SJL 2234, distributed by Arista. Includes recordings of "Deacon's Hop" and "Artie's Jump" by Big Jay McNeely.
Hound Dog's Original Rock & Roll Memorial. Atlantic Records 8068. Includes the original 1953 recording of "Hound Dog".
Joe and Jimmy Liggins. Speciality (U.K.) SNTF 5020. Includes "The Honeydripper" and "Pink Champagne".
Lloyd Glenn: After Hours. Pathe Marconi 1546641. Includes the original recording of "Old Time Shuffle".
Old Time Shuffle. Black and Blue Records (France) 33.077 B. Recordings by Lloyd Glenn, made in France, including "Old Time Shuffle" and "Yancey Special".
San Francisco Blues Festival. Solid Smoke Records SS-8009. Includes recordings of "Blue Shadows" and "Reconsider Baby" by Lowell Fulson.

CHAPTER 4

Sit Down and Listen
The story of Max Roach

BY CHARLES FOX

Paradoxes abound in jazz, a very proper state of affairs for any art claiming to reflect the realities of life. Which means that nobody should be surprised to learn that Max Roach, one of the most buoyant and joyful-sounding of drummers, a man whose life spans a sizeable stretch of jazz history, was born on the edge of Dismal Swamp, an area of great natural beauty on the border between Virginia and North Carolina, yet bearing a name that Bunyan might easily have snapped up for one of the hazards in *Pilgrim's Progress*. Jazz encyclopaedias and other reference books have erred consistently in stating that the event occurred in Brooklyn in 1925. In fact it happened a year earlier, the place a farm in the hamlet of New Land, so-called because it had been purchased by newly-freed slaves at the end of the American Civil War.

Max Roach went into more detail while being filmed at Dismal Swamp for the television series. "The area where I was born is off the major swamp," he said, "but there are little swamps all through, which are even more dismal. And of course the men would go into these swamps and hunt. My father would stay three or four days, then come out with bear meat, possum, coon and so forth. And it's all farm territory. Where I was born it would be like Harlem but only of farm territory, inhabited completely by blacks. And all of them farmers." It was, too, an area full of Roaches. One of them, Mr Ivy Roach, founded the nearby Mount Carmel Baptist Church. And church-going played a significant part in the boy's musical as well as his spiritual development. His mother, a fervent gospel singer, was perhaps the earliest contributor to a career that makes Max Roach an unusually representative figure in black American music.

But the 1920s were hard times for farming. The boll weevil attacked crops. It was expensive to borrow money to buy food for animals. "That's why my dad and his brothers and cousins fanned out and came North," Roach explains. When Max was four the family decided to move to New York, his parents going ahead and then sending for Max and his brother. His father found a job washing cars and eventually turned himself into a self-taught automobile mechanic. Bedford-Stuyvesant, where the Roach family lived, was smaller than Harlem but bore roughly the same relationship to Brooklyn that Harlem did to Manhattan Island. It was, Roach recalled, a tougher district than Harlem, which at that time was still a centre for black writers and artists and intellectuals, the *dramatis personae* of the "Harlem Renaissance" that flourished during the 1920s and into the early 1930s, involving poets such as Langston Hughes and Countee Cullen, novelists like Zora Neale Hurston, artists such as Aaron Douglas and E. Simms Campbell. Upon the heights of Sugar Hill and along Strivers' Row dwelt Harlem's black well-to-do, including A'Lelia Walker, whose family's sizeable fortune had been founded on the Walker System, a method for taking the kinks out of black people's hair. Not long before, Harlem streets had witnessed processions by the Universal Negro Improvement Association, the first back-to-Africa campaign, organised by a Jamaican, Marcus Garvey. But by the time the Roaches reached New York the Depression was about to settle upon America, making life harder in Harlem – and in Bedford-Stuyvesant too.

"When parents went out to work," Max Roach explains, "the younger children would be left at local storefront churches, to be looked after by older women. My mother's aunt was one of those. She had been the pianist at the Carmel Baptist Church in North Carolina. Now she taught my brother and me the fundamentals of piano: scales and how to read church music. That would be when I was seven or eight." It was about that time that Max and his brother, who was two years his senior, joined a Boy Scout troupe attached to Concord Baptist Church. "They let you take instruments home to practice for things like that. I brought a bugle back but couldn't get a sound out of it. So I told the Scout master I would rather play the drums." Those were, too, years when house rent parties were a regular part of life in the black community. "A person would give a party and cook some pig's feet, potato salad, and maybe have some bath-tub gin. People would come in from around the block, contributing maybe five or ten cents each, helping people to pay a bill, or the rent, or to get some food for the family. So there was always a drum set and things like that around. During the day, when the older folk were out looking for work, we'd come home from school and fool around with those instruments."

After the family had moved to Gates Avenue they had a player piano as well. "It had been left because the family living there before us couldn't afford the couple of dollars needed to shift it. There were piano rolls too, of ragtime and stride piano. My brother and I would look to see where the keys went down and put our fingers in the spaces. Our aunt didn't approve of that kind of music, of course. She wanted us to play hymns and gospel songs." Max got his first drum kit when he was twelve, to mark his graduation from Public School 54. "It was just before Christmas," he remembers. "Dad went over to a store in Park Row in the Bowery. He bought two Chinese tom-toms, one cymbal, a high-hat, a snare-drum and bass drum. All the kids stood outside and listened to me play, all of them as cold as hell as I banged away on the drums. I didn't know what I was doing."

But in addition to "banging away", Max Roach had begun listening hard, especially to the radio. In Dismal Swamp he had heard blues ("I had a cousin, 'Cool Breeze', a guitar player who would walk up and down the roads singing songs, blues songs."). And there was hillbilly music, the precursor of country and western. But in Bedford-Stuyvesant he and his friends became fascinated more and more by the big bands whose music came out of the loudspeaker. And what they played, of course, was jazz.

*   *   *

A four-letter word in more ways than one, a bawdy euphemism for the act of sex. Quite why jazz – or jass, as it was spelt originally – was chosen as a name for the lively, syncopated music that sprang up soon after the start of this century is unlikely to be revealed at this late stage. The likelihood is that both activities were seen as signifying vitality. Yet that linguistic affiliation was only one reason why jazz was for many years despised, even feared, by a great many upright Americans, denounced in newspapers as a moral blot, ignored by musicologists and folklorists, even though they had documented the songs of the slaves. Among other things that made the music obnoxious to many respectable white Anglo-Saxon Protestants (the acronym W.A.S.P.S. had still to be invented) were its identification with blacks, the people on the bottom rung of American society, its employment of instrumental techniques that seemed perverse by European standards, and the way in which it encouraged dancing far removed from the formal movements of the waltz or even the polka, dancing that involved much gyrating of hips and torso.

Each of those characteristics was part of the African legacy that jazz inherited. White musicians were playing jazz at a very early stage, yet the origins of the music lay in the methods and the approach of musicians who were either direct descendants of the slaves or else of mixed blood, the Creoles. Perhaps the most distinctive of those instrumental techniques was a kind of vibrato eschewed in European music, yet common not only in Africa but in other cultures around the world, a way of paralleling some of the inflections of the human voice. The dancing, too, sprang from a different tradition to that found in Europe, but one set very firmly at the centre of the black American experience, just as it had been within the societies of Africa. Much was to happen to jazz. It was to expand its scope, to move from being a social music to become almost the dynamo behind the American entertainment industry; eventually it would be accepted as an art form, shedding at least a layer of the disrepute that had clung to it for over half a century. Yet throughout that transformation the music always retained a sizeable part of that African legacy, deriving from it a great deal of its identity.

Nevertheless, the European contribution mattered too. The harmonies used by early jazz players had their origins in the nonconformist hymns that were sung on the plantations. The rags which formed a significant proportion of that early repertoire had a symmetry and structure directly reflecting those of the military march, even the classical sonata. The most enduring, certainly the most symbolic element, the blues, came about precisely through the confrontation of two cultures. The "blues scale", with its optional flattening of the third and seventh notes – the fifth, too, quite often, usually in the minor scale – was what happened when slaves accustomed to African scales adjusted to European melodies based on the "well-tempered" system. So, at any rate, runs the most popular argument, although it may, like all this sort of speculation, be too simplistic. But in these and in other details jazz revealed itself as a fusion, decidedly Afro-American, ineluctably part of the New World rather than of Europe or Africa.

Conjecture occupies a good deal of early jazz history, even though the music began well within living memory. In the absence of first-hand documentation, the scholar falls back on the testimony of musicians who were around at the time. Not all witnesses were as wayward as Willie "The Lion" Smith, a sparkling pianist and composer but a maverick historian, who claimed that the blues were born in the brickyards of Haverstraw, New York. How both blues and jazz came about no longer seems such a tidy matter as was once thought. All the same, ragtime was being heard throughout America at the start of the century, and jazz – slightly younger – would seem to have surfaced first in the Southern states, taking on a precise identity, a set of formal disciplines, in and around the cosmopolitan seaport of New Orleans. The front line of trumpet, clarinet and trombone, borrowed from brass and military bands, first embellished melodies, then began improvising together more boldly. And the music was used for very functional purposes, reflecting the preoccupations of an entire society.

"There were countless places of enjoyment that employed musicians," recalls the guitarist Danny Barker, "as well as private affairs, balls, soirees, banquets, marriages, deaths, christenings, Catholic communions, confirmations, picnics at the lake front, country hay rides and advertisements of business concerns." Similarly, the musicians were often not full-time professionals but had day jobs. Zutty Singleton, one of the first great drummers, remembered that "they were bricklayers and carpenters and cigar makers and plasterers. Some had little businesses of their own – coal and wood and vegetable stores. Some worked on the cotton exchange and some were porters." It was not, needless to say, always as idyllic as it seems. There were, as Louis Armstrong and Jelly Roll Morton have testified, knifings and shootings and other sorts of violence in many dance halls and around the red-light district. Yet the music, whether played by blacks, whites or Creoles, had its place within something distinctly akin to an organic structure.

Ragtime pianists had already wandered across America. Jazz musicians were to do the same. In their case the movement was often linked to major shifts within the society, notably unemployment in the South during the First World War, which sent many black workers to Chicago and other Northern industrial towns in search of jobs. Chicago provided the outstanding example of musicians and entertainers catering for the needs of the black working-class ghetto that sprang up on the south side of the city. Blues were cultivated there by country singers and players; the piano-blues called boogie-woogie put down roots there too. And jazz underwent a major change: individualism set in. Louis Armstrong shifted the emphasis from collective improvising to solo virtuosity; Jelly Roll Morton imposed a composer's discipline upon the vitality of the New Orleans ensemble. Both trends were to be followed up elsewhere, notably in New York, always a key city economically, the headquarters of the song publishers and other manipulators of public taste. By now jazz had largely stopped being a social music, becoming instead an accomplice of show business, played behind drinking or dancing, in clubs or theatres or dance halls.

One development was typical of New York itself, where black musicians tended to be schooled, even middle class. That was the rise of big bands. In Chicago at the start of the 1920s, King Oliver's Creole Jazz Band had perfected a species of collective improvising, yet by 1926 Oliver had taken aboard a section of three saxophones. Black ensembles, in fact, followed the lead of popular white dance orchestras, adopting harmonised section work. Jelly Roll Morton, the first authentic jazz composer, had the ill-luck to excel at devising pieces for the classic New Orleans ensemble just as it was on the way out. Duke Ellington, on the other hand, the coming man, was learning how to create orchestral jazz that was both romantic and theatrical, just as Fletcher Henderson developed an interlocking pattern, brass vying with reeds in a kind of antiphony that some scholars have seen as foreshadowed by African practices – and, in the United States, by the to and fro between the black preacher and his congregation. Henderson also used that formula in the scores he wrote for Benny Goodman's Orchestra, thereby providing a matrix for the entire Swing era. Goodman's band, incidentally, was the first to make a star personality out of a drummer, Gene Krupa, who had grown up in Chicago and been influenced – just like Dave Tough, the even more remarkable drummer in Tommy Dorsey's band – by Zutty Singleton and Baby Dodds, two New Orleans drummers who had been part of that migration from the South. Among the finest black drummers around in the 1930s were Sid Catlett, playing with Fletcher Henderson and later with Louis Armstrong; Chick Webb, hunchbacked and diminutive but adulated at Harlem's Savoy Ballroom; and Jo Jones, using his high-hat cymbal and his bass drum in ways that allowed the Count Basie Orchestra to float in a way no big jazz band had ever done before.

*   *   *

Learning to play jazz is very much a matter of listening to what other people do. Whether that is done from radio or records or in the flesh, the process remains part of the oral tradition, a way of handing down the music; the way blues singers and folk singers – and, undoubtedly, African performers too – have always operated. It was how Max Roach set about his apprenticeship to jazz drumming. A gleam still comes into his eyes when he recollects some of the musicians he listened to on the radio and saw onstage. It happened again when he talked to Geoffrey Haydon about drum techniques. "Baby Dodds and some of those other early percussionists, they would play the song. They weren't trying to show how fast and loud they could play. And there were a lot of polyrhythms in New Orleans drumming." And he praised the old masters of brush techniques: "O'Neil Spencer with the John Kirby Sextet, he did wonderful things with brushes. And Gene Krupa, one of the finest brush players. You know, the brush was never supposed to leave the skin of the snare-drum. It's not used so much today because the record industry thinks it sounds like surface noise, so drummers use sticks instead." One thing he admired about Duke Ellington's man, Sonny Greer, was the elaborate kit he took on to the bandstand. Another hero was Cab Calloway's drummer, Cozy Cole: "He brought my attention to the rudimental military style. He was the technical man."

Sid Catlett (far left), Chick Webb and (above) Jo Jones – three of the major influences on the young Max Roach

Roach and his friends would stay up until the early hours of the morning, the radio switched on, listening to the bands – and especially to Count Basie's. "That would be around 1935, 1936, 1937. Perry Dubonski lived across the street. His father owned a little tailor shop around the corner. We used to have drum battles. His room was in the front too. So we'd open up the windows and just go crazy. I'd be Chick Webb, he'd be Jo Jones. Mother loved it because it kept us off the street. So she'd sweep away the neighbours when they'd knock on the door and say 'Mrs Roach, please!' Later on, when we moved to Monroe Street, our apartment had a small storage bin in the basement for belongings. I turned it into a little studio and put my drums down there. That's when I really began working hard." And foremost among the drummers he learned from were Chick Webb ("the first major drum soloist I know of"), Sid Catlett ("he had fast hands but what affected me was how he played the character of a piece, structuring a solo in almost a classical manner") and, most of all, Jo Jones.

"Jo Jones was the first drummer that I heard who played broken rhythm," Max Roach said. "He'd break the rhythm behind Prez – that was Lester Young, Basie's tenor man. You'd hear that bass drum breaking up the time. That was long before we started experimenting with all those different polymetres and superimposition of time, things like that."

By now Roach was attending Boys' High School. He was also drumming in teenage rehearsal bands that played Glenn Miller arrangements in addition to Basie and Jimmie Lunceford numbers. He even got gigs working behind fire-eaters and in sideshows on Coney Island, where Brooklyn confronts the Atlantic Ocean. One place he worked was the Darktown Follies: "We would literally play eighteen shows a day. We'd be on stage half an hour and off half an hour. At weekends we'd start at ten in the morning and go until four or five the next morning. Then you'd get off and look for some place to jam."

Roach was still only fifteen or sixteen, too young to get into some of the places he wanted to visit. He'd borrow his mother's eyebrow pencil and draw a moustache on his upper lip in order to get into Kelly's Stables or, later on, Minton's Playhouse. But no such problems prevented his attending the two big Harlem institutions: the Apollo Theatre, with maybe Basie or Ellington or Lunceford onstage, and the Savoy Ballroom, where Chick Webb ruled. Meanwhile he had begun studying privately: "He was a Scottish man who would never actually play the drums, except once in a while, but he could sing everything that was written and he'd say 'Play that'." The range and calibre of Roach's jobs had begun expanding too, particularly after America's entry into the Second World War, when many drummers, including Jo Jones and Shadow Wilson, got called into the U.S. Army.

"I could read music because I worked hard at it," says Roach, "and so I had a lot of gigs." By then he had enrolled at the Manhattan School of Music ("the poor kids' Juilliard") in East Harlem, only to have the percussion teacher tell him that his technique was incorrect. "The way he wanted me to play would have been fine if I'd been after a career in a symphony orchestra," Roach explains, "but it wouldn't have worked on 52nd Street. I knew that, so I switched to majoring in theory and composition." In any case, things were starting to happen. Jazz was moving towards a new phase, a way of playing that was more complicated in every sense. And the name it got tagged with may not have been bawdy but was decidedly offhand, even jokey.

*   *   *

Accidents have a way of achieving permanence. That was how the new kind of jazz came to be called bebop. A spontaneous quip, an onomatopoeic description of a rhythmic figure, turned into a label for the most momentous happening in jazz since Louis Armstrong burst upon the scene in Chicago twenty years before. And, once again, like so much in jazz history, it contained a paradox. Most bebop themes tended to be simultaneously rhythmic and melodic, a coincidence of purpose entirely in accord with African practices. The emergence of bebop also took place when black Americans – partly because of the United States' entry into the Second World War – were experiencing a new self-awareness, moving away from automatically aspiring to white values (the Walker System for straightening kinky hair is a splendid example), predicating a future where there would be no dubiety about black being beautiful. Yet in one respect at least bebop explored a musical element that was characteristically European. For alongside the new complexity of rhythm went an elaboration of harmony, a complication of chord sequences (the "changes", as jazz players call them). The ground-plan for improvisation became more demanding but also more stimulating, a situation calling for greater virtuosity.

Another aspect of that paradox concerned the way that jazz, which up to that point had been largely a functional music, satisfying particular needs while pursuing higher aesthetic ambitions of its own, now began moving towards the status of an art form, a decidedly un-African stance. Jazz began to be listened to more and more and danced to less and less, a trend accentuated – in New York, anyway – by clubs being asked to pay an extra tax if dancing took place on the premises. Among the new musicians were such extrovert personalities as Dizzy Gillespie, every bit as much of a natural showman as Louis Armstrong or Fats Waller had ever been. Yet Gillespie, too, adhered to the unspoken policy, a psychological shift on the part of the musicians, that performers should create the kind of music they wanted to play. If audiences liked it, so much the better, but that was no longer the first priority. "Sit down and listen" not only provides the film and this chapter with a title; it also sums up how many young musicians felt halfway through the 1940s.

What happened inside the bebop rhythm section had a great deal to do with the broken rhythms that Max Roach had heard Jo Jones using on those Count Basie broadcasts. Between the wars most drummers employed their bass drums for marking the basic four beats within the bar. That responsibility now got handed over to the string bass player and to the drummer's top cymbal, his bass drum being used for accenting, for sudden explosions ("dropping bombs" was the contemporary – and topical – phrase). Drummers found themselves with greater scope for reconnoitring.

The transition was largely engineered by Kenny Clarke, who had in fact worked alongside the youthful Dizzy Gillespie in Teddy Hill's Orchestra just before the Second World War. Hill fired Clarke from the band (it was not the kind of drumming he felt he needed), but when he retired from music and began managing a club – largely patronised by musicians – at Minton's Playhouse in Harlem, Clarke was the man he chose to lead the resident group. It was Hill, too, who described Clarke's accenting as "klook-mop music" (another venture into onomatopoeia), thereby providing the drummer with the permanent nickname of Klook. Minton's and Clark Monroe's Uptown House became places where, after hours, the more adventurous of the swing players, including the guitarist Charlie Christian, would trade ideas with such newcomers as Gillespie and Charlie Parker and Thelonious Monk. What went on was not so much deliberate exploration as a process of finding out where the fresh methods would lead.

Max Roach sat in at both places. Musicians around at the time suggest that his use of the so-called broken rhythms was lighter than Kenny Clarke's, seemingly more casual and less studied, as might be expected from a drummer who was ten years younger and for whom the new development seemed a starting point rather than a latterday discovery. Roach already had an individual style. Even when he was fifteen it had been recognised by Cecil Payne, a boyhood friend who later became a notable saxophonist; Payne claimed he could tell if it was Roach playing merely by listening from outside a club or hall. And Roach did in fact take Kenny Clarke's place in Coleman Hawkins's band at Kelly's Stables when the older drummer was called up into the U.S. Army. Hawkins had dominated tenor saxophone playing until the arrival of Lester Young, his tone warm, his approach based upon a keen awareness of harmonic potentials. That obsession with harmony made him the first player of his generation really to understand what the young musicians were up to. Roach made his recording debut with Coleman Hawkins's Quintet (it included the bassist Oscar Pettiford) in December 1943. He was nineteen. Apparently he became upset by the way the recording engineer insisted on muffling his bass drum by spreading a rug over it ("I objected to the theory that drums should be felt but not heard"). Two months later he was back in the studio again, this time with a Hawkins group that included Dizzy Gillespie, Don Byas and Clyde Hart as well as Pettiford. Two pieces from that session – "Woody'n You" and "Buh-Dee-Daht" – have some claims to being considered the earliest bebop recordings.

That year saw Roach consolidate his position. He worked at the Onyx Club in Dizzy Gillespie's group, then went on tour with Benny Carter's Orchestra (J.J. Johnson, the first bebop trombonist, was there as well). Carter's was the first big band Roach had worked in, apart from the teenage rehearsal groups and a couple of days when Sonny Greer fell ill and Roach took over the drum chair in Duke Ellington's Orchestra ("It was at the Paramount. Of course Sonny Greer had absolutely everything in his kit, but when I looked for drum music there wasn't a sheet of it anywhere. I was scared to death. Mr Ellington saw the panic on my face. He smiled and said, 'All you have to do is keep one

eye on me and one eye on the act and everything will be all right!' And then I realised he was a great conductor"). The job with Benny Carter had come about because Carter's drummer, George Russell, had respiratory problems and did not want to travel. "So he stayed in my bedroom at Monroe Avenue, working on his musical theories while I went on tour." That house saw other visitors too. "Miles Davis and Charlie Parker often crashed there. My mother always thought Bird was a nice boy because whenever she came in the room he opened the Bible and began reading it. He was great at sweet-talking her."

In the spring of 1945 Roach was playing in a quintet at the Three Deuces led by Parker and Dizzy Gillespie. By the autumn he was working alongside Miles Davis in Parker's Quintet. That must have been when Parker demonstrated his phenomenal command of rhythms. As Roach told Geoffrey Haydon, "He was sitting behind my drums and said, 'Tojo, can you do this?' (He called me Tojo because I wore these thick, horn-rimmed glasses.) And he did a quarter note on the bass drum, a Charleston beat on the sock cymbal, a shuffle rhythm with the left hand and a jazz beat with the right hand, all at the same time and comfortably, still with the saxophone lying across his lap. I walked over and attempted to do it, but I knew I'd have to practice it." Soon afterwards Roach went on a tour of the Southern states with Dizzy Gillespie's first big band, as part of a road show called "The Hep-sations of 1945". "They weren't ready for us," Gillespie recalled, "they wanted bands that played blues and that they could dance to. They said they couldn't dance to our music. But I could dance to it. I could dance my ass off to it." Roach

Max Roach with Charlie Parker and Kenny Clarke

remembers that they worked on what used to be called the chitterlin' circuit. "We'd go down to Baltimore, to Washington D.C., through Maryland, Virginia, the Carolines, Alabama, Texas, playing all black theatres and dance halls. There was segregation then, of course. But the only problem really arose if we had to get some food in an area where they didn't serve blacks. Otherwise we stayed in black homes everywhere. Everything we came into contact with was black."

When Charlie Parker returned to New York from California in 1947 he once again recruited Miles Davis and Max Roach. Both received $135 a week, less than they could have earned elsewhere, yet the honour and challenge of working with Parker meant more than money. "Bird's approach demanded new drum concepts," Roach recalls. "He set tempos so fast that it was impossible to play a straight Cozy Cole four-style, so we had to work out variations." And the first piece would always be the fastest. ("I guess it was one way of keeping us in our place.") The experience was so chastening that when Parker died, in 1955, Miles Davis made a wry joke: "He should have stayed around long enough for us to get even." But it enabled Roach's playing to enter into its full maturity. Part of the achievement was due to those leaders he had worked for who would not overlook anything that seemed imitative or too cocksure. "The night may have gone good," Roach told a radio audience in 1981, "you might have played a solo and everybody cheered, and you were playing your Jo Jones tricks and your Sid Catlett tricks. And you might act a little haughty about it all. You'd say 'Good night Prez' or 'Goodnight Mr Hawkins', and they might say 'Don't stumble, you might fall and hurt yourself.' Or 'You can't join the throng till you write your own song'." By the end of the 1940s Max Roach had done exactly that.

*   *   *

One danger of chopping jazz history up into decades, each reflecting a phase of the music's development, is that it ignores a great deal that was going on at the time. To describe the 1950s as "the cool era" makes sense when the musicians being cited are Miles Davis, the Modern Jazz Quartet, Gerry Mulligan with Chet Baker, or that flock of session men who earned their livings in the film, T.V. and recording studios of Los Angeles but also became identified with West Coast jazz, notable for its concern with European formality and purity of tone and the introduction of instruments – the flute, cello, French horn – previously uncommon within the music. Yet before the end of the 1950s Charles Mingus had begun his combative merging of blues and gospel rhythms, using fiery young soloists like the saxophonist Eric Dolphy. And two groups that emerged during those years, both led by drummers, could be regarded as an extension of the Charlie Parker Quintet, but using a tenor instead of an alto saxophone. Hard Bop was the name given to this latterday traditionalism. The Jazz Messengers were led by Art Blakey, six years older than Max Roach, a drummer whose aggressive personality comes through in the intensity of his playing and the way he dominates his sidemen. Roach, every bit as much a virtuoso, was prepared to be self-

effacing when backing up a soloist, a drummer who could respond as well as dictate. Those qualities became more noticeable when he began leading his own group.

Like Blakey, Roach has always delighted in working with trumpet players who possess strong musical personalities. Kinny Dorham played on the first record made under Roach's leadership, recorded in France in 1949, while Dorham and Roach were both in Europe with Charlie Parker for the Paris Jazz Fair. Roach crossed the Atlantic again three years later, as a member of Norman Granz's package show, Jazz at the Philharmonic. But at least part of the 1950s was spent working in California, with the guitarist Howard Rumsey, and, later on, drumming in Otto Preminger's film *Carmen Jones*. His appearance in that film was so fleeting that, so the story goes, whenever Charlie Parker visited a cinema to see his former drummer make his screen debut he invariably fell asleep and missed the vital few seconds. But quite a while before that film was made, the West Coast promoter Gene Norman had approached the drummer. "Why don't you form a band?" he asked. "So," says Roach, "I came to New York and got Brownie and we returned to California."

"Brownie" was Clifford Brown, once described by Dizzy Gillespie as "A cat down in Wilmington, Delaware, who plays piano and blows hell out of the trumpet." He had perhaps more potential than any other trumpeter of his generation, using a clean-cut tone to improvise solos that were both lyrical and impetuous. "He loved to practice," Roach told a *Down Beat* interviewer in 1958. "If we worked every night he'd practice every day." Roach's admiration for Brown was so great that he shared leadership with him, the group being known as the Max Roach–Clifford Brown Quintet. The alto saxophonist Sonny Stitt was in the earliest line-up, but his place was soon taken by Teddy Edwards, who in his turn was replaced by another tenor player, Harold Land. When Land had to return to California for family reasons while the quintet was on tour in 1955, they recruited Sonny Rollins,

Above left: Clifford Brown. Miles Davis (left) and Kinny Dorham at that moment on the brink of becoming one of the most outrageously inventive saxophonists in jazz. Roach and Brown asked him to join the quintet in Chicago, where he was living at the Y.M.C.A. They had to wait in the lobby, for when they arrived Rollins was in the basement practising with a seventeen-year-old trumpeter from Memphis, Booker Little. That meeting acquired a retrospective poignancy soon afterwards, for Little was to be one of the trumpet players who worked with the quintet after Clifford Brown – only twenty-five years old – was killed in a car crash on the Pennsylvania Turnpike, a crash that also caused the death of the quintet's pianist, Richie Powell, and his wife, Nancy, who was driving the car.

"The band wasn't making enough money for us to fly," Max Roach told Geoffrey Haydon, "so we used two cars. There were times when we would close, say, in Chicago around four o'clock on a Sunday morning and have to rush to Philadelphia, about a thousand miles away, to be in time for a four o'clock matinee. Oddly enough, the last job we played together was in Norfolk, Virginia, just a stone's throw from Dismal Swamp. Now I had no idea, prior to arriving there, that it would be a segregated club. We'd never ever played in a segregated club before. My relatives had never seen me work, so they came up – and of course we refused to go on until they let my folks in. Anyway, they were given a good table. In fact, they turned up every night – about five nights altogether. You could say we broke the colour line in that town at that time.

"After that we had two days off. Clifford, who lived in Philadelphia, had been asked by a trumpet manufacturer near Chicago to endorse some instruments. So he rang me in New York, telling me that he'd be leaving earlier. Which is why we weren't travelling together when the tragedy occurred. Usually we'd be watching one another in case somebody fell asleep. We'd blink lights and pull over and change drivers, things like that. It wasn't until I arrived in Chicago that the agent told me of the accident. Joe Glaser phoned and said: 'Well, Miles is in Chicago, and so is Roy Eldridge. Do you still want to make the job?' I said, 'No, I don't think so.' And we all packed up and came back East."

Roach was devastated by Brown's death, seeing himself as partly responsible. If he had been there, he argued, Nancy Powell would not have been allowed to take the wheel ("She wore glasses five times as thick as mine"). Sonny Rollins, George Morrow and Max Roach worked as a trio to finish off the bookings. Donald Byrd took over on trumpet and stayed six months, after which Kinny Dorham joined the group.

But Roach's grief was so intense that he began drinking more and more, to such an extent that he eventually went into hospital to be cured of alcoholism. "Around 1958," Roach says, "I got a phenomenal young player, Booker Little (the trumpeter who had been practising with Sonny Rollins in Chicago three years earlier). That was when I dropped the piano and added a tuba player, Ray Draper. But Booker had leukemia and died when he was only twenty-four. It was then I began to think I was a jinx on trumpet players. In fact, I stopped using them until years later, when Charles Tolliver asked if he could join the band.'' Both Clifford Brown and Booker Little had been active in jazz for relatively short periods, yet because of their exceptional talent and their youth the death of each took on a tragic stature. Perhaps, too, those events played a part in deepening Max Roach's character, causing the drummer to become more aware of the world around him. The 1960s were to find him taking up attitudes about issues that lay outside music.

*   *   *

Dismal Swamp was not simply a part of the scenery of Virginia and North Carolina. It was there, in 1831, that Nat Turner and his followers retreated after the failure of their slave insurrection. And the drawbacks of being black in the United States have not remained matters of purely historical significance. Bud Powell, one of bebop's pioneers, an early friend of Roach's, and the brother of Richie, suffered brain damage that was later to wreck his life when he was no more than eighteen. It happened, Roach claims, in Philadelphia, where Powell had just finished playing at a dance with Cootie Williams's band. It was 1943, a year when black protests about segregation in the U.S. Army and Navy caused serious rioting in Harlem, which spread to other parts as well. The authorities became edgy. ''When they saw black men congregating in groups of more than three or four or five the police would say, 'Okay, break it up.' Bud took issue with them and they beat him to the ground.''

The 1950s had already seen Roach joining forces with Charles Mingus. Together they ran a record company, Debut Records. And they organised an Alternative Festival to George Wein's official Newport Jazz Festival, using musicians whom they accused Wein of ignoring. They drew up a list of New York clubs that expected musicians to work in degrading conditions. They

Charles Mingus

also independently composed pieces that the French at that time would probably have described as *jazz engagé*. Charles Mingus devised "Fables of Faubus" after Orville Faubus, Governor of Arkansas, had defied a Supreme Court ruling and refused to desegregate schools in Little Rock (Louis Armstrong, normally a peaceable character, was stung into describing Faubus as "an ignorant ploughboy"). Roach occasionally went in for direct action, as when he sat onstage at Carnegie Hall in 1961 carrying a placard during a Miles Davis concert in aid of the African Research Foundation, an organisation with whose policies he disagreed. What have endured are the compositions reflecting social or political themes.The *Freedom Now Suite*, for example, was originally intended to celebrate the centenary of the Emancipation Proclamation of January 1863. Abbey Lincoln, the singer who at that time was Roach's wife, had put him in touch with Oscar Brown Jnr, a singer who was also a songwriter. "We never finished the work," Roach told *Cadence* magazine in 1979, "because Oscar and I were at odds politically about how things were at that moment in time. Historically we could deal with it, but where we were going we were at odds. His view was very ideal, mine was a bit more pragmatic – at least I think so." An L.P. containing the admittedly incomplete *Freedom Now Suite* was followed by *Percussion Bitter Sweet*, including "Tender Warriors", written for those children of Birmingham, Alabama, who had been killed by a racist's bomb, and "Garvey's Ghost", paying tribute to the Jamaican whose efforts at inciting Harlemites to be African rather than American ended in his being framed, deported and eventually dying in obscurity in wartime Britain.

"From about 1963 to 1968 I would talk a lot in clubs," Roach recalled. "I remember Max Gordon at the Village Vanguard would say, 'Max, I want you in the club, but I wish you wouldn't make those speeches. All we want you to do is play your drums and that's it.' I guess we were all kind of caught up in the fever of the moment." Nevertheless, Roach has continued to comment on events and activities that strike him as being important. On an L.P., *Chattahoochie Red*, recorded by his quartet early in the 1980s, he supplied a context of percussion for Martin Luther King's famous speech ("I have a dream"). "I didn't know Martin Luther King," Roach says, "but I was at many of his rallies and he was an inspiring human being, just to hear a speech or just to see his demeanour and the way he dealt with things. To me he was much like Paul Robeson, who had the same kind of magic." When Roach performed a version of this work for our film, *Sit Down and Listen*, he commented on the very musical approach that Martin Luther King took to speech ("I look on this version as a two-part invention, with genuine equality between drums and voice"). And the title of the L.P. refers to the Chattahoochie river that runs through Atlanta, Georgia, in which were found the bodies of black teenagers who had been murdered.

Roach, Mingus and other committed musicians of the 1950s and 1960s were not the first to be preoccupied by the history and condition of black Americans. The premiere of Duke Ellington's *Black, Brown and Beige*, extolling the achievements of Afro-Americans, took place in 1943, the year of the Harlem riots and not all that long before beboppers set about making their idiosyncratic stands against conformity: sometimes frivolous, like the wearing of berets and the growing of goatee beards; sometimes more profound, like the embracing of Islam (William Evans adopted the name Yusef Lateef long before Cassius Clay became Muhammad Ali). Not that Roach sees himself as anything other than an American. For him, too, jazz is an example of genuine democracy in action: "You know, a guy introduces a thing and we all get a chance to say something about it, to make something. That's what democracy is all about. Our music is a reflection of that."

*   *   *

Bebop proved to be not so much a musical revolution as a coup d'etat, a takeover by musicians with fresh ideas about rhythm and harmony. But the forms and disciplines remained very much the same, still employing 16- and 32-bar patterns (the layout of popular songs, in fact) as well as the 12-bar blues. Most performances continued to be in common time, with only occasional digressions into triple time (Sonny Rollins's 1956 recording of "Valse Hot", using a line-up identical to the Max Roach–Clifford Brown Quintet, is an outstanding example of the latter). The instrumentation stayed the same too, the prime differences being the virtual elimination of the clarinet (perhaps it was linked too closely with the Swing era) and the amplified guitar's arrival as a solo voice.

That state of affairs began changing towards the end of the 1950s. The major shift, pioneered by Miles Davis and the saxophonist John Coltrane, was towards the use of scales and modes rather than chord sequences – which had become tighter and trickier as bebop was replaced by hard bop. One result was a greater sense of space, also reflected in the drumming: Elvin Jones's polyrhythms, revolving around a basis of eight beats to the bar rather than four, were to influence young drummers everywhere throughout the 1960s. There were also innovators who at first seemed iconoclastic: Cecil Taylor, a pianist whose approach was both virtuosic and – for much of the time, anyway – atonal; and Ornette Coleman, ignoring chords altogether, playing free melodic lines on his alto saxophone, yet acknowledging a blues tonality and – another traditional touch – regularly using bassists and drummers who swung with quite old-fashioned fervour. On the whole, though, the rhythm section ceased to be a self-contained unit (Mingus had done a great deal to demolish that convention), bass and drums now assuming greater equality with the horns. The paraphernalia of rock music – electric pianos, fuzz-boxes, synthesisers – were also being accepted and integrated into jazz. By the 1970s it would not be extraordinary to find the saxophonist John Surman exploring technology in order to duet with himself onstage. Bassists launched into purely solo recitals and recordings. The notion of jazz having to be performed by trios, quartets, quintets or big bands was supplanted by a wider range of options. Similarly, the *lingua franca* that had prevailed in earlier decades, enabling musicians from different periods to jam with one another, was replaced – in the case of many of the newer performers, anyway – by autonomous activities, the players discovering new forms and disciplines through working together. Most significantly, perhaps, jazz no longer had its roots primarily inside the black community or even within American society in general. It now extended far outside, for the music had become a genuinely international art form.

The most publicised toyings with time signatures were those made by Dave Brubeck, whose quartet recorded in 1959 the popular "Take Five", as well as other pieces using unfamiliar metres. Max Roach has claimed, however, that in 1958 his quintet was already featuring a blues in 5/4, "As Long As You're Living", written by two members of his group, Tommy Turrentine and Julian Priester. Roach subsequently recorded that blues in 1960. Soon afterwards he moved on to a much more ambitious project, the album entitled *It's Time*, using 5/4, 7/4 and 7/8 as well as common and triple time, and employing an ensemble that included a sixteen-voice choir.

Roach has always been conscious of the political role that the church has played throughout black American history ("They organised the 'underground railroad' for getting escaped slaves out of the South. And the songs all presented a vision of freedom"). But he also felt the black church had rejected jazz. At the same time, Atlantic, his record company, was urging him to record material that would reach a wider public. His response was *Lift Every Voice And Sing* (the title came from a poem by James Weldon Johnson), an L.P. that also involved more choral singing, this time by J.C. White's Brooklyn Gospel Choir. The songs, pieces such as "Motherless Child", "Let Thy People Go" and "Were You There When They Crucified My Lord?", were either spirituals or gospel songs and each bore a dedication – to Martin Luther King, Medgar Evers, Malcolm X, Patrice Lumumba or Paul Robeson. That L.P. was also the first on which Roach worked with the trumpet player Cecil Bridgewater, whom he came across in Vienna, when Bridgewater was touring Europe with the band from the University of Southern Illinois.

Bridgewater was not only to become a key member of Roach's quartet, but also composed "Bird Says" (based on themes by Charlie Parker), a piece for double quartet – jazz quartet plus a classical string quartet – that is included in the film. Other pieces for that instrumentation include Roach's "A Little Booker", composed in honour of his former trumpet player. "Survivors", devised for classical string quartet and jazz drummer ("an abstract stop-time piece," says Roach, for whom it was written) is the work of Peter Phillips, an associate of Gunther Schuller, the composer and academic who was in fact responsible in the 1950s for coining the term Third Stream to describe music that more or less bridged the gap between European forms and jazz techniques. The original impetus for Roach's venture into this confluence came from his mother. "She was always saying 'When are you going to do something with your daughter?' That's Maxine, who took up string playing at high school and nowadays works as a session viola player. The first time we performed together was in a jazz mass at the cathedral of St John the Divine, here in New York, the largest Gothic cathedral in the world. She did Duke Ellington's "Come Sunday" as a solo."

The past decade has also seen Max Roach engage in a series of improvised duets, even though he denies that there is anything especially new about that. "It really all began back at the start of the 1940s, when I used to have jam sessions in the basement at Monroe Avenue. I'd be there with just Cecil Payne, or maybe Leonard Hawkins on trumpet. There wasn't room for more than two of us in that little cubbyhole." The latterday involvement began when Roach was in Paris at the same time as Charles Mingus and Archie Shepp. "Mao Tse-tung had died, so the Left all over Europe wanted to pay tribute. The three of us were asked to perform as a trio in Rome, but Mingus had to go back to New York. So Archie and I did it as a duo. I wrote 'Sweet Mao', in three parts. About that time there had also been a slaughter of students in South Africa, so I wrote another piece, 'Soweto '76'. We did another concert in Paris afterwards and recorded together." Partners in subsequent duets have included the multi-instrumentalist Anthony Braxton, the South African pianist Abdullah Ibrahim, formerly known as Dollar Brand, and another, very different pianist, Cecil Taylor, a confrontation as much as a dialogue, demanding stamina as well as inspiration. "With Dollar it's a love affair in a way," Roach says, "sympathy, empathy, politeness. But with Cecil it's more like war, although a kind of love-war. Very demanding, very physical. We never rehearse, we just talk. And I went to his house and looked through his record collection: Muddy Waters, Tatum, Miles, Monk – he listens to everybody. And he loves to go disco dancing."

But the musical enterprise closest to Roach's heart is probably M'Boom Re:Percussion. "I wanted to have a percussion ensemble," he says, "that reflected what we call American music, or jazz if you will – the improvisational thing. Not like Stockhausen, which is wonderful, but the way we deal with our music, with Charlie Parker, Duke Ellington, that style of thing. When I first approached C.B.S. with the idea, they said, 'What! Eight guys on drum sets! You gotta be out of your mind!' and I said, 'Well, it's not drum sets. We're going to play the total percussion family, all the mallet instruments – xylophone and marimba and those – as well as tympani and all the rest.'" Roach had first got his ensemble together in 1970, selecting percussionists who were not only expert on their instruments but could also compose and arrange. "It was my good fortune that I found the right people the first time round," he says. They were, and still are, Ray Brooks, Joe Chambers, Omar Clay, Fred King, Ray Mantilla, Warren Smith and Roach himself, with Kenyatta Abdul-Rahman added for the group's L.P. Over 100 percussion instruments are drawn upon, including many from the Third World. The result, as Max Roach puts it, "moves into new melodic and harmonic variations". Examples were filmed for *Sit Down and Listen*.

*　　　*　　　*

Earlier decades saw remarkably few Afro-American musicians strolling through the groves of academe. True, Percy Grainger inveigled Duke Ellington into playing for his students at Columbia University in 1932. And there were, at the start of the century, plenty of self-styled "ragtime professors", typified by Jelly Roll Morton, performing their elegant music in the dubious parlours of New Orleans's Storyville. It was also the habit of jazz musicians who admired a fellow player's expertise in musical theory to dub him "Fess", short for Professor. That happened to Buster Smith, Charlie Parker's early mentor. Only since the acceptance of Afro-American or black studies on American campuses has there emerged a body of authentic professors who are also jazz performers of repute, even of genius. Max Roach is one of those, on the faculty of – but no longer resident at – the University of Massachussetts at Amherst, where he lectures regularly.

That academic career began in 1971, at a moment when work for jazz groups was becoming harder to find. Roach still toured with his quartet in Europe and in Japan ("They still had a taste for straight-ahead music") but was disenchanted with the way many of his contemporaries hurried to play cross-over, that fusion of jazz and rock. "It was all right for players like Stanley Turrentine, a saxophonist with a natural sound for that kind of music," he says, "but there were others who pretended to be what they were not. It was like a conspiracy. What was frightening about it was that all you could hear was this one dimension, totally. Then the disco thing came in, and that's where we are today." Perhaps Roach's extreme antagonism towards cross-over sprang at least in part from the fastidiousness of a drummer who had perfected a style that now seemed to be threatened by coarser, more simplistic approaches. By 1977, however, the situation had changed, more work was to be found, and Roach returned to regular playing and touring.

Most of the time he remains faithful to the pattern of the quartet, using musicians who have worked with him over many years, such as Cecil Bridgewater and the saxophonist Odean Pope. Roach's attachment to earlier heroes often surfaces at the start of a set, when he is likely to sit alone with his high-hat cymbal and perform "Papa Jo" (sometimes he calls it "Mr High-Hat"), a dazzling tribute to Jo Jones. (Roach has also been instrumental in organising an annual Jo Jones Award, a gilt high-hat presented to a promising young drummer.) His own devotion to his craft and to Afro-American music in general was celebrated in the spring of 1981, when a New York radio station, WKCR, broadcast 200 consecutive hours of the drummer's music in chronological order. Over 1,200 separate tracks were involved, presenting Roach both as sideman and leader.

Nowadays Max Roach lives in the New York apartment he has had for many years, in a block of flats on the edge of Harlem, overlooking Central Park. Two of his children work in the music business: his daughter Maxine as a viola player; his son Raoul as road manager for Wynton Marsalis. Roach likes playing in the present, yet is still surrounded by the past, including tapes of Charlie Parker conversing about every subject under the sun, and un-released "live" performances by the Max Roach–Clifford Brown Quintet (he still gets close to tears when he hears Brownie's voice announcing a number). Throughout the world he is recognised by truly knowledgeable listeners as the greatest living jazz drummer, never an exhibitionist, even making a fetish out of appearing cool. He does not sweat or grunt or lash his arms like many

celebrated performers. Instead, he sits almost immobile, moving neither head nor torso, ensuring there is the shortest possible distance between sticks or brushes and skin or cymbal. Apart from playing the organ, being a drummer is the only job in jazz that calls for the co-ordination of all four limbs. You need to keep in condition as carefully as a boxer or athlete.

Roach's concern with the true nature of his craft and art came through when he was reminiscing to Geoffrey Haydon. He recalled how, in 1939, he had been taken to the New York World's Fair, where he was overwhelmed by the playing of an Haitian drummer, Tiroro. So much so, that at the end of the 1940s, he took the opportunity to spend a couple of weeks in Haiti, where he sought out the drummer who had amazed him a decade earlier. Tiroro could not read or write and he taught with a partition between himself and his student. "It was rather like the way we had learned from listening to records by Jo Jones or Catlett or Webb or Krupa. So you get an idea, you hear the sound, but you have to figure out yourself how to make that sound. So you work out an original technique. But Tiroro did astonishing things with his hands, skin on skin. He would say, 'Me Tiroro, I am the world's greatest drummer.' So the whole time I was there I never told him that I was a drummer too." (Roach also invited Tiroro to visit him in his small hotel: "But they wouldn't let him in. That's when I realised there was a caste system between black and black as well as white and black.")

Design is a word that keeps cropping up when Max Roach gets talking. It explains the way he approaches drumming, whether taking a solo or backing up one of his musicians. Some critics have called what he does "melodic drumming", but Roach considers that to be inexact. "You know, when I started making records they'd say to me, 'OK Max, how long are you going to

Max Roach today

play?' I didn't cotton on to the fact that the drummer just played as he wanted to do, then gave the cue – bop-bop-de-bop-da-bop-boom – and the band would start up again. I've always insisted that I'm going to play thirty-two bars like everybody else.'' That meant providing different textures for each 8-bar section, fitting everything inside a wider design.

It is, perhaps, evidence of a composer's instinct as well as a drummer's imagination. Roach's concern with balancing parts, with letting the listener know exactly where he is, surfaces too in all his music, whether filling in behind Clifford Brown or Sonny Rollins in the old quintet or jousting with Anthony Braxton or Cecil Taylor. One can do worse than think of European music as resembling a cathedral, very decidedly a structure, while African music moves like a river, open-ended, flowing for as long as the players want it to. Combining those two metaphors is not only a suitable task for a genuine Afro-American like Max Roach, but another of the paradoxes that help to keep jazz alive.

BIBLIOGRAPHY
ANDERSON, Jervis. *Harlem: The Great Black Way 1900–1950.* London: Orbis, 1982.
COLLIER, James Lincoln. *The Making of Jazz: A Comprehensive History.* London: Granada, 1978.
GILLESPIE, Dizzy, with Al Fraser. *Dizzy.* London: W.H. Allen, 1980.
GITLER, Ira. *Jazz Masters of The 40s.* London: Macmillan, 1966.
RUSSELL, Ross. *Bird Lives.* London: Quartet, 1976.
SHAW, Arnold. *Fifty-Second Street: The Street of Jazz.* Da Capo, 1977.
TAYLOR, Arthur. *Notes and Tones: Musician-to-Musician Interviews.* London: Quartet, 1983.

RECORDINGS
Charlie Parker 1945–8, *Bird/the Savoy Recordings* (2 L.P.s), Savoy SJL 2201.
Charlie Parker on Dial 1947, vol. 4, Spotlite 104.
Charlie Parker on Dial 1947, vol. 5, Spotlite 105.
Max Roach/Clifford Brown Quintet 1956, vol. 1, Elektra/Musician MUSK 52. 388.
Max Roach Quintets 1954–9, *Standard Time* (2 L.P.s), Emarcy 8141901.
Sonny Rollins plus four (1956), Prestige SMJ 6586 IMS.
Max Roach Again (1960–1) (2 L.P.s), Affinity AFF 32.
Max Roach Quintet (1958–62), *Conversations* (2 L.P.s), Milestone M–47061.
Max Roach (1960), *We Insist: Freedom Now Suite*, Columbia JC 36390.
Max Roach Orchestra (1961), *Percussion Bitter Sweet*, Impulse AS-8.
Max Roach sextet with choir (1961–2), *It's Time*, Impulse AS-16.
Max Roach Quintet (1965), *Drums Unlimited*. Atlantic K50519.
Max Roach with J.C. White Singers (1970), *Lift Every Voice and Sing*, Atlantic 2400 167.
Max Roach – Anthony Braxton (1978), *Birth and Rebirth*, Black Saint BSR 0024.
Max Roach – Archie Shepp (1979), *The Long March* (2 L.P.s) Hat Hut 2 R 13.
Max Roach – Cecil Taylor (1979), *Historic Concerts* (2 L.P.s) Soul Note SN 1100/1.
Max Roach Quartet (1979), *Pictures in a Frame*, Soul Note SN 1003.
Max Roach Quartet (1982), *In the Light*, Soul Note SN 1053.
Max Roach (1981), *Chattahoochie Red*, Columbia FC 37376.
Max Roach (1980), *M'Boom Re:Percussion*, Columbia JC 37066.

CHAPTER 5

The Drums of Dagbon

BY JOHN MILLER CHERNOFF

In African societies, music fulfils functions which other societies delegate to different types of institutions. In Africa, musical events provide a focus for personal character and encourage the socialisation of indigenous philosophical and moral ideals: respect, patience, flexibility and adaptability, collectedness of mind, composure in the exercise of power and in the toleration of powerlessness, a sense of pluralism, and a sense of balance in the perception of personal character and generational filiation. Music serves a crucial integrative function within many types of institutionalised activities, and musicians perform a complex social role in community occasions. Music and dance sometimes provide the generative dynamics of large- and small-scale social movements. In many African societies, musicians are the acknowledged authorities on history and custom, and particularly in the Western Sudan, the area south of the Sahara Desert and north of the coastal forest, musicians often have important political functions. Among the Dagbamba of northern Ghana, these musicians are drummers, with their own distinct lineage groupings and hierarchical chieftaincy organisations. Drummers undergo formal training for years, and they continue their acquisition of knowledge throughout life.

For more than a dozen years, I have been apprenticed to a Dagbamba drummer named Alhaji Ibrahim Abdulai, a great master who is addressed in his area of Tamale as M'ba Lunga, literally, My Father Drummer. I report some details of our relationship in my book of African music, *African Rhythm and African Sensibility*,[1] but my apprenticeship as a drummer has obliged me to obtain a broader knowledge of Dagbamba society. In addition to teaching me how to beat drums, Alhaji Ibrahim has lectured to me about all topics essential for a comprehensive understanding of the Dagbamba cultural heritage, and we are collaborating on a forthcoming book entitled *A Drummer's Testament*.[2] Extremely articulate and knowledgeable, Alhaji Ibrahim has witnessed the significant transformation of Dagbamba society during this century. He grew up in Dagbamba villages and has lived in the major cities of Ghana, and he balances a great respect for the Dagbamba tradition with a sensitive worldliness.

I once asked a son of Alhaji Ibrahim what sort of person he thought his father was and why we should be interested in him. His answer was, "He always knows what is good and how to do things in a correct way, and he knows what is bad, too. And it is because he knows that he was trained by some very great people in the past." And a fellow sitting nearby said, "You see, his way of living is something like tradition." What a wonderful society, I thought, where a musician can represent the whole tradition. Dagbamba drummers respect themselves and understand their traditional social significance. In addition to their role as artists, Dagbamba drummers devote themselves to learning with the same dedication that characterises most Western scholars. Drummers have a disciplined approach to learning, a concern for sources of information, and an awareness of their responsibility to educate; they are self-conscious of their relative erudition within their society; they are occasionally prone to the pride and foibles of scholasticism, but the majority of drummers exemplify the temperance and continence of intellectual life. As a drummer, a householder, a farmer, and a Muslim, Alhaji Ibrahim is well qualified to represent Dagbamba customs and tradition.

The Dagbamba people number about 300,000. They live in a traditional state called Dagbon about 400 miles north of Accra, and they speak a language called Dagbani. Dagbon's principal towns are Tamale, the administrative centre of Ghana's Northern Region, and the traditional capital Yendi, about sixty miles to the east. The Dagbamba entered their present traditional area more than 500 years ago as conquerors. With horses, spears, and arrows in their military technology, they subjugated the indigenous tribes under an elaborate hierarchy of chieftaincies and consolidated one of the earliest centralised political states south of the Niger bend. The dynastic line of their paramount chiefs has been unbroken throughout this period, making the Dagbamba dynastic chieftaincy certainly one of the oldest among currently ruling royalty.

The Dagbamba gradually intermingled with the indigenous inhabitants and became agriculturalists. Their staple crop is yams, but they do multiple plantings in their fields, and they rotate crops. Their other main food crops are sorghum, corn, millet and beans, though recently intensive rice cultivation has been encouraged by the national government. They are

Alhaji Ibrahim, a great Dagbamba master drummer

polygamous, and descent is traced through the father's line. Just over a majority of the Dagbamba are Muslim, and the rest are involved in animism and ancestor worship, relying to a great extent on local shrines, land-priests, soothsayers and medicine men. Funerals are elaborate, and there is an annual cycle of festivals. There are several craft-guild lineages, drummers being one such group. The Dagbamba have assimilated and made their own a number of customs from other tribal groups. For example, the Ashanti influence on Dagbamba music can be seen in the two large atumpan drums – called timpana by Dagbamba – which are beaten outside the houses of Dagbamba chiefs. Ashanti influence is also visible in the customs and dances of the Dagbamba soldiers – called "Kambonsi", the Dagbani word for Ashantis – whose organisation evolved under Ashanti tutelage; the elders who are leaders of the soldiers sit on chairs instead of on animal skins, and they wear multicoloured Ashanti kente cloth instead of the traditional smocks and gowns.

A sense of history is central both to Dagbamba culture and to the Dagbamba musical heritage. The paramount chief of Dagbamba drummers, the Namo-Naa, is an important elder of the paramount chief of Dagbon, the Ya-Naa. A Dagbamba drummer is a political figure whose influence extends from conferring varying degrees of respect on chiefs to discriminating the status of individual lineage identities at social gatherings. As such, drummers acquire high respect not only for their historical erudition but also for their very detailed knowledge of the kinship patterns of their local communities.

Dagbamba drummers do not gain their knowledge easily. First, according to the movement of the drumming tradition, a drummer learns from another drummer, to whom he incurs many obligations. Second, soliciting the information takes time and patience because elder drummers do not give it up easily or at once. As the Dagbamba say, "An old man will not vomit out everything in his stomach for you to see." Third, some topics in Dagbamba history are "forbidden". Such topics deal with war and death or with wickedness and betrayal, aspects of history in which the foundations of sociable living were broken; or they deal with individuals who were so great that they seem to be more than human beings. "Forbidden" topics can be discussed only on particular days and when accompanied by appropriate sacrifices to acknowledge and give respect to the seriousness of the topics, and the sacrifices required by some topics can be quite expensive.

In such a context, although it is not forbidden for a drummer to learn anything, most drummers have no interest in learning everything. The procedure for soliciting information involves greetings and gifts before one can even begin to ask for what one wants. Those who know the most about the tradition also know the most about its taboos. A drummer who thirsts for knowledge will cite the proverb, "You should continue visiting a dry well. If you don't visit it when it's dry, you won't go to visit it when it has water." Because of the difficulties of learning and the slow acquisition of erudition, drummers are not a homogenous group in terms of the extent of their

knowledge; they are certainly better informed than most other Dagbamba, but their search for knowledge remains a lifelong task to which they subject themselves with the same varying degrees of commitment as do Western scholars. But for a drummer who seeks knowledge about his heritage, performing the sacrifices and following the tradition is a way of ensuring that his work will have beneficial results. The relevant Dagbamba proverb is "Somebody with horns cannot enter a hole." All in all, it is a remarkable achievement that drummers have been able to preserve their history so well without the aid of writing. From generation to generation in Dagbon, there have been drummers who have cared enough to learn with thoroughness and to pass on their knowledge. As they say, "You don't bury a person and leave the legs sticking out."

At a time when our understanding of traditional cultures is being redefined, we can find a unique representation of traditional culture among Dagbamba drummers, professional musicians whose lives partake of that union of historical and aesthetic sensibilities which may perhaps be best described as classical. Indeed, the recitation of the Dagbamba drum history is an event that recalls no art form more clearly than it does a Homeric epic. At certain times during the year, drummers beat and sing morally edifying stories from Dagbamba history outside the house of their town's chief, who sits with his wives and elders while the populace assembles around. The Dagbamba drum history has a function in its own context quite different from the function history serves in Western scholarly and political contexts. Within the orientation of Dagbamba scholar-drummers, to point to something and call it tradition is not the same thing as to live and act in a way that respects and is consistent with the wisdom of past generations. Tradition is something that exists only in the living commitment of people, and because Dagbamba drummers acknowledge the fact that different types of people have to live together in Dagbon, they tend to use their knowledge with a focus on moral themes of community integration. Their spiritual inclination, therefore, is towards complementarity and the balancing of conflicting traditions in a way reminiscent of the balancing of conflicting musical elements in their aesthetic style. The institutional context of history in Dagbon is an indigenous tradition of knowledge focused on the human content of culture. Dagbamba refer to history and their traditional way of living as "old talks", and as drummers say, "In Dagbon, old talks do not die."

A Dagbamba drummer with a reputation for learnedness, asked to consult on a given situation, would typically tell a story or cite a proverb rather than sermonise from a general principal and, indeed, Dagbamba say, "It is proverbs that a person takes to do work." If not that, the drummer would prescribe a step-by-step series of appropriate actions that would be "following the way" of custom for that particular situation. In contrast to the legalistic and metaphysical focus of Western social thought, the situational focus of the Dagbamba historical orientation is ethical and aesthetic. It is interesting that, among the Dagbamba, the most profound grasp of social realities resides within a tradition of artistic genius. Dagbamba drummers are moralists with an elaborate conception of history and human relationships. And yet again, they are musicians, and one of the most intriguing aspects of Dagbamba culture is the image of music that emerges within a portrait of a society where music plays an important role in political and family affairs.

Tourists occasionally visit the north of Ghana. Whether the journey is worthwhile or not depends on the sensitivity of the traveller. African towns do not have the usual European kind of tourist attractions like churches or museums, but someone who enjoys meeting different types of people and seeing how they live can have the experience of a lifetime. The lay of the land and the local architecture are typical of the African savanna. The land is mostly flat with a few trees. Houses are built as complexes of round rooms with thatched roofs. There are plenty of charming vistas with small villages, a tree or two, and perhaps a farmer riding his bicycle home from the farm.

Tamale is a typical small town in the Third World, and there is not much to see if one is just passing through. The kind of dynamic energy that exists in a major city like Lagos is not at all there, and the contradictions of modern Africa have only begun to make their appearance in Dagbon, symbolised by the presence of petrol stations and international banks side by side with the traditional round-roomed, thatched-roof houses. There are still many sights which Westerners consider typical of Africa. The women, of course, carry their babies on their backs and their loads on their heads. They carry corn, millet, and sorghum to the grinding mills. The young girls carry firewood from the market. Some parts of the town are without water pipes, and women and young girls still carry water on their heads in large metal containers, walking single file to their houses. On market days, if one arrives early enough, one can see the villagers arriving and carrying their loads. Some of them arrive crowded into large trucks, and others arrive on foot or bicycle. Around the lorry stations and by the roadsides are women cooking local types of snack food. At local food bars, one can also see groups of three or four women rhythmically pounding yams.

Market days are a time of entertainment and visiting as well as business. The market at Tolon, about thirty miles from Tamale, is one of the biggest around. Dagbamba markets are held every six days in market towns, and the market moves from town to town every day. At the market, people buy and sell various foodstuffs and craft goods. The market is well organised in rows and sections. The women sit behind their wares and greet potential customers with postcard smiles. One notices how hard the children work. There are a lot of handsome faces and wonderful characters to look at: old people, young people, chiefs, peasant farmers. A number of musicians will be around, notably market-drummers who roam alone and beat praises for tips, and fiddle players as well, and maybe a few other musicians like a singer with a local type of guitar called a moglo. Usually the musicians can be found at the entrance to the market and in the part of the market where friends sit and drink pito, a local beer brewed from sorghum.

One of the loveliest sights a tourist will notice is the Dagbamba manner of greeting. As people pass each other in public, they greet one another, and the young women and young men squat to greet their elders. The cadences and sounds of Dagbamba greetings are very pleasant to the ear. As the young person squats, smiles and greets, the other person will take his hand and gently pull him up. The laid-back style of Dagbamba life and work and human relationships shows through beautifully in greetings. Even at a working place, every craftsman sits and works steadily and patiently, but he always has time for an opportunity to chat and greet and receive people.

Many of the artisans and craftsmen can be seen around the markets and the petrol stations. The vulcanisers are always busy with their footpumps and with their patchkits made from pistons. The local watch repair places are also interesting – little tables with hundreds of tiny parts spread all over them. The local blacksmiths make all kinds of things that one would not believe possible out of scraps of metal. They repair buckets and pails, but they also make castanets and leg-rattles and jazz drum kits for use in certain types of drumming and dancing. They work on a small open hearth with charcoal made from kernels of oil-palm nuts. Watching the weavers is also nice: they use their hand looms to weave narrow strips of cloth with distinctively African multirhythmic patterning. The local barbers have a little kit with an assortment of blades for shaving, complemented with a tube of penicillin ointment for circumcisions and minor operations. They go around to their customers and shave them on the verandas of the houses.

Dagbamba drummers are among the craftsmen whose work of making and repairing drums is something one can observe with enjoyment. The Dagbamba play a type of drum which they call "lunga": it is a tension drum shaped like an hourglass, with thin drumskins over each mouth. The skins are sewn onto bound reeds and laced together so that a drummer, holding the drum under his arm, can squeeze the drum and change its pitch and resonance. Westerners often call this type of drum a "talking drum" because the modulation of the drum's voice can duplicate the speech patterns of human language. There are several sizes of lunga in an ensemble to provide a supporting beat for solo playing, and to a Dagbana, a Dagbamba drum ensemble sounds as if the lead drum is singing while the supporting drum chorus hums harmonies. To a Westerner, the pulsating overtones of the drums might resemble the breathing of the wind, and when the sound of the drumming dies, it moves away like exhaled breath. The Dagbamba also play a large tomtom which they call "gungon". It has a single snare made from a string of hide that adds a buzzing rattle to the booming bass sound of the drum. A gungon player uses his hand and stick near the snare to lend a delectably rough edge to the sound, and he uses his stick in various ways on the centre of the drum, muting and altering the bass beat so that it seems as if the drumming is vibrating inside the earth. Because both drums extend outward from the drummer's body, they are beaten with a curved stick.

The making of a drum is a fascinating process. The drum-maker offers a sacrifice to the tree he is about to cut down, then he cuts the wood into logs of the appropriate length. He uses a variety of adzes and scraping tools, first making a hole through the centre of the log and then working with the adzes and scrapers to shape the wood. It takes an expert half a day of hard work to carve a drum. Once carved, the drum is ready for sewing. When Alhaji Ibrahim has not gone to work on his farm, he is usually seated outside his house working on drums. He does not carve the drums himself, but he finishes them and makes the drumheads. The drums he uses are carved in a village not far from Tamale called Tampion, where one of the Tampion drum chiefs, Mahama Alhaji, is an expert carver. To sew the drumhead, Alhaji Ibrahim uses a goatskin which he buys from butchers. He buys about three or four skins, brings them home and trims off any excess meat with a curved knife. When he is ready to sew some drums, he soaks the skins and lets them get soft. Chemicals from a local type of melon and from ashes further soften the skin and remove the hair. After a few hours, he spreads a skin on a board, where he scrapes it again with a knife to make it clean and even. Then he washes it to remove the smell. It is now ready to be sewn.

The preparation of the ring that holds the drumskin is a very interesting process in its own right. The ring has to fit exactly over the mouth of the drum, and it has to be made very evenly or the continual flexing of the drumstrings will cause it to separate or break. There are two types of materials used. The first is a type of mat which is not woven but is made out of long reeds. Alhaji Ibrahim buys one of these mats from the market, and he separates the reeds. Then he takes a knife and splits each reed by holding it against his foot and pulling it in one smooth movement that strips the outside part and leaves a thin flexible strip. The other material for the ring is made from dry grasses about four or five feet long, and Alhaji Ibrahim uses a knife to slice them to the right width. When trying the ring, he takes a reed and hoops it round the mouth of the drum, leaving a little extra space as an allowance for the grasses as he wraps the ring. He builds up the ring concentrically and secures his work by wrapping the grasses round the reed. When he is done, he has a perfectly circular ring about one-quarter of an inch thick and one inch across which fits exactly over the mouth of the drum.

He then takes a skin and spreads it and cuts it so that it is a little wider than the ring, and he pulls it round the ring and secures it roughly with a string of leather. To sew the skin onto the ring, he uses thread made from an old broken drumhead. He takes a blade and cuts the old drumhead concentrically into a long quarter-inch strip, he wets it, then rolls it against his leg to make a very fine but strong thread. He uses an awl to punch a hole through the skin at an edge of the ring, and then he makes his stitch, coming back through the same hole and leaving a loop for lacing the outside strings. When he has sewn one drumhead, he does the same thing for the other drumhead, which will be finished with almost exactly the same number of loops. The strings for lacing the drum are made from a goatskin which Alhaji Ibrahim prepares the same way he prepares the thread. After he laces the drum, going through each loop, he ties the drum and lets it sit overnight to seat the skin. By the next day, the drum is ready.

For a visitor to Dagbon who has time to spend with local craftsmen like drummers, blacksmiths, tanners, or weavers, or who has the patience to sit quietly and observe the daily life of people in markets and in neighbourhood streets and lanes, at work or at prayers, the visit can begin to evoke deep feelings about the importance of interpersonal respect and the beauty of community living. After a while, overwhelmed by the magnificence of the treatment one receives and the poignance of the things one witnesses, and bolstered by the intimacy of personal contact, one may not notice much about the poverty of the people or the level of material life. "Wealth" becomes a relative concept, and in the depth and unity of the local culture, a Westerner will find an admirable and even enviable lifestyle which is difficult to achieve in a modern, technological society. If one stays long enough to establish friendships with some of the great people who live in Dagbon, one will know why the Dagbamba are proud. People are attuned to the quality of a person's character, ready to respect the judgment of the wise, old chief of Nanton, who has never been to school, just as much as they respect the judgment of the learned chief of Tolon, who was formerly Ghana's Ambassador to the United Nations and whose praise-name is "Wisdom is too much; one person cannot hold it alone".

Watching a performance of the drum history is a good way to get an introduction to the spiritual foundations of Dagbamba culture and musical life. The "old talks" of the drum history performance provide the centre for the whole cultural complex of music and dance, family and chieftaincy in Dagbon. I went to a drum history with a poet once; his eyes glazed, and he kept repeating in a numbed voice, "This is incredible." I am sure that every poet hungers for such a forum. A whole village comes outside to spend the

night listening to poetic oratory and song. The crowd is attentive and responsive, laughing at verbal excess, sighing at pathos.

Most of the drum history tells of Ya-Naas and their accomplishments, lending meaning to traditional Dagbamba social dances, which are based on the proverbial praise-names of the paramount chiefs of Yendi and the chiefs of other traditionally important towns such as Savelugu and Karaga. Although a Dagbana's preference in dancing is not necessarily political, different dances have associations with family origins, since most Dagbamba trace their ancestry to former chiefs. The relationship of commoners to past chiefs is based on the simple fact that not every son of a chief can become a chief, and although the Ya-Naas represent a continuous dynasty, many branches of the lines of former chiefs are by now far removed from potential succession. Nonetheless, someone for whom the "door" to chieftaincy closed generations ago may still respect his family's line by dancing to the name of a great forefather.

A dance called Nantoo Nimdi can serve as an example. Nantoo Nimdi is a praise-name for Naa (Chief) Yakubu, who ruled Dagbon in the mid-nineteenth century. "Nimdi" is meat, and "nantoo", defined by Dagbamba as a very poisonous flying creature, is a vector of anthrax. The praise-name means that meat which has been touched by nantoo cannot be eaten or approached. In addition to obvious respect for the power of chieftaincy, the name implies that whatever a chief's hand touches becomes a dangerous thing; thus the name cautions that citizens should not do anything bad or become involved in a matter that will come before the chief. The name the drummers gave Naa Yakubu is not only appropriate to his violent career; it has a good dance beat. Drummers beat the name Nantoo Nimdi and improvise on its rhythm, and people dance to it.

Dagbamba drummers beat Nantoo Nimdi

Zhim Taai Kurugu is another such dance. *"Zhim taai kurugu, ka jangbarsi wolinje"* means that when blood touches iron, rats will try to eat it but will fail. Zhim Taai Kurugu is a proverbial praise-name of Naa Alhassan, who ruled Dagbon in the early twentieth century. The praise-name shows that Naa Alhassan's strength was too much for others who wanted to get the chieftaincy instead of him, and it shows as well that once he had his chieftaincy, his rivals could not disturb him. When the drummers beat the dance, a chorus of drums will beat sounds which resemble the words *"Zhim taai kurugu"*, and lead drummers will beat the rest of the proverbial phrase.

Dances such as Nantoo Nimdi and Zhim Taai Kurugu are danced individually inside a circle of spectators. Drummers inside the circle approach each dancer individually. One drummer squats in front of a person and beats praise-names of his or her forefathers. When someone comes out to dance, the rest of the people in the circle watch. The lead drummer turns to his ensemble and beats an introduction to the beat. The drummers fall in with the beat, and the dancer comes out. After the dancer dances a few steps, his or her relatives and friends come from their sitting places to press money onto the forehead or into the hands of the dancer in appreciation of the dance. Giving the money is a way of showing respect and demonstrating relationships before the public at a social occasion. It is also a way of paying the musicians for inspiring the dance, and children of the drummers gather the coins and bills as they fall to give them to an elder who will later share the money among the musicians. Then the dancer goes back to sit down, and the whole sequence is repeated with another dancer. At a typical Dagbamba community celebration — whether a funeral, a wedding, a festival, a chief's installation, or a newborn baby's "naming" — music, dance, and proverbial praise-naming are integrated with status encounters, concerns of social control, and genealogical and historical elucidation.

The drum history which is the foundation of the various social dances is beaten at two times during the year, though it can also be beaten when a new chief is installed in a town. The two occasions are the night the new moon comes out at the end of the Ramadan fast and the night before the holiday that coincides with the sacrifices of animals during the month of the Islamic pilgrimage. The drum history is an all-night affair, beginning in mid-evening and continuing till dawn. One man will carry the whole show, standing up with his drum under his arm, gesturing with his stick, his voice strong throughout. Behind him, seated cross-legged, are the drumming chiefs and elders, and as many as forty to one hundred drummers can play the supporting chorus. Younger drummers assemble at around eight or nine o'clock and beat what is called "sweeping the compound" or "pounding the soup vegetables". This drumming is preparatory to the event, and a younger drummer will sing about his ancestors and his drumming elders in the town. Meanwhile, the whole range of the town's population assembles, from the chief and his elders to young mothers with their sleeping infants to petty traders selling oranges, cough drops, or whatever. Young men of the town set up their tape-recorders in front of the singer. Illumination is provided by

Coleman or kerosene pressure lanterns. The actual singing of the history gets started around ten, when the chief of drummers or his representative, perhaps his son or one of the other drum chiefs, takes over and begins singing about one of the ancient chiefs. The drum history is a very leisurely event which builds for about six hours to its climax, usually the dancing of a dance called Bangumanga.

The mood of the crowd throughout all this is relaxed. Nobody gets upset if somebody coughs. Nobody thinks the less of someone who gets up in the middle of a story to go to urinate. Those assembled all have plenty of time. The drummer who is singing will be entertaining them with the way he sings the stories, and he will be playing the audience for laughs. But there is also something awesome and dignified about the power of those many drums beating. The drum history rings out through the night air, and it is sure to make anyone who sees it nostalgic for a bygone time.

The dancing of Bangumanga usually comes at about three or four o'clock in the morning. There are two chiefs for whom the Dagbamba dance Bangumanga: Naa Luro from the seventeenth century, and Naa Sigli from the early eighteenth century. Alhaji Ibrahim told me, "As for the way they dance Bangumanga, you should not let it surprise you, because truly, it is for war. You know, when we sit for the drum history, we look at the olden days talks, and so it is something like reading. We beat the history, and when we come to the place where the war was fought, then we have to beat Bangumanga. When we come to beat that history, the chief will slaughter a sheep or a cow, because on the day of the war people died, and there was blood. If we beat the drum history and come to the point where blood was coming out from the war, the chief has to let blood come out too."

When the drummers finish the story about how Naa Luro killed the enemy chief, there is a story of the starting of the dancing of Bangumanga as a victory dance. Naa Luro asks musicians to play for his victory, and the drummers beat a song to celebrate Naa Luro's greatness in saving Dagbon: "They will look for me, but they will not see me again." That is the meaning of the Bangumanga drumming. As Alhaji Ibrahim describes it, "If the leader of the drum history sings about Naa Luro's time, that was when Bangumanga was first beaten. When they start beating Bangumanga, the women in the chief's house – the chief's wives and sisters – they all tie baskets and carry them on their heads. They are the ones who dance it, and when the story of the war is being sung, they go into the chief's house to prepare themselves. They will be inside and waiting until the time comes. The meaning of tying and carrying the baskets is that when war is coming, people pack their things and move with them, and they will be carrying supplies and carrying the spoils of victory. All the small children in the chief's house will put bells on their necks and be making noise. The young men and old men in the chief's house will hold bows and arrows when they dance. And they will be dancing and running outside the house while Bangumanga is being beaten. Everybody will be happy. They will be blowing flutes and whistles, and the guns will be shooting: Kpa!! Kpaa!! Kpaa!! And that Bangumanga is Naa Luro's

Bangumanga. After they finish dancing Bangumanga, the chief will bring food for the drummers, and they will eat. That food is prepared with the meat of the slaughtered animal. When they finish eating, they come back to start the history from where they left it, and they continue the drum history until they come up to the present, unless day breaks." Needless to say, Bangumanga is a wonderful sight. When one sees the chief's housepeople rush out of the house dancing and ululating, one will know that definitely it is a war dance. The beat, by the way, is nearly the same as a "soul" beat at a disco.

Stories from the drum history as well as songs based on proverbs and folktales can also be heard in the music of singers who accompany themselves on two local string instruments: jenjili and moglo. These instruments are also present in Mali, Guinea, Gambia, and Upper Volta, and they exemplify some of the continuities in the music of the vast savanna area. The vocal and performance styles are very similar to American blues singing. Jenjili and moglo are instruments typically played by older men to relax in the evenings and entertain themselves and their families. Recently, jenjili and moglo singers near the larger Dagbamba towns have been taking their instruments around to houses during festival times, and they play and sing to entertain in people's compounds. By and large, however, someone who can play jenjili or moglo will just play it inside his house.

Jenjili is a musical bow with a single wire that sounds like a jew's harp. A half-calabash mounted on the back of the bow resonates the sound as the musician moves it against and away from his chest. People who are familiar with the whole range of African-American musical idioms will recognise that the jenjili is another form of the Brazilian birimbao. Fuseini Tia of Tamale is one of the best jenjili players in Dagbon, and in recent years he has been trying to popularise the instrument. He has made records, and he is occasionally featured on the radio. Fuseini is a very nice and pleasant fellow, extremely modest, who works at the Public Works Department in Tamale. He has a plaintive voice, and he performs with support from a friend who plays a steady 12/8 beat with metal rings on a beer bottle. Fuseini also sometimes gathers a few people to sing chorus. He usually sings stories and proverbs. Sometimes he tells a story in a style like a "talking blues", using the Dagbani language for extraordinary counterrhythms.

One moglo player who sings detailed songs from the drum history is Issahaku Abdulai, who is the chief of drummers in the village of Zhiong. He has also recorded for the radio. He is blind now, but when he was playing the drum as a young man, he also learned the moglo, and he sings drumming songs on it. Issahaku has a reputation for learnedness, and it is only a few drummers who can challenge him on knowledge. Issahaku is an exciting performer, very soulful, and his neck bulges out when he opens up his voice. The moglo he plays is an interesting-looking instrument. He attaches a metal disc with small rings through it to the neck to add the sound of a rattle to his playing. Jenjili and moglo show some of the diversity of musical activity in Dagbamba culture.

The Dagbamba also have a type of fiddle called goonji. It is another interesting-looking instrument, made from a half-calabash covered with a lizard skin, with a horsehair string and a curved bow. A young person or two accompany the goonji on gourd rattles called zaabia. Sometimes one sees a goonji player sitting outside his house with some children around him. One generally sees the goonji players at the markets, at weddings and funerals, and at the pito houses where Dagbamba drink their locally brewed beer. At the pito houses and the markets, the music is generally provided by one goonji player with one rattle player, often a pre-teenage girl or boy. Like the market-drummers, the goonji players stroll from area to area.

When the goonji musicians play for dancing at a major function, they use about two or three goonjis and at least two rattles played by strong young men. They can lead a chief coming from his house and going somewhere like a festival or funeral. At the wedding houses they also play for the women to dance. They sometimes have their own circle at a funeral house, but usually they are inside a common circle with the drummers. They will have their time to play for dancers, and they interact with the dancers in the same way as drummers: they have a singer, and they praise people and invite them to dance. The dancer comes out and dances in the midst of the goonjis. The musicians who really punch out the beat are the rattle players, who shake the rattles all around the dancer. Like the drummers, the goonjis give quadrophonic sound. The goonji music may sound strange until one makes an adjustment to the harmonic structure. The rattles add a lot of definition to the

Nyoglo drum chief, Issahaku Abdulai – moglo singer

12/8 beat, and the way the musicians turn the rattles around with their wrists and slap in accents with the free hand is quite amazing.

One place to see the diversity of Dagbamba musical culture is at a funeral house. A Dagbamba funeral is in several parts. The first parts are the burial followed by prayers during the week after the death, but the main part of a Dagbamba funeral is actually performed a number of months after the burial. The final funeral is a way of giving respect to the deceased, and it is a happy occasion. Family, friends, and neighbours assemble for several days. The artistic culmination of the final funeral has to be seen to be believed. Circles are formed for people to dance the popular dances based on praise-names from the drum history, and a town's drummers often have to divide themselves into several groups. If there are several dance circles, sometimes the women will be in their own circle and sometimes they will be mixed with the men, with younger people having their own circle. Goonji players come with their groups and join the drumming circles. In addition to fiddlers and drummers, other traditional dances are performed by groups who specialise in dances like Baamaaya, Takai, Tora, Jera, Simpa, and others. Apart from all that, it is also likely that there will be a circle of people dancing Mamprusi or Mossi dances or the dancing from any of the many tribes who live in the town, just because the dead person may have been from that tribe, had some family from that tribe, or merely had a friend from that tribe. If the dead person was a chief or an important person, chiefs or their representatives will come with their own entourage of musicians and followers. A moglo player like Issahaku might come and be moving among these important people, singing and praising people and collecting money as a gift for his songs.

Goonji players

With all this activity, a Dagbamba funeral covers a large area around the funeral house. The dancing begins in the late afternoon, and after a dinner break the funeral resumes in force in the evening, continuing until dawn. When the Baamaaya, Simpa, and Jera groups arrive in the late evening, a large funeral can spread out through the cluster of houses to fill a whole neighbourhood with music and dance. Other people gather to watch the dancing, and through the lanes petty traders set up their tables to sell their wares. Drummers move around beating the praise-names of people's ancestors, and inside the dance circles drumming groups beat the praise-name dances for the solo dancers.

A good dancer often comes out quite dramatically to begin his or her dance. Dagbamba dancers use the whole body, and they accentuate their movements with their clothing. Often, male dancers plant a foot on the beat, then reverse their direction to spin away; alternatively, they spin into the planting of the foot. Personal expression in dancing reaches high points through relatively sudden shifts in style, much like the rhythmic movement of Dagbamba drumming. A male dancer who is moving within a small area will suddenly expand his movements and enlarge his dancing space, or he may just start running with quick steps in a large circle. But the other side of dancing is a kind of concentration: Dagbamba dancers maintain a look of composure, like the expression on an African mask. A dancer can freeze his or her body and bring the focus of movement into the face and the head. The most beautiful example is a dancer who, sometimes nose-to-nose with the drummer, moves only the eyes from side to side. Thus there is a double movement in Dagbamba dancing, inward and outward. The eyes and the facial expression form one focal point for the demonstration of personality, and then the body movement carries the personality outward.

Nantoo Nimdi, the praise-name of Naa Yakubu, is a wonderful dance. There are a variety of styles in it, but the basic one is a sideways jumping movement in time with the gungon, the big bass drum. Then the dancer locks eyes with the drummer and goes into a crouched walk with his fingers and arms pointed as if he is taking aim at the drummer. Other praise-name dances that are popular, like Zhim Taai Kurugu, Naanigoo, Nagbiegu, Damduu, and literally dozens more, have different types of beats and dance styles. Some are slow and majestic, others are quick and precise. The variety of dances allows an individual to find a favourite dance beat or two that are well suited to his or her taste. Dancing is an occasion for the demonstration of character, where artistic command parallels maturity and public focus acknowledges community relationships.

It is not until the evening, when the Baamaaya, Jera, and Simpa groups get going, that the wealth of Dagbamba musical culture is in full display. The drum history, the praise-name dances, and the various string instruments do not exhaust the musical repertoire of the Dagbamba. These other dances are danced for recreation and also as a part of funeral and festival activities. Baamaaya is one of the best of these dances, and it is one of the most important for the general musical culture. Along with Damba, it is the most famous

Dagbamba dance. It is generally danced by every Ghanaian folkloric dance troupe, including groups in Britain and America.

As Alhaji Ibrahim describes the dance, "Every Dagbana knows Baamaaya. Today when they dance Baamaaya, it is a funeral day or a festival day, but formerly, when I was a small boy growing up in the village, Baamaaya was the music of Dagbon in the night. It wasn't a funeral day, and it wasn't a festival day. At that time, anywhere they were playing it, the village boys would eat their night food and go to the playing. And even the girls too used to go. And at that time they were lighting our local lamps, the ones they used to make with clay. Sometimes they would light four of the very big ones and put them in four places where they gathered. It was not anything that was making them dance. We gathered and we didn't know what to do, and we couldn't be sitting quietly as if somebody had died. And so we played it to enjoy ourselves. As for the songs of Baamaaya, they are only to make people laugh. 'If you say that the person who catches fish is bad, what of the basket that catches the fish?' This is one of the songs which the Baamaaya dancers sing.

"What brought Baamaaya? How we drummers know Baamaaya, Baamaaya comes from mosquitoes and the way they want to bite us at night. When it is the time of many mosquitoes, you will play Baamaaya. When you finish eating and you enter the room, the mosquitoes are inside. When you are outside, it's the same thing. And you will hear people say, 'Let's play Baamaaya.' Someone will take a drum, and you will hear the gungon coming out: 'Kwa kwom, kwom kwa'. That was how they used to beat. They will take cloths to tie on their necks, and part of the cloth will hang and be rolling on the legs. And they will be holding fans and fanning themselves. They will make a line, and they will be going round, twisting their waists. How the dance of Baamaaya is, you are fanning yourself, and shaking your waist, and making noise: how will mosquitoes get you? And you will see that all the small children will come. And the very small children who are about five or six years will be standing aside and wrestling and jumping around, and their hearts will be very white with happiness. And you will see that some of the small children will be lying at one side sleeping. Sometimes they will play Baamaaya until it's two o'clock in the night. The time of mosquitoes, the villagers don't sleep early."

Modern Baamaaya groups are locally organised in neighbourhoods or villages wherever there is interest. Baamaaya is a recreational dance, though nowadays it is almost always present at any funeral, and it is danced during official visits to entertain dignitaries. The leading group in the Tamale area is led by Harruna Alhassan, one of the best Baamaaya dancers in Dagbon. He is an older man who dances with a beautiful smile on his face. Baamaaya dancers are the last to get going at a funeral, generally starting after one or two in the morning and finishing at dawn. The Baamaaya group arrives after midnight at the house where they will change into their costumes. One of the reasons for Baamaaya's popularity is the beautiful and outlandish costumes the dancers wear. They wear earrings and headdresses, T-shirts and skirts, with baubles and bells hanging from their waists, and with metal shakers tied round their

ankles. When the dancers are ready, they get in line according to age and height, and they come out dancing and move straight to the dance area to form their circle, already dancing Baamaaya.

The actual Baamaaya dance is divided into different dances with non-stop playing. The beat and the dance just change from one to the next. The dancers move counterclockwise in a circle as large as the particular group requires. Within the circle are the musicians, who also move counterclockwise but at a slower pace than the outer circle of dancers. The metal shakers that the dancers tie to their feet add tremendously to the overall sound of the beat. Generally there is only one lunga drum beaten, and it is overpowered by two or three gungons beating in synchrony. The lunga drummer moves slowly from dancer to dancer, leaning towards the dancer he is next to, and the gungon beaters lower their drums nearly to the ground to beat more strongly when they get a dancer who is doing well or needs energy. Someone will play a double rattle, shaped like two cones, with one held in each hand. In front of the drummers, another musician plays a flute. The traditional type of flute in the area, called yua, is still played by some people, but often one sees plastic flutes or little fifes. Right at the centre of the circle might be an older woman or two who ululate. These women also spread water on the ground to prevent too much dust from rising.

The actual movement around the circle is very slow, with the dancers following the leader and passing the leader's movements down the line, their feet and body movements sychronised. Most of the Baamaaya movements are in the continuous twisting of the hips, with the fringe and bells swinging about the waist, the feet in a shuffling two-step, one arm extended outward

Baamaaya dance, with gungons, Tamale

and the other holding a fan with which the dancer fans himself, smiling and holding his head stationary and coolly relaxed. At first, the dance seems wildly funny, and the dancers seem to be laughing at a joke. As the dance progresses, the sweat pours down and the muscles bulge, and the smiles of the dancers seem to be projecting a challenge of strength and rootedness to the earth.

Jera is another dance like Baamaaya, but it is not as common. In their rootedness to the earth and in the amulets that the dancers wear, both dances seem to reach back to the culture of the original inhabitants of the Dagbamba area. Alhaji Ibrahim said, "As for Jera, we all grew up and met it. They don't dance Jera for nothing. If not a funeral house, they won't call Jera people. If a person who becomes very old dies, or if a chief dies, they can go and dance it. If it is not something that happens, I have never seen those who dance Jera go and dance it in a town. They will never just get up and say, 'Let's go and dance Jera.' How they beat, they beat gungons, and their gungons are just small ones, and they pull the skin very tight. They have one lunga drummer, and he beats along with the gungons. We have something we call feenga: it is a castanet made of metal, and it is blacksmiths who make it. They hold these and knock them when they are dancing. And when they are dancing, they sing their songs. They don't sing about chiefs. They only sing the songs that will make people laugh. This is how it is. If you see them coming to dance Jera, you will be happy, because how they dress and dance, it is very interesting."

Befitting its ancient origins and instruments, Jera is more prevalent in the villages. The Jera group from the village of Changnayili is one which often dances at occasions around Tamale. The lead dancer is a strikingly handsome man and a great dancer. Jera is rustic and unpolished, but it is another dance that takes strength and endurance. The Jera dance circle is like that of Baamaaya but slightly more intimate. The drummers move counterclockwise inside a circle; the women ululate; the castanets click; and the dancers sing while they dance. The dance of Jera is in the hips, a forward and back movement, and in the feet, with the hands extended and working the castanets, and the head steady, as usual.

Takai is one of the central dances of Dagbon. It is a beautiful men's dance, a great artistic achievement which cannot fail to give a genuine aesthetic thrill to anyone who sees it. It was Alhaji Ibrahim's group who popularised Takai throughout Ghana during the Nkrumah regime and who play Takai whenever it is called for a dignitary or a special function. Among the fine musicians in the group is the gungon drummer, Fuseini Alhassan, a complete showman who jumps around and does fantastic things with the gungon.

Takai and its female counterpart, Tora, are generally danced in the afternoons during the week of a final funeral. Dagbamba do not dance these dances on the night of a funeral, though sometimes they arrange Tora for young girls as a recreational dance. At a typical performance the people from the funeral house sit outside the house, and the Takai or Tora dancers will come and dance in front. The dancers come after work, and they usually arrive and get going by about five o'clock. They dance for about forty-five

minutes or an hour, and then they dance individually to the praise-name social dances, and the people from the funeral or wedding house may also dance. They close at about six. The housepeople sit with their family elders in the central positions, along with their friends and neighbours who are also elders, all of them either on chairs or on mats. The rest of the people from the house, like the children, will be where they can be. When the dance starts, many people from the area also come and look, forming an outer perimeter, but those who have called the dance will have a relatively unobstructed view.

Alhaji Ibrahim says, ''As for Tora and Takai, we have all grown up and met them. And our forefathers met them. If an old man or an old woman dies, we will take Takai or Tora and play it in front of the old person's house. A chief can be happy and he will call Tora or Takai. Or someone's daughter will be married, and he will call Tora. Tora and Takai have come for happiness and they have come for when you are not happy. If there is a festival, we can take Takai and play it. Tora is the same. It is only white people who call it any time, and they call it because it is wonderful.

''Tora is a dance only for women; it's not for men. If you are a man and you are as useless as anything, you will not dance Tora. As for women, they dance men's dances, but we men don't dance Tora because how the dance is, it will not add to us. And so Tora has come because of women. If a woman says she does not know Tora, then we don't count her into Dagbamba. If a woman does not know any dance, at least she will know Tora. Our old drummers say that if you go to some place and they cannot dance any dance, you should beat Tora for them. And it's true, too. You will see that they will dance. Tora and Takai follow one another. I can say that Tora is the Takai of women. And when you go to watch it, you yourself will know, because how we beat it, many of the

Tora dance, Tamale

dances inside Tora are in Takai, too. And so Tora is the Takai of women, because the beating is moving in one way.

"As for Baamaaya, Takai, Tora, and Jera, everybody knows them. Even children play and dance them, and we look at them, and the old people don't stop them. By the time a Dagbana child is about six years old, he can start learning Baamaaya or Takai. Children take broken pieces of calabash or they pick up things and they beat the dance. How the small boys start dancing Takai, that is how the small girls also start dancing Tora. When children are small and they gather and sit, they will get up and say, 'Let's play Tora', or 'Let's play Takai'. And they will clap their hands and start singing, '*Sagsi zani ka nin kpem' zugu, kpai! Dim pa taali*' – 'Stand and shift, and knock an old person on the head, kpai! It doesn't matter.' And the others will sing, '*Sagsi zani ka nin bii zugu, kpai! Dim pa taali*' – 'Stand and shift, and knock a young person on the head, kpai! It doesn't matter.' And they will play and dance it. Tora has not come from children, but when they are playing, they dance it. And women like it, too, and they will be dancing it and laughing. Or when children get up and play, they can bring Jera. And as for our children, when they can speak and when they can hear the playing of any music, at that time even they already know Baamaaya. My son Osmanu is about four and a half years now, and he knows Baamaaya, and Takai, and Jera. And so even children play all these dances, but they are not the dances of children."

Takai is a dance of elegance and dignity. The dancers maintain the graceful billowing of their smocks and the equilibrium of their heads. Takai dancers arrange their line from the older dancers down through the younger dancers, like Baamaaya dancers. Takai is a much cooler dance than Baamaaya. The movement of the Takai dancers as they spin and knock iron rods is extremely

complex. Although the general movement of the Takai circle is counterclock-wise, the individual dancers spin both clockwise and counterclockwise. They alternate every four bars. The iron rods they carry are knocked on the ending beat of a phrase: a dancer spins one way and knocks rods with the one in front of him, then he reverses himself and spins the other way and knocks rods with the dancer behind him. The whole dance is like a chain: when a dancer reverses direction and spins away from the one in front of him to knock rods with the one behind him, the one in front of him reverses and spins to knock rods with the dancer in front of him. Then they reverse themselves and come back to each other, knocking the rods and reversing themselves again. The logical grouping for following the dance is therefore in groups of three. All this is accompanied with rather intricate footwork. Given the complexity of the dance, one of the best things to look at, apart from those who are dancing it with elegance and grace, is the children at the end of the line. They get confused. Sometimes they dance together well, but then they get out of phase and start bumping into each other, tripping over their feet, and missing each other's rods. Since they're spinning, they sometimes get dizzy and start laughing and even fall down. It can be hilarious.

Tora is linked to Takai both musically and socially. There are some dances that resemble Takai in other cultures, and there is no oral tradition of its origin, but the origin of Tora, more than 200 years ago, is described in the drum history. Unlike Takai, Tora does not have a circular movement. The drummers are to the side, as are some women who sing and ululate to encourage the dancers. The dancers make a line, and the first woman comes out with the dance step. The dancer spins or turns until the beat hits its accent, when she plants a foot. She then turns and comes back towards the centre, still dancing, and by the time the beat reaches its second accent, another woman has come out dancing in the opposite direction. When the beat hits its next accent, they spin and knock their bottoms together on the beat. Then the first one goes back to the line, and another one comes out. Thus there are three women who are actually dancing at any one time, the two who are out and the one getting ready to come out and who is picking up the beat.

The Tora dancer leans with her body as she is moving and doing the dance, accentuating her body movements to convey the change of direction when she marks the beat or bumps her bottom. It is interesting to watch the different styles with which the women move into the accent, and this movement towards a danced definition of the accented beat is the clearest aesthetic parallel with Takai. There is a great deal of variety to the way they hop, turn, and reverse direction. The interest of their dance also comes from the way they move to bump each other: they come towards each other fairly fast, and they cover a lot of ground, yet each somehow manages to know where the other is going to be so that they knock their bottoms firmly and cleanly and not roughly or sloppily. Tora is a happy dance. Spectators always get a kick out of it, and general laughter occasionally breaks out. All in all, it is a uniquely wonderful part of the Dagbamba musical heritage.

Young people also come to help in the performance of customs much in the

Takai dance, Tamale

way that Baamaaya or other groups come, and Simpa is their showcase. Young men and boys play the percussion instruments, and the lead singer is a young man, but the chorus of girls who sing and dance extends in age from teenagers down to five- and even four-year-olds. Almost every urban neighbourhood and every village has its Simpa group. Simpa is played at most of the same types of occasions when Takai or Tora or Baamaaya might be played. If a chief comes to visit an area, the Simpa people will come out to entertain him. If a chief is installed, Simpa will be beaten. At funerals in Tamale there are generally two, three, and sometimes four different Simpa groups. When they come, they set up and do their thing. On days when they are not playing, they practise in preparation for playing, and one hears the drums and songs of Simpa every night. It is nice to walk through the quiet moonlit streets following the sound of the music to the area where this or that group is practising. Though the young people certainly understand that music is better when it is well organised, the practices are not totally goal-orientated because the young people enjoy themselves so much. For them, practising is basically another way of getting together and making music and dancing.

There are fluctuations in the number of active groups at any time. Almost as in a pop music scene, new people come up, and older groups fade away as their personnel changes. Among the great current Simpa leaders is a handsome young man from the village of Kumbungu. His popular nickname is Gowon. His Lion Boys group and his dancers are always musically disciplined, and his own singing and dancing have made him a local star. At a village Simpa, the quality of the performers may not be as polished, but the whole village will come out to support the group, including most of the mothers. The cuteness of the kids is one of the reasons why Simpa is so entertaining. They will be dressed to the hilt: all the little girls will be made up with lipstick, and wearing their best dresses, women's co-ordinated blouses and bottoms, with scarves, purple dots on their foreheads – an idea they get from watching Indian movies – and even plastic sunglasses and watches. They are totally adorable.

Simpa is not really the name of a beat. Simpa people play a variety of beats. The most common beat is highlife, but Simpa groups have other beats for various songs – agbadza, soul, blues, merengue, pachanga – all the beats they hear from the radio. Simpa drums are of several types. The traditional drummers can even play Simpa if it is requested. Originally, Simpa was played on square-frame drums. Each frame drum in an ensemble has its pitch, and the beat is built in layers from the combination of the different drums, usually at least four, plus a bell and a rattle and maybe a lunga drum. The drums common since the sixties are more like a modern Western drum set. These instruments are made of metal by local blacksmiths. There is a double or triple conga, behind which one drummer stands. Dagbamba kids are wizards with the conga drum, which functions as the lead drum. They get more types of sounds from these drums than people playing more traditional African wooden hand drums, and they use the metal rims for a special ''ping!'' that cannot be obtained even from a fibreglass conga drum. A second

drummer plays what is the essence of a jazz kit, also made by local blacksmiths: there is a bass drum with a foot pedal, a snare, a standing tomtom, a bell, and a cymbal. Someone will play maracas made out of an aerosol can with wooden handles attached. Finally, someone may be playing a harmonica or a flute. And, of course, there is a lead singer and the chorus. The song lyrics are sometimes difficult to interpret. They can be silly satire, or they can be sweet homilies.

The dancing for Simpa is done by one or two pairs of girls at a time. They come from the chorus, and they take turns. The dance is in essence a cool highlife with a downward focus, movement centred in the hips. A Simpa girl dances with her partners, barely moving and generally looking downward, her face a mask of coolness and concentration, her body a model of control. Simpa is truly one of the most beautiful low-key types of dancing one can see in West Africa. Almost all of the girls are good dancers, but there are some outstanding ones in terms of sheer beauty. The whole scene is both exciting and charming. As interesting is the way the young people and children invent their songs, scout other groups, and try to top each other with their performances. The most impressive thing about Simpa is the way the children give their all to the music. They are conscious from an early age of presence and projection in musical expression, and the general artistic awareness of the young people who grow up in Dagbamba society is one of the critically important factors in the greatness of Dagbamba musical culture.

As Alhaji Ibrahim said, "Children are wonderful, because they can talk and their talk will do some work. And so the children can start something and it will come to stand as something for the old people. When the children start a dance, if there is another village where there is some playing, sometimes these children will say, 'Let's take our playing and go and show to the chief of that village.' And so children bring good things into a town."

Simpa

We can be sure that whatever transformations occur in the course of modernisation, Dagbamba children will grow up to love and preserve their musical heritage. The Dagbamba have a proverb that says, ''When an elephant gives birth to a child, if the child is not up to the size of an elephant, at least it will be up to a hippopotamus.''

Many of the dances one can see at a funeral can also be seen at the Damba Festival. The Damba is the biggest of the five major community festivals that the Dagbamba celebrate each year. The Damba Festival celebrates the birth of the Prophet Mohammed, but it seems more like a festival for chieftaincy. As is evident in the drum history and in the praise-name dances, respect for chieftaincy is truly at the heart of Dagbamba society. ''In everything'', Dagbamba say, ''there needs to be a leader''. Throughout the year, one can observe the way the Dagbamba respect their chiefs on Mondays and Fridays, when townspeople assemble with their chief to discuss the problems of the town. These biweekly town meetings are augmented by consultations among the chief and his elders to deal with any problem or issue that comes up. But it is in the Damba Festival that the respect for chieftaincy takes a different and more visually spectacular form.

From the first day of the Damba month, drummers go to the chief's house every evening and beat for people to dance. On the eleventh day, there is a big afternoon dance at the chief's house. The seventeenth and eighteenth days are the culmination of the event. Many of the dances are the same dances one sees at a funeral, though there is more dancing of the Damba dance than usual. On the seventeenth day, a huge dance circle is formed in front of the chief's house. At one side the timpana drummer beats his two Ashanti double-drums and calls the names of the visitors. Every chief comes with his drummers, and other drummers go around drumming praises and collecting tips. It is not rare for people to break into spontaneous dances at this time. Those coming on

horseback have their horses elaborately decorated, and they make their horses dance as they approach the dance circle. The dance circle is wide enough to accommodate everybody who has a right to sit down, and spectators gather around the perimeter. Everybody is dressed up. The men dress in typical Dagbamba smocks, pantaloons, hats and boots. Some wear robes. The women wear wax-print cloth dresses and scarves, though the chief's wives and some others may wear locally-woven cloth and head-ties. As the other chiefs arrive, they start taking their places.

When the dance circle is forming, the place for the chief and his most important elders and visitors is in one part of the circle opposite the door to the main entrance hall of the chief's house, and the majority of the chief's wives and children find places in other parts of the circle. There is also a section for the Kambonsi, the soldiers, who arrive dressed in their kente cloths, preceded by children carrying their chairs. When the chief comes out of his house to take his place in the circle, the chief's people hold an umbrella over his head and move it up and down when he comes out, employing it as the Akans do during their processions. The chief comes out with a dignified walk to a special type of drumming which is telling him, "Walk gently and coolly. The earth is yours." Sometimes, as he reaches his place, he breaks into the Damba dance. The Kambonsi fire their muskets, and the spectators crowd around. The drummers who are inside the circle go to each chief or prince or princess individually to invite the person to dance, and the assembled spectators and guests watch when the dancer comes out to dance. To one side, the Kambonsi, a truly colourful bunch, dance their own special dance, an energetic and aggressive dance befitting soldiers. They beat double-bells and drums, and the dancers leap about. The dancing continues for several hours before people go back to their homes.

On the eighteenth day, the chief sits outside his house, and everyone comes to greet him before they "lead the Damba home". Those who are riding horses display their horsemanship, and after the greetings, the people make their procession. In every town, the Damba has its resting place for the year, usually a short distance from the town. When the procession reaches that place, there is another dance. A special favourite is a women's dance called Lua. The Lua dancers form ovals to one side of the main dance circle, singing and clapping their hands. At one end of each oval are the drummers. At the other end, three women arrange themselves. A dancer comes into the open space, does a few steps, then jumps back into the arms of the three women, who pick her up and throw her to the other end of the oval. She lands just as the drummers hit the main beat. When all the dancing is finished, the Damba Festival is truly over, and the people go back to their homes, saying to each other, "May we all last to see another Damba."

Alhaji Ibrahim described the significance of the Damba in the following words: "On the day of the Damba, you will see wonders in Dagbon. On that day, you will know whether Dagbon is Dagbon, or Dagbon is not Dagbon, because you are going to see wonders, wonders that are many. You will see how they dress, how they dress with foolishness and how they dress with

Dance circle at the Damba Festival

sense. There is beauty inside it, and there is ugliness, too. There is good inside it, and there is doing of bad things, too. As for the Damba day, unless you are there to see it before, you will know what is Damba. When the last Damba days come, all our people, even if they are at Kumasi or Accra, they will all come home and dance Damba. All the roads are full of people. On every road, you will see young girls, young boys, old men, old women, all of them coming to dance Damba. Damba is our leading dance, and every twelve months we dance it, and nothing comes to prevent us from beating it. And so Damba is a big thing in Dagbon, and it is something on the part of our chiefs. As for chieftaincy, on that day, when you see a chief, his heart is too white with happiness. Chieftaincy is what makes our Dagbon go forward, and Damba makes also our chieftaincy to become strong. And Damba also shows the respect of drumming, because if there are no drummers, then no one will know a chief. And so Damba is a big thing in Dagbon. On the Damba day, everybody is happy, and it's like when the white people say Christmas. And when we reach Damba, it's a new year, and we greet each other, 'You have got a new life, and may God bless us to have health and long life, and may we greet each other again at the Damba Festival.' This is how Damba is.''

The Dagbamba have a remarkable culture indeed. They are lovers of music, and the richness of their musical heritage has helped them hold their culture well, year after year, for centuries. They have had the wisdom to give proper respect to musicians and to let music play a profound role in their lives, and for that wisdom, they have received the benefits of happiness and beauty. Ultimately, we must recognise that the Dagbamba are not significant because of any relevance to our own social forms. Their history and culture are relevant to their own situation. What is relevant to us is their deep humanism, the inspiration that has led to a style of life in which art has been elevated to become the necessary complement to the important stages of a life and the important events of a community. The reality of this achievement is something the Dagbamba experience all the time, and it is no wonder that they are proud of their great heritage and committed to the perpetuation of their tradition in Dagbon. As the Dagbamba say, "The place where water is good will gather water-drinkers.''

NOTES

1. John Miller Chernoff, *African Rhythm and African Sensibility: Aesthetics and Social Action in African Musical Idioms* (Chicago: University of Chicago Press, 1979).
2. John M. Chernoff and Alhaji Ibrahim Abdulai, with the collaboration of Kissmal Ibrahim Hussein and Benjamin D. Sunkari, *A Drummer's Testament: A Dagbamba Drummer Talks About His Culture*: vol.1, *The Way of Drumming*; vol.2, *In Our Living*; manuscript in progress, forthcoming, 1986. All direct quotes by Alhaji Ibrahim Abdulai are taken from *A Drummer's Testament*, and much of this essay is based on the introduction to that book, also in progress.

BIBLIOGRAPHY
On Dagbon and Dagbamba Society
BENZING, Brigitta. *Die Geschichte und das Herrschaftssystem der Dagomba*. Meisenheim am Glan: Verlag Anton Hain, 1971.

BLAIR, H.A., and DUNCAN-JOHNSTONE, A.C., eds. *Enquiry into the Constitution and Organisation of the Dagbon Kingdom*. Accra, Ghana: Government Printing Office, 1931.

CARDINALL, A.W. *The Natives of the Northern Territories of the Gold Coast: Their Customs, Religion and Folklore*. London: George Routledge and Sons, 1925.

—— *Tales Told in Togoland*. London: Oxford University Press, 1931.

CHERNOFF, John Miller. *African Rhythm and African Sensibility: Aesthetics and Social Action in African Musical Idioms*. Chicago: University of Chicago Press, 1979.

—— "Music-Making Children of Africa", *Natural History* 88, no.9 (November 1979): pp.68–75.

—— *A Drummer's Testament: A Dagbana Drummer Talks About His Culture*. To be published by the University of Chicago Press, 1985.

FERGUSON, Phyllis, and WILKES, Ivor. "Chiefs, Constitutions, and the British in Northern Ghana", in *West African Chiefs: Their Changing Status under Colonial Rule and Independence*, edited by Michael Crowder and Obaro Ikime. New York: African Publishing Corp., 1970.

LEVTZION, Nehemia. *Muslims and Chiefs in West Africa; A Study of Islam in the Middle Volta Basin in the Pre-Colonial Period*. Oxford: Clarendon Press, 1968.

RATTRAY, R.S. *The Tribes of the Ashanti Hinterland*, vol.2. Oxford: Clarendon Press, 1932.

STANILAND, Martin. *The Lions of Dagbon: Political Change in Northern Ghana*. Cambridge, Massachusetts: Cambridge University Press, 1975.

TAMAKLOE, Emmanuel Forster, ed. *A Brief History of the Dagbamba People*. Accra, Ghana: Government Printing Office, 1931.

Comparative

AMES, David W. "Professionals and Amateurs", *African Arts* 1, no.2 (winter 1968): pp.40–5, 80, 82–4.

D'AZEVEDO, Warren L., ed. *The Traditional Artist in African Societies*. Bloomington: Indiana University Press, 1973.

BANKOLE, Ayo, BUSH, Judith, and SAMAAN, Sadek H. "The Yoruba Master Drummer", *African Arts* 8, no.2 (winter 1975): pp.48–56, 77–8.

BERLINER, Paul. *The Soul of Mbira: Music and Traditions of the Shona People of Zimbabwe*. Berkeley and Los Angeles: University of California Press, 1978.

CUTTER, Charles. "The Politics of Music in Mali", *African Arts* 1, no.3 (spring 1968): pp.38–9, 74–7.

JONES, A.M. *Studies in African Music*, 2 vols. London: Oxford University Press, 1959.

KEIL, Charles. *Tiv Song*. Chicago: University of Chicago Press, 1979.

LADZEKPO, S. Kobla. "The Social Mechanics of Good Music: A Description of Dance Clubs Among the Anlo Ewe-Speaking People of Ghana", *African Music* 5, no.1 (1971): pp.6–22.

MERRIAN, Alan P. "African Music", in *Continuity and Change in African Cultures*, edited by William R. Bascom and Melville J. Herskovitz. Chicago: University of Chicago Press, 1959.

NKETIA, J.H. Kwabena. *Drumming in Akan Communities of Ghana*. London: University of Ghana and Thomas Nelson and Sons, 1963.

—— *Music of Africa*. New York: W.W. Norton, 1974; London: Gollancz, 1975.

THOMPSON, Robert Faris. *African Art in Motion: Icon and Act in the Collection of Catherine Coryton White*. Los Angeles: University of California Press, 1974.

ZEMP, Hugo. *Musique Dan: La musique dans la pensée et la vie sociale d'une société africaine*. Paris: Mouton and Ecole Practique des Hautes Etudes, 1971.

RECORDINGS

African Rhythm and African Sensibility, audio cassette accompanying the book of the same title, order number 0-226-10346-3, available from the University of Chicago Press, 5801 South Ellis Avenue, Chicago, Illinois 60637, U.S.A.

Master Drummers of Dagbon, Rounder Records 5016.

CHAPTER 6

Caribbean Crucible

BY KENNETH BILBY

History has played many tricks on the Caribbean. Subjected for centuries to the whims of European colonisers, depopulated and subsequently repopulated by successive waves of migration drawing from several continents, the Caribbean region has been shaped more than most parts of the world by external forces. This history of conquest and colonisation, of moulding and refashioning, has given to the region an unusual cultural and social complexity. Caribbean societies are multi-layered, and sometimes bewildering in their cultural diversity. One speaks of the "Anglophone", "Hispanophone", "Francophone", or "Dutch-speaking" Caribbean, and each of these is further divisible into clearly differentiated societies displaying their own unique cultural blends deriving from African, European, Asian and Amerindian sources.

Just as one must be careful in generalising about Caribbean culture, one must be cautious when talking about Caribbean music. The remarkable richness of Caribbean musical life is partly the product of its multi-layered complexity and diversity, and in blurring the distinctions between different local musical traditions, one risks losing sight of their individuality and the subtleties that set them apart and give them their special appeal. Yet it *is* possible to speak of a single Caribbean "musical family", for underlying much of the region's diverse music is an unmistakeable family resemblance, a kinship based in history. In most of the islands and territories of the Caribbean, the central, dominating fact of musical life ever since shortly after the Conquest has been the encounter between European and African musical traditions. Across the region, European folk music – whether of Spanish, French, British, or Dutch origin – has for centuries been coming into contact and fusing with the varied musical traditions brought by slaves from West and Central Africa. The specific ingredients have differed from place to place, as have the ways in which they have been combined. But the fundamental similarity of the available cultural materials in the different colonies – for example, the broad similarities between British, French, and Spanish harmonic and melodic concepts on the one hand, and on the other, between the rhythmic and aesthetic concepts held by, say, the Akan or Yoruba of West Africa and the Bakongo of Central Africa – paved the way for a creative process of blending and fusion (sometimes called "Creolisation") that had similar results throughout the Caribbean.

Consequently, one finds today in most parts of the region a broad spectrum of folk musical traditions or styles, ranging from those that have been called "neo-African" to those that are clearly European-derived. In between these two extremes are a large number of "hybrid" traditions that can be placed in neither musical world – whose historical components have become so intricately intertwined that it is difficult to separate with any certainty the "European" from the "African". Such African-European musical spectrums are characteristically Caribbean, existing in places as historically and geographically far removed from one another as Cuba and Trinidad, Haiti and the Netherlands Antilles.

To speak of "Caribbean music", then, is a bit like speaking of "African music" or "Asian music": in spite of the broad variety of styles, techniques, and aesthetic canons lumped together in these categories, certain generalisations can be made, which will hold true for many, if not most, members of each of these musical families. With this in mind, two musical cultures – one from the English-speaking Caribbean, the other Spanish-speaking – are presented here to stand for the kinds of musical experiences one might expect to find in any part of the region. In spite of all that distinguishes them, the citizens of Jamaica and the Dominican Republic and their Caribbean neighbours inhabit similar musical landscapes and lead quite similar musical lives.

Jamaica, like several of the other large Caribbean islands, is rich in "neo-African" traditions. Some of these are directly descended from the "plays", or slave dances, that were once a part of daily life on the plantations (these are well documented in the travel literature of the eighteenth and nineeenth centuries). Contemporary descriptions of these ceremonies leave little doubt as to their religious significance – they were often tied to slave funerals and involved divination and spirit possession – and show the extent to which slaves succeeded in forging their own viable culture, based largely on African-derived principles. Such "neo-African" musical traditions have been carried down to the present and continue to be found in pockets spread across the island. Complex drumming and dance are central to all of these traditions, as are call-and-response singing and a number of other African-derived musical features; in some cases, possession by ancestral spirits is sought.

One of the most interesting "neo-African" musical traditions found in Jamaica is that of the Maroons, descendants of slaves who escaped from coastal plantations during the seventeenth and eighteenth centuries and fled to the forests to form their own societies. In 1739, after nearly a century of guerrilla warfare against the British colonists, the Maroons, who were never defeated, signed treaties of peace which guaranteed their freedom, provided them with their own lands, and granted them a certain degree of political autonomy. Today their descendants live in four separate communities in the interior of the island, and possess governing councils and headmen known by the official title "Colonel". The Maroons are viewed by other Jamaicans as the guardians of the "deepest", most African cultural tradition in the island – and not without reason, for in the Maroon ceremony known as "Kromanti Play" or "Kromanti Dance", a centuries-old African-based musical tradition has been preserved and carried down to the present. (The term "Kromanti" is derived from the name of a historical slave port on the coast of what is today Ghana, from which a large number of slaves were transported to Jamaica.)

The Maroons of Moore Town, located in the eastern parish of Portland, boast the richest and most varied Kromanti tradition of all the present-day Maroon communities. Driving along the single road leading from the coast into Maroon territory, one cannot help but be awed by the rugged beauty of the changing landscape. As one climbs higher and higher into the hills, a striking vista unfolds. The glistening Rio Grande courses through a deep valley, flanked by a solid wall of mountains. Behind the first foothills rises one of the remotest and least touched expanses of land in Jamaica. The thick carpet of rainforest covering the Blue Mountains remains almost completely uninhabited, and is still largely unexplored. It was in this wilderness that the ancestors of the Moore Town Maroons took refuge from the plantations and acted out their heroic resistance against the slave system, settling finally, after many treks, in the protective valley that encircles the present-day village of Moore Town. This stretch of land is still haunted by the ghosts of past Maroons, being filled with historical landmarks – mountain outlooks, precipices, creeks, and gorges – each bearing a name and telling a story.

Kromanti rituals in Moore Town are full of references to the Maroon past, centring as they do on the possession of participants by ancestral spirits, invoked to ceremonies by music and dance. Possessed mediums act as the original "first-time" Maroons are said to have acted. They are hostile to outsiders and behave violently towards them. They continue to have a

"warlike" character – indeed, the ritual specialist and central medium who presides over ceremonies is known as the "fight-man" (*fete-man*) – and retain knowledge of the herbal and magical healing techniques that were so important to the guerrilla fighters of the pre-treaty period. Even today, Kromanti ceremonies are predominantly concerned with the healing of injuries and spirit-caused illnesses.

Given the orientation of Kromanti Play towards the past, it is not surprising that the varied repertoire of Maroon musical and dance styles reflects at many levels the African heritage. Present-day Maroon music bears witness to the historical process through which elements from a diversity of African traditions were long ago fused into new, integrated wholes on Caribbean soil. Many of the general labels once used in Jamaica to refer to the different African regions and ethnic groups from which the slaves were drawn have been preserved in the names of the "deeper", more sacred Kromanti Play musical and dance styles. Among these are Prapa, or Papa (originally referring to slaves brought from the Ewe-speaking region of West Africa), Mandinga (indicating a Senegambian origin), Mongola (referring to Angolan origins), Ibo (pointing to Nigerian origins), and of course the name Kromanti itself (referring to slaves originating from the Gold Coast). The present-day Kromanti sub-styles going by these names are clearly "neo-African"; they incorporate a variety of complex drumming traditions, and show little or no European influence. And yet it would be extremely difficult, if not impossible, to trace most of them to specific African ethnic groups, for in spite of the "ethnic" labels they bear, they are the products of years of inter-mixture between different African traditions. Through a process of blending, they have lost their ethnic specificity and become "African" in a more general sense.

This is not to say, however, that specific African retentions do not abound in the Kromanti tradition. Although influences from several different ethnic groups are present, the Akan-speaking peoples of West Africa have left the most conspicuous mark. The 'Kromanti language" (known also as "Country") spoken in ceremonial contexts is largely derived from Akan. The long cylindrical drums usually played in pairs in Kromanti Play are called printing or aprinting (from the Akan language Twi, "*oprenteng*"); the metallic percussion instrument that is played along with these drums is known as adawo (from Twi, "*dawuro*"). Kromanti drummers are referred to as okrema (from Twi, "*okyerema*"). The cow-horn which is blown and used to send messages and to call Maroons to assembly is called abeng (the word is still used in Ghana as a generic term for wind instruments made from the horn of an animal, which are used in West Africa, as among the Maroons, to communicate messages). The Moore Town Maroons have also preserved a "drum language" similar to that used by the present-day Akan peoples of Ghana and the Ivory Coast. And the specific Maroon musical style known as "Country", which incorporates this drum language, bears a striking resemblance to a particular musical tradition of the Ashanti and Fanti that blends song with proverbs played in drum language. The language of many of

Nanny Mountain near Moore Town

the songs in the more sacred categories is African-derived. The following very sacred "Country" song, for example, often sung during Kromanti Play, is at least partially Akan-derived, although the meaning of most of the words appears to have been lost by the present-day Maroons:

> *manda manda*
> *o siri manda*
> *manda manda*
> *o printing manda*
> *manda manda*
> *o debreku manda*
> *o manpraba jina-eh*
> *eh —*
> *o denkima Kwadjo-eh*
> *o denkima Kwadjo*
> *ma bra, ma bre*
> *osei-oh*
> *Fanti*
> *ma bra, ma bre*[1]

The forceful music and dance of Kromanti Play lend ceremonies much of their dramatic power. Once seen, such a ceremony is not easily forgotten. Summoned by the language of drums, participants gather together, pledged to a common goal — whether the healing of an illness or the resolution of some other crisis. The early hours, dominated by the "pleasurising" sounds of the lighter, recreational styles, help to set the tone for the drama to come. Dancers form a ring or join in couples, while lead singer and chorus spur one another on. The galloping rhythms of the drums synchronise all to create a spirit of co-operation and unity. As the singing grows "sweeter" and the drumming "hotter", enthusiasm increases, until the spirits of ancestors are attracted to come and take possession of dancers, and are persuaded to offer their aid in the struggle against the evil at hand. Eventually, a leading medium thrusts himself onto centre stage, his body now taken over by the spirit of a deceased ritual specialist. The mood becomes more serious. The ancient, more sacred songs and drumming styles are brought into play. The lead dancer and medium ferociously "throws" out one song after another, and is answered by the driving pulse of the drums. He spins and leaps about, brandishing a machete. As he attends to his patient, applying herbal remedies and performing a series of intricately choreographed ritual motions, the drummers and singers continue to build up tension. At last, the ceremony comes to a cathartic peak, with the sacrifice of a fowl or a hog. The cure is completed, the music levels off, and the spirits return for the time being to the world of the ancestors.

In spite of their relative isolation in the past, the Maroons have not been exempt from the process of Creolisation that has long been shaping musical developments in other parts of the island. Their "lighter", less sacred

Kromanti musical styles – such as Jawbone, Saleone, and Tambu – combine "neo-African" drumming with songs in English or Jamaican Creole and melodies that are often clearly European-influenced. And so the Kromanti tradition, though preserving some of the "deepest", most African musical styles in Jamaica, shows the same sort of multi-layered complexity found elsewhere on the island, combining the older and the newer.

Another "neo-African" Jamaican musical tradition is that of the Kumina cults which are found primarily in the eastern part of the island. In St Thomas parish in particular the night air still often vibrates with the compelling rhythms of Kumina. Here, Kumina music remains part of the fabric of daily life, as characteristic of the landscape as the rows of sugar cane, or the aroma of burning palm leaves and white rum. Marketplaces in the larger towns are often livened up by the sounds of visiting Kumina bands, and night-time revelries and gambling tournaments sometimes feature secularised Kumina drumming and dancing as an extra attraction. But the most impressive form of Kumina is that which occurs in the context of religious ceremonies, held for the purpose of communion with the spirits of ancestors. It is in these ceremonies that the overall setting is at its most dramatic, and dance and drumming performances reach their aesthetic high point.

During the later hours of a Kumina ritual, all of the diverse elements that go into the make-up of ceremonies coalesce into one carefully orchestrated communal experience. The warm glow of fire and the play of shadows create an other-worldly atmosphere. At the hub of the action, the drummers sit hunched over their instruments, deep in concentration, eyes locked on one another, but hands unleashed in a flurry of motion. A woman of dignified bearing, the Kumina "Queen", glides across the centre space in a graceful dance, urging the others on. Her fervent chanting is answered by a swelling chorus. A gently undulating ring of dancers, their faces illuminated by the candles they hold in their hands, slowly rotates around the drummers, in perfect time with the rhythms. A goat is brought out, perched on a man's shoulders, and danced around the crowd. When it is sensed that the critical moment has arrived, the goat is sacrificed and, with the respect reserved for those of previous generations, an offering is made of its blood. With renewed vigour, drummers, dancers, and singers celebrate, finally ushering in the first light of day. The ancestors have been shown, once again, that they are not forgotten.

Kumina represents one of the last historical links between Jamaica and Africa, dating from the period just before the transportation of Africans to the island came to a final halt in the third quarter of the nineteenth century. Whereas the Kromanti Play of the Maroons was planted on Jamaican soil centuries ago, the Kumina tradition – according to both recent historical research and many older Kumina devotees themselves – was introduced to the island by "voluntary" post-Emancipation African labourers who came to work the plantations on contract roughly between 1840 and 1865 (emancipation was finalised in Jamaica in 1838). A large percentage of these indentured African immigrants were of Central African origin, and many of them were

concentrated on plantations in the eastern part of the island (particularly St Thomas parish), where Kumina is today most strongly represented.

Kumina ceremonies, like Kromanti Play, centre around ancestral spirit possession. More than anything else, it is this continuing dialogue with the departed ancestors that has helped to keep alive the Central African legacy. Kumina devotees remember the names of a large number of specific ancestors, including several of the original nineteenth-century African immigrants, some of whom are only two or three generations removed from present-day cultists. In ceremonies ranging from memorials for deceased cult members ("Black-and-White" Kuminas) to birth celebrations, from healing rites to "tombing" (entombment) rituals, these ancestors are invoked to come and take possession of the living, whom they join in a renewal and reaffirmation of the "African Bongo" heritage. It is in such contexts that deep "African Country" songs such as the following, sung for my tape-recorder by a Kumina elder in Spring Garden, St Thomas, in 1978, have been passed on. The song is in Kikongo, with a few Creole words added, and the English translation given below was kindly offered by the Zairean scholar Fu-Kiau kia Bunseki, himself a native speaker of the language:

CHORUS: *nki balongo*

   n'dimba kwenda
   nki ba'
   nik'e

CH: *nki balongo*

   nki bilongwa
   gyal, weh you name
   mama

CHORUS: what did they learn?

   going to the valley
   what did they learn?
   what?

CH: what did they learn?

   what are they learning?
   girl, what is your name?
   mama

Kumina singer

CH: *nki balongo*

   musele seh gyala
   Ya Manok'e

CH: *o nki balongo*

   Ma Minott-oh
   from Pera

CH: *nki balongo*

   o 'Cadia-oh
   crossroad way

CH: *nki balongo*

   from 'Cadia-oh
   cross a way

CH: *seh nki balongo*

   mbuta wayenda
   kuna Mbamba

CH: *nki balongo*

   e Nsunga
   wayend'e

CH: *s'eti vo*
   nki balongo

   Nana gyal
   wayend'e

CH: *nki balongo*

   Bongo Eustace-oh
   wayend'e
   Old Kenyon
   wayend'e
   e Mimba
   wayend'e

CH: *o nki baloti'e*

   mbuta, bangial'e
   wayend'e

CH: *nki baloti'e*

   yakala n'nwa wantaba
   sosa yandi

CH: what did they learn?

   my love charm, girl
   Ya Manoka

CH: oh what did they learn?

   Ma Minott
   from Pera

CH: what did they learn?

   oh Arcadia
   crossroad way

CH: what did they learn?

   from Arcadia
   across the way

CH: I say what did they learn?

   the elder went
   to Mbamba

CH: what did they learn?

   oh Nsunga
   went

CH: ask yourself this
   what did they learn?

   Nana girl
   you went

CH: what did they learn?

   Bongo Eustace
   went
   Old Kenyon
   went
   oh Mimba
   went

CH: oh what did they dream?

   the elder, governed by them
   went

CH: what did they dream?

   the man's mouth is to be heeded
   seeking him

CH: *nki balongo*   CH: what did they learn?

   n'kanda ngung'e   the skin of the bell

   wayend'e   went

This song, widely known among Kumina devotees and often sung at ceremonies, invokes the names of several of the original "Bongo" immigrants who arrived in Jamaica during the nineteenth century – Ma Minott (an early Kumina "Queen", or female cult leader), Bongo Eustace, Old Kenyon, and Manoka (Manoka Mvula, one of the most famous and most revered of the original Central Africans) – and asks what they were "dreaming" when they "went", and what they have learned on their journey far from home. Like a number of other "Country" songs, it records in the language of the ancestors the experience of immigration and the encounter with an unfamiliar new world.

The relative youth of the Kumina tradition – its primarily post-Emancipation origins – is reflected in the large number and the "purity" of the African survivals it contains. Some older Kumina practitioners still possess "African Country" vocabularies of several hundred words, most of which are unambiguously traceable to Kikongo. Fundamental religious concepts, ranging from colour symbolism to notions about the proper preparation of the dead, owe much to specifically Central African principles. The music of Kumina is likewise rich in such survivals. The very name of the tradition itself evidences the strength of the Central African musical heritage in Kikongo. "*Kumina*" is a verb that expresses rhythmic motion (the related verb "*kumu*" means "to play a musical instrument", while the noun "*kumu*" signifies "metre, melody, rhythm"). Jamaican Kumina music, played usually on two interlocking drums, the bandu (Kikongo, *banda*) and the "playing cast" (the Kikongo word "*ngoma*" is also sometimes used for both drums), is remarkably similar to a present-day Kongo drumming tradition found in many parts of Zaire, also played on two drums, called kumunu. In both traditions, the drums are placed on their sides and mounted, and the foot of the player is pressed against the head to vary pitch. The ancestral "Country" songs themselves, aside from being sung in Kikongo, make use of a style of delivery, a vocal timbre, and a melodic sense which are palpably Kongo in quality.[2]

The African-influenced musical traditions of the Dominican Republic, like those of Jamaica, show the presence of different historical layers. There is, for example, the music of the congos or palos (a type of long, cylindrical drum), found primarily in the southern part of the country. Tied to celebrations in honour of a number of Catholic saints, these traditions bring us somewhat closer to the middle area of the African-European musical spectrum. Not only the religious observances, but the musical styles themselves are the result of syncretism, or blending, between Spanish and African-derived elements. The Dominican Congo groups, such as the Congos of Villa Mella, play an exciting music with clearly "neo-African" drumming, but with Spanish-influenced vocal techniques and melodic style.

As Fradique Lizardo, the director of the Ballet Folklorico Dominicano and an authority on Dominican culture, has emphasised, it is very difficult to tease out the different threads in the many-stranded ancestry of Afro-Dominicans. Slaves were brought to the country from several parts of West and Central Africa, both "legally" and "illegally", many of them indirectly, via other parts of the Caribbean such as Puerto Rico, Cuba, or Haiti. Blending between the different African traditions represented among these arrivals must have occurred almost from the beginning. Because the Catholic Church began to suppress African religious manifestations among the slaves from early on, these went underground and rapidly merged with Catholic practices (as happened as well in many other Catholic Caribbean colonies). For this reason, and a number of others, the Dominican Republic seems not to have retained the sort of less Creolised, almost completely African-derived musical styles found in some parts of Jamaica and several of the other islands.[3] But in any case, the drumming of several of the Congo groups, if not the songs – which are Spanish both in language and, to some extent, melody – is often extremely African. In this respect, these Afro-Dominican traditions show how subtly shaded the intermediate range of the Caribbean musical spectrum can be, balancing and proportioning African and European elements in different ways and combinations. The syncretic music of the palos/congos – clearly closer to the African than the European end of the Dominican spectrum – is paralleled by similar traditions blending "neo-African" drumming with European-influenced vocals in several other parts of the Caribbean.

Our brief glance at Afro-Dominican musical traditions touches on another important aspect of Caribbean life that has contributed to the multi-layered complexity of the region's music: the long and continuing history of inter-island (or inter-territorial) migration. This constant movement back and forth

Pri-Pri – a relative of Merengue

has helped to circulate many local styles way beyond their places of birth, spreading their influence far and wide. Just as the Atlantic coast of Central America has its Jamaican mento bands, and French Guiana has its Haitian vaccine-players (the vaccine is a wind instrument associated with Haiti's carnival), the Dominican Republic has its British West Indian fife and drum ensembles, brought many decades ago by immigrants from the islands of Nevis and St Kitts. Replete with costumed dancers who parade about the streets and recite passages from ancient British mummers' plays, the "mummies" tradition of San Pedro de Macoris incorporates a fascinating hybrid musical style that gives some idea of how thoroughgoing the fusion of African and European elements in the Caribbean can sometimes be. Here we have an example of a form of music that is clearly of both worlds, and yet belongs to neither. The instruments used are themselves not clearly traceable to either continent; they include a bass drum and type of side-drum (traditionally made from local materials) that are similar in design to European military parade drums, but have parallels as well in West Africa; and a type of side-blown flute (traditionally made of bamboo) that is as African as European in design, but is tuned to an approximation of the scale found in European fifes. The music produced by this ensemble meshes European and African musical features so tightly that the whole can no longer be broken down into its individual parts. Echoes of old European military parade drumming are still there, but they have been spiced up almost beyond recognition by a fundamentally African rhythmic approach. Likewise, the fife-playing is occasionally vaguely reminiscent of certain European melodic conventions, but its rhythmic underpinnings, its emphasis on creative repetition and improvisation, and its overall melodic style all owe a heavy debt to Africa.[4]

There is a similar tradition in Jamaica known as John Canoe (or Jonkonnu).[5] Several theories have been put forth as to the origin of the name "John Canoe". The most likely derivation is from the name of a notorious African, John Conny, who was involved in the slave trade along the West African coast during the 1700s. The Jamaican John Canoe tradition is described in historical writings going back as far as the eighteenth century. At that time, it was tied to island-wide Christmas festivities in which slaves played a central role. Masked dancers made their way through the streets and lanes, accompanied by animated music played on a variety of African and European instruments, occasionally stopping to deliver speeches or perform segments of British folk plays. At a later point, "set dances" were added to the festivities; teams, or "sets", of colourfully costumed dancers competed in the streets, accompanied by a variety of European and Euro-African styles.

John Canoe is still danced from one end of Jamaica to the other during the Christmas holidays. As recently as the 1920s, John Canoe bands in some parts of the island were still including recitations from Shakespeare and passages from medieval mummery plays in their performances (much as the "mummies" performers of San Pedro de Macoris do today). But this aspect of the tradition seems to have faded out. In any case, the costumed characters of

present-day Jamaican John Canoe – Horsehead, Cowhead, Devil Satan, Wild Indian, Belly-Woman, Pitchy-Patchy, Jack-in-the-Green, and others – still betray the dual origins of the tradition. This menagerie blends elements from a number of British folk traditions (pre-Christian "pagan" survivals, such as the Morris and sword dances, as well as the mummers' plays) with the subtly sinuous quality of African dance and the influence of West African masking traditions.[6]

Although the John Canoe tradition seems to have once had religious associations, today it is danced solely for "jollification", to enliven the streets and contribute to the holiday spirit at Christmas time. An energetic John Canoe performance rarely fails to create the proper atmosphere of joy and exhilaration. With the first sounds of the drums off in the distance, people begin to line the streets in anticipation of the approaching spectacle. The masked dancers troop by, their patchwork costumes flashing a blur of colours as they caper about, swerving, twirling, and hopping. Some of the masqueraders leave the earth with athletic bounds, while others remain with feet firmly planted, bodies centred, torsos swaying with contained tension. The drums continue to exert their irresistible pull, and some spectators jump forth and join the surging procession. The rhythms are punctuated by the sharp crack of a whip, wielded by one of the dancers. Another member of the troupe acts out a pantomime with a pair of wooden swords, while a third, encased in a horse-head mask with movable jaws, dashes off to the side and thrills the watching children with mock threats. Although in some parts of the island John Canoe has virtually disappeared, recent years have seen something of a revival of the tradition, and many Jamaicans continue to look forward to the street celebrations as yuletide rolls around. As one seasoned performer averred, "If it weren't for the John Canoe, they wouldn't know that it was Christmas; if the John Canoe bands don't come out, you don't see any liveliness, you don't see any crowd."

Some Jamaican fife and drum bands continue to play, in addition to the hybrid music of the John Canoe dance itself, a number of "set dance" tunes that are clearly of European origin, and are performed in a very European manner; these are immediately distinguishable from the rhythmically and melodically more complex John Canoe music. Some of them are based on old British march tunes, and others incorporate British dance tunes (for example, the various figures of the quadrille). These "neo-European" traditions are related to a larger group of styles that have been crucial to the development of recreational Creole dance music, not only in Jamaica, but in the rest of the Caribbean. I refer here to the pan-European "ballroom" dance styles of the eighteenth and nineteenth centuries, which were diffused over the entire Caribbean. Dances such as the waltz, the mazurka, the reel, the polka, the schottische, and the quadrille, though having their origins in specific parts of Europe, were popular in all of the European countries involved in the colonisation of the Caribbean. They were backed by much the same instrumentation everywhere: guitars, fiddles, flutes, and so forth. Today, rural village bands in most parts of the Caribbean continue to play versions of these dances.

What makes these "ballroom" styles so important is that they long ago introduced to all the far-flung territories of the Caribbean a common harmonic system (based on the European eight-tone diatonic scale) that was quickly grasped and adopted by slave musicians. While the original European styles were sometimes retained in the Caribbean remarkably unchanged – indeed, in many areas, village bands are still capable of producing quite "pure" renditions – a host of Creolised forms began to emerge alongside them, clothed in the same tonality, but driven by a new conception of rhythm. This included not only transformed versions of the "ballroom" dances themselves (versions of the mazurka and quadrille, for instance, that swung and rocked as never before), but a large number of completely new dance styles that were truly indigenous Caribbean creations. Many of the "national" folk and/or popular musical styles of the Caribbean – the Dominican merengue, the Cuban son, the Trinidad calypso, or kaiso – are outgrowths of this process.

The Jamaican counterpart to these indigenous styles is the mento, a musical form that is somewhat reminiscent of the traditional Trinidadian calypso, but grew from distinctively Jamaican roots. In fact, a great deal of variety is encompassed in the mento tradition (sometimes the term "mento" is used in rural Jamaica to refer to folk songs in general). Instrumentation may vary from a harmonica accompanied by a collection of scrapers, rattles, and other percussion to the more typical string band consisting of a rhumba-box (a bass instrument of African design, with three or four metal tongues that are plucked), and sometimes drums and assorted other percussion, topped by a lead melody instrument, often a fiddle or fife. Some modern bands feature saxophones, trumpets, or other horns, and of course there are often vocals as well. The historical connection between mento and the old "ballroom" dances is still retained in the practice, followed by some village bands, of replacing the fifth figure of the quadrille with an instrumental mento (sometimes called a "round dance").

Mento has never really been stylistically homogenous. Even the traditional old-fashioned mento, played by rural village bands, may be either slow and plaintive or bright and up-tempo. Some bands play with a more European flavour than others. In the last few decades, a new version of the style has popped up in coastal areas, played by bands who make their living performing for tourists; sometimes influenced by Trinidadian calypso and other styles — and often referred to as "Jamaica calypso", since this was a name that tourists would recognise – these updated variants of the mento are in a more pan-Caribbean vein, and are often quite interesting. Likewise, the urbanised mentos turned out by the fledgling Kingston recording industry during the 1950s represent another interesting dimension of the tradition, a new development that heralded the coming transition from "folk" to "popular" music in the Jamaican capital. But all variants of the mento remain basically Jamaican, sharing the same rhythmic foundation (particularly the characteristic "off-beat" strumming pattern of the banjo or guitar), as well as a large number of "standard" Jamaican melodies, and a similar style of melodic improvisation. Many of the better known Jamaican folk songs – "Linstead Market", "Solas Market", "Nobody's Business", and so forth – are typical mento tunes. The mento tradition, in characteristically Caribbean fashion, has also long been absorbing elements from the various other folk styles surrounding it; Jamaican work songs, ring-play tunes, and wake songs, for instance, often also exist in mento versons. This absorptive quality makes mento Jamaica's indigenous music *par excellence*, the traditional style most typical of the Jamaican countryside. As one elderly songster once told Louise Bennett, the renowned Jamaican folklorist and poet, *"Every* Jamaican folk song is a mento, we *grow* mento."

Work songs also constitute a vital part of Jamaica's mixed musical heritage. In the recent past, such songs were a ubiquitous part of the Jamaican scenery, providing rhythmic accompaniment to the co-ordinated movements of co-operative labour gangs. As in other parts of the Caribbean, fields were planted, roads repaired, and buildings constructed in time with music. (There is a clear precedent for this tradition in the documented work songs sung by slaves during earlier centuries.) Jamaica's well-known "digging songs" are only one of a large variety of different kinds of work songs, accompanying an assortment of tasks ranging from lumber-sawing to rice-beating. Usually, there is a leader who sings out solo lines and is answered by a lively chorus of fellow workers. Since most of the work songs have a call-and-response structure, there is a temptation to assume they are African-derived. But it must be remembered that many European, including British, work songs are

based on a similar antiphonal structure (perhaps the best known example being the sea shanties, many of which were carried to Jamaica). In fact, Jamaican digging songs, like Jamaican folk music more generally, vary from the more European to the obviously African-derived (the latter often being recognisable by their highly-syncopated, very short choral responses). But many of them fall into that shaded intermediate area where African and European have been fused into something totally new and totally Caribbean. The very popular digging song, "Judy Drownded", belongs to this group:

> LEADER: Judy drownded, Judy drownded
> CHORUS: Woy-oh, Judy drownded!
> L: Judy drownded, Judy drownded
> CH: Woy-oh, Judy drownded!
> L: Judy no drownded, Judy ina bed
> CH: Everybody bawl out, Judy drownded!
> L: Judy no dead, but Judy drownded
> CH: Woy-oh, Judy drownded!

This song, and other popular digging tunes, such as "John Tom" and "Chi-chi Bud" (Chi-chi bird), are known throughout the island, and are sometimes performed by mento bands.

   Game song traditions are also common to the entire country. In some parts of the island, children still assemble outdoors on moonlit evenings to entertain themselves with "ring play" and other sorts of traditional games that depend on musical backing. Many of the songs have a call-and-response form that is governed by the rules of the games they accompany (there are stone-passing games, ring games, memory games, and other sorts, some of them of English origin and others indigenous). There are also adult game song traditions associated with traditional wakes and other death ceremonies. Many of the game songs, particularly the children's songs, such as "Brown

Girl in the Ring" or "Jane and Louisa", appear to be derived from British melodies. But many others have clearly been touched by the African presence. And, as usual, there are those that are wholly indigenous creations, such as "Emmanuel Road", one of the most popular Jamaican game songs. The players rapidly pass stones in rhythm as they sing, attempting to avoid an accidental collision between the circulating objects and their hands:

> Go dung [down] Emmanuel Road, gyal an' bwai [girl and
>   boy]
> fe go bruk [break] rock-stone, gyal an' bwai
> go dung Emmanuel Road, gyal an' bwai
> fe go bruk rock-stone, gyal an' bwai
> bruk dem one by one, gyal an' bwai
> bruk dem two by two, gyal an' bwai
> bruk dem three by three, gyal an' bwai
> bruk dem four by four, gyal an' bwai
> finger mash, no cry, gyal an' bwai
> memba, da play we da play [remember, we're only playing]
>   gyal an' bwai, etc.

Through traditions such as these, children from an early age become imbued with a specifically Jamaican – some would say Caribbean – sense of rhythm and style that is the culmination of a process of cultural blending that began centuries ago.[7]

This Jamaican sense of rhythm and motion is in any case carried in the very language that is spoken in everyday life. Any American or British English speaker who has listened carefully to spoken Jamaican Creole, or "patois", knows that its unintelligibility has much to do with its unfamiliar rhythms. In Jamaica, language and music are permeated by the same rhythmic sensibility, and are shaped by one another. As Louise Bennett put it, in a recent interview: "The rhythm of the language – you find the same rhythm in the mento songs, you find the same rhythm in the Poco [Pocomania, an Afro-Protestant religion], in the Revival, in the reggae, you find that same rhythm of the spoken Jamaican language." It is perhaps at this deep level – in language and movement style, for instance, where behaviour is so ingrained that it is often unconscious and seems almost innate – that the African heritage in Jamaica has had its most profound and enduring impact. And it is in the Jamaican orientation to rhythm that this is most apparent. Rex Nettleford, Artistic Director and Principal Choreographer of the National Dance Theatre Company of Jamaica, has often emphasised the deep-level "Africanity" that pervades Jamaican culture, pointing out that it is present in the whole way that Jamaicans approach movement, from the polyrhythmic use of the body in dance to the very way the body is carried in walking. All of this goes to show that in the complicated, multi-layered cultural mix of Jamaica, even where the drums of Kumina and Kromanti are absent, the rhythm of Africa still prevails.

This is true even of today's urban reggae, which in spite of its North American rhythm and blues roots and its growing cosmopolitanism, is as much a product of the Jamaican countryside and its rich musical resources as any of the folk styles already discussed. Some Jamaican experts, such as Louise Bennett and Rex Nettleford, detect a strong mento contribution in reggae, while others, like Olive Lewin, the founder of the Jamaica Folk Singers and a pioneering folk music collector, believe that the music of the Afro-Protestant Revival cults has played a more important role in the development of the style (through its ancestor, ska).

While the history of reggae has yet to be unravelled in all its complexity, one thing that is certain is that evidence of continuing influence from various traditional styles exists in abundance. A well-attuned ear can clearly make out strains of mento in the "off-beat" rhythm guitar – as well as in the subtle rhythmic interweave between guitar and keyboards – in many reggae recordings. Traces of John Canoe, Kumina, and mento phrasing can be heard in the rolls and carefully-placed accents of reggae trap drummers (whose individual styles vary quite a bit). Louise Bennett has noted similarities between certain modern dance movements popular among young reggae enthusiasts and an "old African step" (the "weak knee" dipping motion, as she puts it) that is much used in mento dancing. The melodic, harmonic, and rhythmic influence of traditional Afro-Protestant Revival music is certainly there as well. Indeed, there are certain reggae ensembles that have always been known for their specifically Revivalist-tinged style (the Maytals and Culture, for example). Other artistes specialise in conscious mento-reggae fusions, such as Stanley and the Turbynes, King Bedbug, Count Lasher, and in a somewhat more progressive vein, the Trinidadian-born Lord Laro. Even the reggae of Bob Marley, which many foreign listeners have assumed to be less "authentic" or true to its roots because of its commercialism, is full of references to traditional styles. There is, for example, a strong mento feel in the loping rhythms of "Bad Card" ("dem a go tired fe see me face, can't we get we out of the race"), one of the last songs he ever recorded; and several Marley numbers, such as "Rastaman Chant" and "Babylon System", are solidly based on the traditional Rastafarian drumming style known as Nyabingi, itself a direct outgrowth of the "neo-African" Buru and Kumina traditions.

The rhythm of the Jamaican language continues to exert a powerful influence on urban popular music, as is most evident in the incredibly rich and lively contemporary Deejaying tradition. The Deejay's art of "toasting" – an indigenous Jamaican style of rapping over instrumental music – is equally popular in the studios of Kingston and in the touring "sound system" dances that draw crowds all over the island. Some raps are carefully thought out in advance, while others are improvised on the spot. Not only do Deejays make the appreciation of rhythm through verbal improvisation an end in itself, but they constantly draw directly from traditional sources, quoting proverbs or snatches of ring-play tunes, digging songs, mentos, or even cult songs. The same has always been true – though perhaps less obviously so – of reggae

Bob Marley

more generally. The Mighty Diamonds, for instance, sing, "If you wan' fe hear duppy [spirits] laugh, go a riverside Sunday morning": a folk song, sometimes performed as a Kumina "bailo". Toots, of the Maytals, belts out, "Thy will be done": a Revivalist song. And in "Who The Cap Fits", Bob Marley intones, "throw me corn, me no call no fowl" – a traditional proverb that forms part of a popular Kumina "bailo" song:

> Marly Clebba, come out a me yard
> Marly Clebba, come out a me yard
> me throw corn a yard, me no call neighbour fowl
> Marly Clebba, come out a me yard

Even when traditional songs and melodies are not directly quoted, the influence of the Creole language of Jamaica runs deep. Take, for example, one of Marley's most powerful and poignant songs, "Dem Belly Full":

dem belly full, but we hungry	their bellies are full, but we're hungry
a hungry mob is a angry mob	a hungry mob is an angry mob
a rain a fall, but de doti tuff	the rain is falling, but the ground is tough
a yot a yook, but de yood no nuff	the pot is cooking, but the food is not much

"De rain a fall, but de doti tuff" is an old Jamaican proverb that poet Louise Bennett set to verse over forty years ago; while the last line – in which "pot", "cook", and "food" become "yot", "yook", and "yood" – displays a Rastafarian adaptation of an archaic, more African form of Jamaican Creole known as "Bongo talk". (This dialect, which replaces certain initial consonants with the "y" sound, still survives in pockets of the island, and is sometimes heard in the African-influenced Anansi stories told throughout the country.) That such traditional elements remain so strong in reggae should not be surprising; they are part and parcel of the daily experience of popular musicians, the sounds they have grown up hearing, day in and day out.

The ongoing alliance between reggae and Rastafari has also helped to keep popular music indirectly, but constantly, in touch with "neo-African" traditions. Ever since the early 1960s, when Count Ossie and the Folkes Brothers merged Rastafarian drumming with the popular ska style in the historic recording "Oh Carolina", the urban Jamaican sound has been receiving continual injections of rural-based cult rhythms from the West Kingston ghettos. As the ska (with its strong rhythm and blues base) progressed through the soul-tinged rocksteady style and came into full bloom with reggae (newly fortified by a dose of mento), it gradually opened itself more and more to traditional Rastafarian musical inputs along the way. By the 1970s, the re-Africanisation of reggae – or a large proportion of it – was complete, with the Rastafarian repeater drum, and often the complete Nyabingi akete (or kete) drum ensemble (bass, funde, and repeater), being regularly featured in Kingston studio sessions. Today, the "heartbeat" throb of the funde drum and the syncopated embellishments of the repeater continue to provide reggae with much of its kick; even when the Rasta akete drums are not themselves present, the rhythms of Nyabingi often assert themselves all the same, in the interplay of traps, percussion, bass, guitar, and keyboards.

It is through its liaison with the Nyabingi drumming style that reggae remains linked with two of Jamaica's deepest "neo-African" traditions, Buru and Kumina; for Nyabingi is a direct descendant of both styles. In the early 1950s, when the Nyabingi tradition was in the process of evolving, West Kingston was home to a number of "neo-African" musical styles that had been carried to the ghetto by rural migrants. Among these were secularised versions of both Kumina and Buru (a drumming tradition going back to the slave period, still practised in the parishes of St Catherine and Clarendon, where it is associated with a type of masquerade dance). There is evidence that in the urban setting, elements from these two styles fused freely, and a number of new combinations resulted, sometimes called by either name. From these Buru-Kumina hybrids, urban Rastafarian musicians, who had previously been without drums, took what they needed in order to create their own new dance-drumming style, which they christened Nyabingi. The three-part drum ensemble of Buru – the bass, funde, and repeater (or pita) – was retained in modified form in Nyabingi, but the music played on it was neither Buru nor Kumina, combining as it did elements of both. It was this new fusion that was later brought to the recording studios of Kingston by the Rastafarian master drummer, Count Ossie, and a large number of others who followed in his footsteps.

But the influence of the deep, "neo-African" music of Kumina apears to have reached Nyabingi (and thus reggae) via other pathways as well. It has only recently come to light that the early Rastafari prophet Leonard Howell (alias "Gong" or "Gangunguru Maragh"), a key figure in the development of the Rastafari movement, was thoroughly immersed in the Kumina tradition. Early in his preaching career, during the 1930s, Howell concentrated his activities in the Kumina "heartland" of St Thomas parish. In 1940, he founded his famous commune, named Pinnacle, in St Catherine, which was one of the first and largest Rastafarian communities in Jamaica. Throughout his years at Pinnacle, Howell used Kumina drumming, dance, and the Kongo-based "African Country" language in his ceremonies.[8] When Pinnacle was raided and broken up by the police in 1954, Howell himself was jailed and then, after his release, retreated into semi-retirement; but many of his Kumina-steeped disciples, suddenly finding themselves homeless, headed en masse for West Kingston, where they helped to swell the numbers of the urban Rastafarian community, and undoubtedly contributed to the nascent Nyabingi tradition. Through channels such as this, the rhythm of Kumina, once grounded in a specific rural African-based religion and way of life, has travelled into the mainstream and come to occupy what Rex Nettleford has called "a centrality in the complex of Jamaican music".

Over and over, this same pattern has repeated itself in different parts of the Caribbean. Wherever one looks, one finds that the musical riches of the rural folk have continued to feed urban popular traditions, with the result that, no matter what stylistic fads and transformations they undergo, they always retain a strong indigenous ("típico", "typique", "roots") character. The cadence (*kadans*) of Haiti and the French Antilles, the soka (*soca*) of Trinidad, and other recent Caribbean innovations have, like reggae, remained in close touch with the local folk musical spectrums – the full range of "neo-African", hybrid and Creolised European styles – that surround them. And so the

Steel Pulse

various current Caribbean popular musical styles, like their rural predecessors, have maintained their strong family resemblance; they are, after all, extensions of the same creative process of blending that has been shaping Caribbean musical life for centuries. The process continues and, indeed, has begun to widen in scope, as popular musicians in different parts of the region increasingly recognise the musical affinities that link them not only to one another, but to the immense burst of creativity now emanating from urban Africa (whose popular music styles have themselves sometimes been heavily influenced by those of the Caribbean). In short, it can be said that Caribbean popular music – busy as ever absorbing, blending, and re-creating – has never been healthier or livelier than it is today.

But the story does not end with the Caribbean itself. For the Caribbean diaspora of the last few decades has been sending out musical shoots to the capitals of Europe and North America, from which have sprouted a number of fresh contributions to the Caribbean musical family. Even as reggae has managed to win increasing popular acceptance among Europeans and North Americans, and has influenced Euro-American pop styles, Caribbean immigrant communities – Antilleans in Paris, Surinamers in Amsterdam, West Indians in London, and mixed Caribbean enclaves in Toronto, New York, Miami, and other cities – have continued to make and use Caribbean music very much for themselves. In Europe, reggae, often subtly transformed by its meeting with other popular traditions, has become a sort of musical *lingua franca* for Caribbean peoples in the diaspora. Perhaps the most influential branch of this new family of transplanted Caribbean styles is that which has grown up in London and a number of other English cities; in this new setting, young Jamaicans, Trinidadians, Guyanese, Grenadians, and

Misty in Roots

other West Indians (as well as British-born children of immigrants from these and other parts of the Caribbean) have joined forces to create their own form of "Brit reggae", reflecting their experiences in the metropolis. The vitality of this British tradition – represented by bands such as Steel Pulse, Aswad, Matumbi, Misty, and the pioneering group Cymande – has carried its reputation way beyond the borders of the United Kingdom, and has inspired young Caribbean immigrants in other parts of Europe to follow suit.

The truth is that Caribbean music can no longer be defined by geographical boundaries. Wherever Caribbean peoples have gone, they have brought their rich musical heritage with them. The process of Creolisation that has given birth to so many vital new forms in the past continues to do so, both at home and abroad. As is made clear by the British experience, Caribbean musicians in the diaspora do not hesitate to borrow whatever they find pleasing from the ever-widening stream of foreign musical currents confronting them. But even in Britain, several thousand miles and an ocean removed from the original Caribbean "crucible", the rhythm of Africa – whether in the electrifying "dub poetry" of the London-based Jamaican poet Linton Kwesi Johnson or the Nyabingi drumming of a Rastafarian religious service in a Brixton basement – is still there, loud and clear. And there is every reason to believe that, whatever may befall the various members of the Caribbean musical family in the future, it will continue to be there.

NOTES
1. "Printing" is from the Akan language Twi, *oprenteng*, referring to a particular type of drum. "Kwadjo" is a West African "day-name" given to boys born on a particular day of the week (the day varies from place to place); this name is common in Akan-speaking and neighbouring areas. "Osei!" is a war-cry used by Ashanti and Fanti warrior associations (and is also the name of an important figure in Ashanti history). "Fanti" is the name of an Akan-speaking ethnic group located on the coast of Ghana. Several other of the words in this song are probably derived from Akan, and closer analysis by a native Akan speaker might well permit a full translation into English.
2. It should be mentioned that Kumina music, like that of Kromanti Play, also has its more Creolised, European-influenced component, in the "lighter" songs known as "bailo"; though backed by the same style of drumming as the deep "Country" songs, they are in English or Jamaican Creole and show European melodic influence.
3. This view may eventually have to undergo revision, for research into Afro-Dominican music – owing to the traditional denial of things black and African in that country – is still quite young, and much exploration of the African heritage remains to be done.
4. It should be noted that rather similar traditional flute and drum ensembles, uninfluenced by European military music, are not uncommon in West Africa.
5. Other similar Afro-American folk traditions going by variants of the same name have been documented in Belize, the Bahamas, North Carolina, and several other parts of the New World.
6. It should be added that the music of John Canoe and "mummies" fits into a larger family of syncretic Afro-American fife and drum traditions that stretches from northern Brazil through Haiti and into the southern United States. That these traditions are so widespread in the New World tells us something about the ease with which African and European musical forms could be fused, given the right conditions.
7. Very similar game song traditions are found in Guyana, the Lesser Antilles, and many other parts of the Caribbean.

8. Although he died in 1981, a small group of Howell's original followers, based in St Catherine, continue to hold gatherings in which they praise Rastafari to the traditional songs and rhythms of Kumina, played on the bandu and playing cast; in 1983, an American anthropologist, Elliott Leib, visited one such meeting and made a recording of the music, which includes – in addition to several standard Kumina "bailo" songs – a version of the very same Kumina "Country" song, *"nki balongo"*, quoted earlier in this chapter. For further information on Howell's involvement with Kumina, see the sleeve notes to the L.P. phonograph recording *From Kongo to Zion: Three Black Musical Traditions from Jamaica* (Heartbeat Records, 1983).

BIBLIOGRAPHY

BAXTER, Ivy. *The Arts of an Island*. Metuchen, New Jersey: Scarecrow Press, 1970.

BECKWITH, Martha. *Black Roadways: A Study of Jamaican Folk Life*. Chapel Hill, North Carolina: University of North Carolina Press, 1929.

BENNETT, Louise. *Jamaica Labrish*. London: Collins, 1967.

BILBY, Kenneth. "The Kromanti Dance of the Windward Maroons of Jamaica", *Nieuwe West-Indische Gids* 55(1/2), pp.52–101, 1981.

—— *The Caribbean as a Musical Region* (forthcoming).

BILBY, Kenneth and Fu-Kiau kia Bunseki. *Kumina: A Kongo-Based Tradition in the New World*. Brussels: Cahiers du Centre d'Etude et de Documentation Africaines, 1984.

BRATHWAITE, Edward Kamau. *Folk Culture of the Slaves in Jamaica*. Boston: New Beacon Books, 1970.

—— "Kumina: The Spirit of African Survival in Jamaica", *Jamaica Journal*, no.42, pp.44–63, 1978.

CASSIDY, Frederic G. *Jamaica Talk: Three Hundred Years of the English Language in Jamaica* (second edition). London: Macmillan, 1971.

CLERK, Astley. Extract from "The Music and Musical Instruments of Jamaica", *Jamaica Journal* 9(2/3), pp.59–67, 1975.

DALBY, David. "Ashanti Survivals in the Language and Traditions of the Windward Maroons of Jamaica". *African Language Studies* 12: pp.31–51, 1971.

DAVIS, Martha Ellen. *Voces del Purgatorio: Estudio de la Salve Dominicana*. Santo Domingo: Museo del Hombre Dominicano, 1981.

HERNANDEZ, Julio Alberto. *Música Tradicional Dominicana*. Santo Domingo: Julio D. Postigo, 1969.

HURSTON, Zora Neale. *Tell My Horse*. Berkeley, California: Turtle Island, 1981 (originally 1938).

JEKYLL, Walter, ed. *Jamaican Song and Story*. New York: Dover, 1966.

LE PAGE, Robert. *Jamaican Creole*. London: Macmillan, 1960.

LEWIN, Olive. *Some Jamaican Folk Songs*. Kingston: The Oxford Group, 1970.

—— *Forty Folk Songs of Jamaica*. Washington, D.C.: General Secretariat of the Organisation of American States, 1973.

LEWIS, Maureen Warner. "The Nkuyu: Spirit Messengers of the Kumina". *Savacou* 13: pp.57–86, 1977.

LOGAN, Wendell and WHYLIE, Marjorie. "Some Aspects of Religious Cult Music in Jamaica", *The Black Perspective in Music* 10(1): pp.85–94, 1982.

MOORE, Joseph G. "Music and Dance as Expressions of Religious Worship in Jamaica", *In the Performing Arts*, John Blacking and Joann W. Kealiinohomoku, eds. The Hague: Mouton, 1979.

NETTLEFORD, Rex M. *Identity, Race and Protest in Jamaica*. New York: William Morrow, 1972.

O'GORMAN, Pamela. "An Approach to the Study of Jamaican Popular Music", *Jamaica Journal* 6(7): pp.50–4, 1972.

RECKORD, Verena. "Rastafari Music – An Introductory Study", *Jamaica Journal* 11(1/2): pp.4–12, 1977.

ROBERTS, John Storm. *Black Music of Two Worlds*. New York: Praeger, 1972.

RYMAN, Cheryl. "The Jamaican Heritage in Dance: Developing a Traditional Typology", *Jamaica Journal*, no.44: pp.2–14, 1980.

SCHULER, Monica. "Alas, Alas, Kongo", *A Social History of Indentured African Immigration into Jamaica, 1841–1865*. Baltimore and London: The Johns Hopkins University Press, 1980.

WHITE, Garth. "Reggae – A Musical Weapon", *Caribe* (New York), pp.6–10, December 1980.

— "Traditional Musical Practice in Jamaica and Its Influence on the Birth of Modern Jamaican Popular Music", African-Caribbean Institute of Jamaica *Newsletter*, no.7: pp.41–68, 1982.

RECORDINGS

BILBY, Kenneth, ed. *Bongo, Backra, and Coolie: Jamaican Roots* (2 volumes). New York: Folkways Records, 1975.

— *Music of the Maroons of Jamaica*. New York: Folkways Records, 1981.

BILBY, Ken and LEIB, Elliott, eds. *From Kongo to Zion: Three Black Musical Traditions from Jamaica*. Cambridge, Massachussetts: Heartbeat Records, 1983.

BROOKS, Cedric. *From Mento to Reggae to Third World Music*. Kingston: Institute of Jamaica, no date.

COURLANDER, Harold, ed. *Caribbean Folk Music* (2-record set). New York: Folkways Records, 1960.

GILLIS, Verna, ed. *Music of the Dominican Republic* (4 volumes). New York: Folkways Records, 1979.

LEIB, Elliott, ed. *Churchical Chants of the Nyabingi*. Cambridge, Massachussetts: Heartbeat Records, 1983.

LEWIN, Olive, ed. *From the Grassroots of Jamaica*. Kingston: Dynamic Sounds, n.d.

— *More From the Grassroots of Jamaica* (2-record set). Kingston: Jamaica Information Service, n.d.

MALM, Krister, ed. *Music of the West Indies: The Lesser Antilles* (3-record set). Stockholm: Caprice Records, n.d.

MARKS, Morton, ed. *Afro-Dominican Cult Music*. New York: Folkways Records, 1983.

Mystic Revelation of Rastafari. *Grounation* (3-record set). Kingston: Dynamic Sounds, n.d.

— *Tales of Mozambique*. Kingston: Dynamic Sounds, n.d.

ROBERTS, John Storm, ed. *Caribbean Island Music*. New York: Nonesuch Records, 1972.

— *Black Music of Two Worlds* (2-record set). New York: Folkways Records, 1979.

SEAGA, Edward, ed. *Folk Music of Jamaica*. New York: Folkways Records, 1956.

SIMPSON, George Eaton, ed. *Jamaican Cult Music*. New York: Folkways Records, 1954.

WHYLIE, Marjorie, ed. *Heritage* (2-record set). Kingston: Jamaica Broadcasting Corporation, 1979.

CHAPTER 7

Africa Come Back
The popular music of West Africa

BY JOHN MILLER CHERNOFF

The popular music of the contemporary world is increasingly becoming an African musical idiom. From Asia to Europe to the United States to Latin America, people are dancing to music that has its roots in Africa. This music originates in many places where people of African descent have carried on their traditional approach to music and developed new forms. Latin American musicians have developed rumbas, sambas, mambos, cha-chas and many other dance beats out of the swinging rhythms of Afro-Cuban and Afro-Brazilian styles of drumming. Haitians and Dominicans have developed merengue music, and the people of Trinidad and nearby islands have developed calypso. Jamaicans have developed reggae out of their own roots music. And most important, black Americans have developed jazz, soul, funk and disco music from the many rich strands of gospel music, ragtime, boogie-woogie, and rural and urban blues. At the moment, on the pop music charts of any country in Europe and America, it would be difficult to find a song that has not been heavily influenced by these musical idioms, and even much of the music played by white musicians for white audiences, like rock 'n' roll, is patently derivative of African-American forms. A clear musical continuity can be heard from the African savanna to the Mississippi Delta to the Chicago blues of Muddy Waters and Howlin' Wolf to the music of the Rolling Stones and Eric Clapton.

Many modern Western musicians, from the Talking Heads to Peter Gabriel, seeking fresh inspiration, are looking beyond the music of the African diaspora to the traditional music of Africa. At the same time, many Western musicians are looking at contemporary African musicians who are building upon their traditional music to create a wealth of new music. In Ghana, Nigeria, Benin, Zaire, Mali, Guinea, Upper Volta, Kenya, everywhere on the vast African continent, modern African musicians are making popular music in situations that are removed from the enveloping cultural matrix of traditional music. Modern African musicians are using guitars, saxophones, trumpets, jazz drum kits, organs, and all the electronic instruments and equipment that Western musicians use. The rhythmic diversity and innovative formats of African pop music are a new addition to the resources of Western musical creativity, and African musicians are beginning to tour Europe and America, winning fans and admirers with their new sound. Their music seems familiar to Westerners who are up-to-date with contemporary

trends in American and European music, but it has developed in the nightclubs of African cities for African audiences who are sophisticated music-lovers and who dance many of the same steps both to electrified African pop and to village drumming and singing. Modern African musicians look inward and outward, backwards and forwards, and they have expanded their traditional music and adapted it to modern social contexts and modern musical technology. In typical African fashion, they have seen the new and the different as a means of adding to themselves, and they have turned adaptation into an agent of increase and not abandonment. The source of their musical vitality is their connection to their own African roots.

In Ghana, highlife music has developed from Akan and Ga prototypes to become one of the most characteristic West African styles of music. In western Nigeria, musicians like Sunny Ade, Ebenezer Obey, Dele Abiodun, Segun Adewale and Shina Peters are current exemplars of Juju music, built upon traditional Yoruba Apala and Sakara rhythms merged with Ghanaian highlife. In Afro-beat, Fela Anikulapo Kuti has built upon the same base to create an incredibly rich fusion of Yoruba rhythms, highlife, jazz and funk. Fuji music, a kind of folk revitalisation of Juju music, is currently the rage among some Lagos audiences. In eastern Nigeria, a brand of highlife has developed that blends indigenous rhythms, Ghanaian highlife, and Zairian and Congolese music, exemplified by the music of Stephen Osadebe, Prince Nico M'barga and Oliver de Coque. Sonny Okosun from mid-western Nigeria has blended highlife and reggae beats to make a type of music he calls Ozziddi. In Mali and Guinea, groups like Ambassadeurs, Super Boiro, Bembeya Jazz, Horoya Band, 22 Band, Sidi Yasa, Super Djata, Orchestre le National Badema, Balla et Ses Balladins, Super Rail Band, and many others have rearranged and modernised the lovely Malinke, Bambara, Wolof, and Dioula rhythms and

Above left: Sunny Ade and (right) Segun Adewale

harmonies of the savanna. The great saxophonist of the Cameroon, Manu Dibango, famous as the Makossa man, has been based in Paris for many years, where his bands mix indigenous rhythms of the Cameroons with jazz and funk. From Zaire and the Congo to Abidjan, Dakar and Paris, soukous has emerged as a lively blend of BaKongo and Afro-Cuban rhythms, played by current stars like Sam Mangwana, Rochereau, Tabu Ley, Franco and the Orchestre O.K. Jazz, Theo Blaise Kounkou, Lokassa ya M'Bongo, Pamelo, Orchestre Mass-Media, Orchestre le Peuple, and countless others. Orchestre Polyrhythmo of Cotonou, Benin, has blended Yoruba and Fon rhythms with Afro-Cuban and funk beats.

Most of these musicians and their music will remain obscure for the majority of Western listeners, though their influence will be felt indirectly through the music of many leading Western musicians. It is likely, however, that at least a few of the popular musicians of Africa will make their mark directly on the Western musical scene, and it is certain that in the near future some of the new talents coming out of Africa will promote their musical ideas in collaboration with European and American musicians. Advances in the recording and mass communications industries have made it possible for musicians around the world to hear each other, and the branches of the African musical tradition are no longer related only by their roots. A new flowering of Western popular music is coming, and one of the seeds is the modern popular music of African cities. Where has that music come from and how did it develop?

In the emerging nations of Africa, rapid and dynamic growth has brought many changes in the past fifty years. Almost every institution of the traditional societies of the pre-colonial era has been affected, but there has not been a wholesale adoption of Western social forms. Instead, contemporary Africans are trying to maintain the best features of their traditional ways of

Chief Ebenezer Obey

life and blend them into those Western institutions that they feel can be of value to their economic growth and development. Modern African cities are somewhat like European cities in the late nineteenth century. There is a tremendous amount of construction: residences, public and private offices, industrial facilities, schools, hospitals and clinics, stores, as well as urban infrastructure like roads, water, sewerage, electrical and communications systems. The physical creation of a modern urban landscape has been accompanied by a monumental movement of population from rural to urban life. Forty years ago, Accra, Ghana, had a population of about 30,000; today more than 1 million people live in its metropolitan area. African cities are growing rapidly, filling up with migrants from the countryside.

Modern African cities, however, are developing much faster than European cities did, and the kind of energy needed for such growth almost crackles through the urban atmosphere. The twentieth century, with its global economy and technological advances, demands such an effort. The change from tribal society to a pluralistic national society is happening rapidly, and there is little time to waste. From the time of Ghana's independence, the motto of the new era has been "Move or Die", and young and old Africans alike have responded to the challenge of modernisation. Of course, the rapid growth of African cities, like that of all major cities, has often been disorganised. An astounding number of makeshift occupational categories have sprung up to manage the discontinuity of growth: while many people are employed in mainstream industrial, administrative or distributive occupations, a large number of people make a marginal living providing services and short-term maintenance for aspects of the modern system threatened by temporary shortages of supplies and resources. Charles Dickens would have felt at home moving among those who are creating their own economic opportunities by recycling goods and designing and manufacturing spare parts out of scrap. These people have refused to be discouraged by the personal obstacles of their historical dislocation, just as their leaders refuse to be discouraged by the monumental task of modernising their means of production in the face of a world economic order still orientated towards the exploitation of African resources and markets. The limited vision of Africa held by the former colonial rulers has required Africans to restructure not only their own traditional societies but frequently also the foundations of the colonial legacy. Needless to say, the modernisation of Africa is one of the most exciting historical dramas of our time.

Informed observers of Africa have long abandoned the notion that modern African history reflects a process of replacing indigenous traditions with Western ones; it is clear that current developments reflect a process of working out multiple syntheses of available options. Contemporary African urbanites are denied the luxury of merely thinking about this process. For them the modern situation is fraught with both opportunities and difficulties; their decisions and attitudes are crucial to the quality of their lives, and they are the first to experience the validity or inadequacy of the values they bring to their social behaviour. They are certainly well informed about points of breakdown, weakness, and ineffectiveness in the institutions of competing systems. Problematical status values, potentials for verbal and physical abuse, economic constraints, exploitation of labour and political powerlessness, human failings, the dilemmas of sickness and death: all these are the negative stuff of life both in traditional and in urban or modern systems. Young urbanites in Africa are concerned with survival and dignity, the antipodal elements of compromise, but they project a sense of adaptability, strength, and resourcefulness that exemplifies much of what is best about African traditions in the throes of radical change. There is no lack of volunteers to experiment with and develop the new lifestyles which social changes both depend upon and demand.

Modern African music, with its strong foundation in tradition, has been a focus for the creative vitality of modern African societies. In the nightclubs of African cities, modern adaptations of African musical idioms provide the beat for a cross-section of urban society in a setting that is an occupational focal point for contemporary African musicians. They attain success by their ability to mediate, through their music, the disparate lifestyles of their pluralistic social environment. Their music tells much about the life of people in African cities, and at the same time their music establishes continuities to African traditional life that also serve to remind people of the values of traditional societies. The nightclub audience is for the most part young office-workers and labourers who come out in the evenings to socialise, drink, dance, and "refresh" their minds. Like young people everywhere, they sometimes bluff each other in matters of fashion, but they have an essential optimism and a live-and-let-live attitude, and they respect people's differences. A popular motto is painted in two parts on some Ghanaian trucks and buses. On the front of the vehicle a sign declares, "Observers are Worried", while on the back the message concludes, "Believers are Enjoying". In the bars, nightclubs and discos of African cities, it is the "believers" who set the social tone and dance to the music. In Ghana, the music the bands play for them includes soul, reggae, and soukous, but the main beat that inspires happiness is highlife. To get a better idea of the spirit of modern Africa, we can use Ghanaian highlife as a way of looking into the contemporary world of African music, tracing it from its diverse roots to its current forms and finding in its development a model for understanding the continuity of African traditions in the face of change. Every tribe in Ghana has its own music, but highlife is music for everyone. It is the music of a nation, and it has found admirers and influenced musicians throughout black Africa.

Highlife music has so many roots that no single traditional style can claim to be its progenitor. At the same time, every Ghanaian culture has some form of music that can be considered prototypical highlife. Highlife music in a modern guitar band is essentially a rhythm ensemble with the different instruments providing rhythms that formerly would have been provided by percussion instruments. A typical line-up features bell, claves or sticks, rattle, conga drums, trap drums, bass guitar, rhythm guitar, and occasionally an organ or second rhythm guitar; the lead guitar and the vocal chorus are

Ko Nimo, renowned palmwine guitarist

also usually providing rhythmic lines. The beat itself can be played in a variety of ways, and we can consider highlife something of a generic rhythm that encompasses many beats, somewhat as rumba does in Afro-Cuban music. The freedom in highlife's rhythmic form makes it different from typical traditional beats that are tied to specific occasions and instrumental ensembles. The various rhythmic lines that make up the highlife beat, however, appear as units of traditional beats, and highlife has a characteristic feeling and movement that invites comparison particularly to rhythms in 4/4 time. Ko Nimo, one of the most famous highlife guitarists, counts at least twenty-five forms of Ashanti music alone that he considers to be roots of highlife. These forms cover a range of music from recreational drumming to stringed instruments like the seprewa. Even Kete, the court drumming of the Ashanti chiefs, has some rhythms which resemble highlife. In the midst of the complex 12/8 rhythms of Kete or Adowa, the music might shift into a version of the lighter 4/4 beat called Akatape that exists in a number of Ashanti musical types. The town of Techiman is the home of the god Tano, and there is a rhythm called Techiman that is generally played for priests and priestesses as part of Ashanti Akom religious music: the Techiman rhythm is another 4/4 beat that has found its way into recreational contexts.

In the early part of the twentieth century, areas of Ghana, particularly along the coast, had a more thorough introduction to Western institutions as the colonial contact of preceding centuries was expanded. Many Ghanaian farmers had become venture capitalists in the cocoa industry, and the

production of cocoa became the major source of revenue for the development of the Gold Coast colony. As the cocoa economy began to boom, more schools were built to add to the few schools built in the nineteenth century. More colonial workers came to supervise the construction of roads, the adminis- tration of local government, and the activities of trading enterprises. Along with Western goods imported for sale came other imports. Western musical instruments and styles of playing began to have an impact. Full-scale dance bands were organised to entertain the upper classes of society, and it is generally thought that the term "highlife" originated in reference to Ghana's early dance-hall music.

But there were other points of contact between African and Western musical traditions. Around the twin port city of Takoradi-Sekondi, seamen from the West African coast and the West Indies played their guitars, harmonicas and accordions in local bars. The new schools formed marching bands and drum-and-fife corps. Regimental brass bands and church choral groups offered other opportunities for the local population to learn Western songs and Western instruments. Quite naturally, indigenous rhythmic styles gradually found their way into the musical arrangements. One wonders about the expression on the face of a British headmaster reviewing the school band when a precocious youngster decided to add a little flash on the snare-drum, or the expression on the face of a British officer when a few members of the brass section in the marching band decided to improve the music by bending some notes into more traditional harmonic conceptions, or the expression on the face of a British missionary whose choir decided to introduce a local spirit to the spirit of Presbyterianism or Methodism and decided to swing the hymns ever so slightly to make the local spirit feel at home.

Through the 1920s and 1930s, the foundations of modern highlife were laid. The situation is perhaps comparable to that of the Mississippi Delta when the roots of modern blues began to sprout. Local musicians undoubt- edly had a diverse repertoire to please diverse audiences, and while they were conversant with musical styles that could be played for white audiences, they also found ways to experiment with their creativity before more indigenous gatherings. Most modern fans of highlife probably are as unaware of the obscure progenitors of highlife styles as fans of contemporary Western music are of early blues singers. Only a few aficionados know the names of people like bandleader Teacher Lamptey and guitarist Kwame Asare, but they and many other musicians helped spread and popularise the new forms. In towns, villages, and cities, in cinema halls and dance halls, at public gatherings and elite social events, new instruments and new types of songs found their way into common usage, and most important, new institutions provided additional support and additional contexts for musical expression.

The instruments and the social contexts may have owed much to contact with the West, but the evolving music became more and more African through a slow process of organic growth. Musical instruments are only the means of musical expression, and just as one would not expect European symphonic musicians to make authentic African music if they were given a set of African drums, so one should not overemphasise the Western influence on highlife. In the same way that Afro-American musicians found "blue notes" that bent the tonality of the Western harmonic system, African musicians played Western instruments in ways they had not been played before. Even the Latin American and Caribbean percussion instruments that found their way into highlife ensembles after the Second World War did not turn highlife into a variety of rumba. When Ghanaian musicians became familiar with other types of music, they worked from their own roots to find the inspiration that could solidify their aesthetic command of different musical forms. In the early part of this century, the Gold Coast was already changing rapidly, and there was increased contact between Westerners and the indigenous population of the future nation of Ghana. Highlife developed as a generic rhythm that these people could share, that they could use to express what they had in common and to help their music cross cultural boundaries.

We can still glimpse something of early highlife in modern Ghana. At festivals particularly, it is not uncommon for brass bands to play. Though some of the band members may be old, the music retains a youthful swing. At posh hotels in Accra and other major cities, outdoor dances on Saturday afternoons are an opportunity for people who normally avoid the crowds at busy nightclubs to relax to the music of such famous highlife bands as Jerry Hanson's Ramblers International. In keeping with the times, the Ramblers have a diverse repertoire that includes soul and reggae music, but they play highlife with a full complement of brass that recalls the time when dance orchestras performed for the colonial elite; the Ramblers' string of hits goes back more than twenty years. The hotel setting also recalls less complex days: an afternoon breeze rustles the palm trees; waiters rush around with beer; heavy-set rich men dressed in African cloth walk majestically from their tables to dance serenely to mellow highlife arrangements. But perhaps the most pleasant images can be seen in Ghanaian villages in the type of prototypical music that is still popular in Ghana today. It owes its name, "palm-wine guitar music", to its social context, and for many Ghanaians, the idyllic setting of palm-wine drinking is a major component of any nostalgic idealisation of village life.

Palm wine is obtained in Ghana by cutting down a palm tree and by simply placing a big pot to collect the palm wine being tapped. Nigerians tap palm-wine trees with taps that are like the ones used when tapping rubber or syrup, but the Ghanaians do not use that technology. Once the tree is felled, the tapster trims excess branches and chops a small hole through the tree. He inserts a tube through the hole to tap the sap, and he digs underneath the trunk and places a pot to collect the drippings of the tap. It is necessary to apply heat during the process, and a light fire around the pot aids the collection. After the tree is cut down and the tap is made, the tapster leaves the place and returns the next dawn to collect the palm wine. A tree can yield several days' worth of palm wine. Palm wine is usually drunk as is, but it is also used by local distillers to make "*akpeteshie*", the Akan name for local gin.

Palm wine ferments quickly during the course of the day, and it can pack quite a wallop by the second day. It is often transported to the cities in large plastic drums, but in its village setting, it is carried to the drinking place in a clay pot and served in calabashes. Typically, in an open area of a village, under the shading of a big tree, the palm-wine drinkers seat themselves on wooden benches in something of a circle. In its most rustic locations, palm-wine drinkers simply set their half-calabashes on the ground, but in many palm-wine locations, shorter benches in front of the drinkers become a kind of table: these benches are gouged out at intervals to provide places to put a calabash.

Palm wine is usually drunk in the afternoon. A typical West African farmer gets up early and begins work just after sunrise. He works steadily until about twelve or one o'clock, and then he goes home and eats lunch. Farming with a cutlass is strenuous and seasonal work. Occasionally the farmer goes back to the farm, but often he is finished for the day because the weather is just too hot. Thus, especially during the hot dry season, or when the fields have already been cleared or the crops planted or the farm weeded, farmers are free in the afternoon. They bathe and go to the drinking place, where they are also joined by friends who have been working on their farms and are on their way home in their work clothes. These new arrivals are greeted in the traditional Akan, "*Adwuma-o-o. Akwaba*" – "How is your work? Welcome!"

Management of the drinking place is often in the hands of the tapster's wife assisted by a young girl who serves the drinkers and washes used calabashes. Usually, customers are given some of the palm wine to taste. Palm wine sent to the cities is often cut with water and sugar, and there the reason for the tasting is often to affirm that the palm wine is fresh, but in the villages, the gift is primarily a welcoming greeting. People who are gathered buy amounts measured in large calabashes which can then fill a number of the smaller calabashes that the drinkers use and rest in front of them. The palm wine in the large pot may be transferred to a gourd or a pot so that drinkers can serve themselves. The proprietor serves the first round of any new purchase and then leaves the balance with the drinkers. Generally, when friends are assembled, they buy successive rounds for each other. When one person serves himself, he will also serve anyone near him, filling up the calabash. Most drinking begins with a libation: some of the palm wine will be poured on the ground by tipping the calabash, and some words will be said to call the names of God and to remember the ancestors. In the modern cities, when urban young people who consider themselves "believers" gather to drink palm wine imported from the villages, the libations are cut slightly short; the believers are not all that liberal about throwing the precious stuff away.

We can imagine the scene in colonial days when some of the villagers came dressed in wide knickers with white shirts and broad-brimmed hats, others in traditional kente or adinkra cloth. A few older people set a tone of eldership, maturity, security and wisdom. The atmosphere is informal. A relaxed community of friends pursues life at a leisurely pace. Someone brings out an acoustic guitar. There may be various small percussion instruments for the drinkers to play, and the group sings choruses in a congenial call-and-response fashion. The music follows whatever the mood calls for.

The renowned palm-wine guitarist Ko Nimo has played a major role in keeping this nostalgic vision and its lovely music in the mind of the Ghanaian public. Ko Nimo works in the Department of Biochemistry at the University of Science and Technology in Kumasi. The beauty of his voice and his guitar playing have earned him an international reputation as Ghana's foremost exponent of acoustic guitar highlife, and he has performed in Europe and America. Ko Nimo is currently the president of the Musicians' Union of Ghana, and his countrymen hold him in high esteem not only for his music but for his respect for and love of tradition. He welcomes and assists any student of African culture who comes his way. Despite his education and his career at the university, he is straightforward and modest, and he has spent years travelling to villages to do research and to learn various guitar styles from older musicians. His love for people and for old-fashioned lifestyles extends to every aspect of his being. He prefers to walk rather than to ride; when he must ride, he prefers buses to taxis. He even prefers to maintain an ancient wind-up gramophone on which he plays his priceless collection of early highlife recordings, and one can often find him sitting outside his house, his gramophone beside him on a table, practising his guitar and increasing his vocabulary of highlife guitar styles. He shifts effortlessly from Odonso to Yaa Amponsah to any of a myriad of rhythmic forms, and he sings ballads and proverbs, stories and folktales, all in a gentle voice.

Another example of a prototypical highlife form that has maintained its vitality is Nnwonkoro singing among the Ashanti. "Nnwonkoro" literally means "song-go-around". The name derives from its traditional role as recreational women's singing, a kind of intimate neighbourhood entertainment in which a song would go around from singer to singer in a vocal group. The singers would make up verses and name their loved ones and relatives, and an Ashanti proverb maintains that, "If your sister is a member of a Nnwonkoro group, your name never gets lost." If a person's name was mentioned by a Nnwonkoro singer, it was customary for him or her to go and greet the singer the next day and reward her with a gift. Traditionally, Nnwonkoro groups sang without instrumental accompaniment, although handclapping provided some rhythmic accentuation, and there was no dancing, either. In the past thirty years, however, Nnwonkoro has found a role in formal traditional contexts, and the music has expanded its original form by borrowing features from other types of Akan music.

Perhaps the most influential figure in this development has been Madame Efua Abasa of the Manhyia Nnwonkoro of Kumasi. It was Efua Abasa who introduced Nnwonkoro to the Asantehene, the paramount chief of Ashanti, to give Nnwonkoro a role in the traditional morning waking-up greetings to Ashanti chiefs, and her group has also expanded the use of Nnwonkoro into other traditional contexts, like funeral observances. Among the musical innovations Madame Abasa has introduced are her own role as a featured soloist, the use of recitative song introductions borrowed from hunters' association music, the use of two-part leading harmonies, and the use of supporting percussion instruments. The songs of the Manhyia Nnwonkoro also encompass a broad rhythmic repertoire, some resembling the 12/8 beat of Adowa, while others, like the 4/4 Techiman and Akatape beats, resemble highlife. Madame Abasa has earned praise for the wisdom and depth of her lyrical poetry, and she has earned respect for her more prosaic skills of formal organisation. She keeps a register of her song repertoire as well as her patrons and her associated artistes. Many of Efua Abasa's innovations have been adopted by other Nnwonkoro groups, and Efua Abasa, much like other highlife innovators, has been credited with revitalising this traditional musical form by expanding its musical range and leading it into new social venues. In the Manhyia Nnwonkoro as we see it today, the other women of the group sing chorus, provide rhythmic accompaniment by handclapping, and dance gracefully. Many of these women are well-to-do traders in the gigantic Kumasi market, and they sing not merely for the joys of musical expression but primarily as a way of participating in the respect for custom. Their lovely harmonies, typical of Akan vocal styles, are augmented by a calm rhythmic back-up provided by a bell, by a small traditional hand drum called apentima, and by a large bass thumb-piano called aprempremsewa.

The flexibility of highlife rhythms is due perhaps to the fact that highlife has always been a recreational form of music. In contrast to types of African traditional music that accompany ceremonial religious and political events, recreational music, with the somewhat informal character of its performance settings, changes gradually as musicians bring new ideas or as popular tastes shift. In traditional African societies without television, movies, or radio,

people enjoyed themselves by getting together and making music. Nnwonkoro was only one type of recreational music among many. Singing or playing a string instrument helped to pass a few quiet hours; drumming, singing and dancing were a means for the people of a village or neighbourhood to entertain themselves. Such recreational music often became a part of major social events like funerals or festivals or the installation of chiefs, as musicians or dance groups performed to give respect to an occasion or as loosely organised spontaneous dance circles attracted anyone with an inclination to participate.

Many of highlife's roots can be found among such styles of music, and highlife itself has inspired many similar types of informal tribal styles. Borborbor, played by the Ewe people of the south-east of Ghana, is one such style. Kpanlogo has been played by the Ga people of Accra and its environs since the Second World War. Sikyi is an Akan dance that goes back to early decades of the twentieth century, and as Sikyi has developed, the original musical repertoire has been expanded to include beats like Akatape and Techiman. To the accompaniment of a battery of drums, with bells, rattles, and singing, Sikyi features a slightly more formalised type of couples dancing than seen in traditional events. Couples dancing is rare in most traditional societies of West Africa, where group or solo dancing is the norm, but the Akan have traditionally augmented their solo dances with the notion of a supporting dancer because, as they say, no one should be left to dance alone as if he or she has no relatives. In Sikyi dancing, the tendency was elaborated as the supporting dancer became part of a more formalised danced dialogue, and although the dance steps resemble traditional Akan Adowa dancing, Sikyi dancers jokingly pantomime flirtatious behaviour. Thus, to a Westerner, Sikyi looks familiar, like a village version of Western dancing, and though the visual parallel is somewhat misleading, Sikyi's rhythms and recreational style certainly make it one of the obvious roots of highlife. Among the Fanti of the western and central coast, a fisherman's dance called Osibi resembles highlife in many aspects. In the north of Ghana, a style of music and dancing called Gumbe has evolved into the Simpa music of today. Gumbe groups originally used square-frame drums with bells, rattles and occasionally a squeeze drum, but modern Simpa groups use locally made versions of conga and trap drums with maracas and bells. Simpa groups are organised by young people in a neighbourhood, and a pleasant rivalry exists among Simpa groups who strive to outdo each other in drumming, singing, and dancing. Young people in the Western world have their basketball and sporting teams, scouting and church groups, but young people in Africa express themselves and compete with each other in musical endeavours.

A closer look at the Kpanlogo drumming and dancing of the Ga traditional area can give us a further idea of the musical range and varied contexts from which highlife developed. Actually, Kpanlogo drumming started after the Second World War, but Kpanlogo undoubtedly developed from a more archaic beat that is no longer played but has been transmuted rather than significantly transformed. When one hears how naturally and endlessly

Nnwonkoro, prototypical highlife form

inventive a Kpanlogo drummer is, it is difficult to think that the early Kpanlogo groups organised themselves by saying, "Hey, let's play highlife on our drums!" Rather, Kpanlogo is an old beat with a new name. In its rhythmic structure, Kpanlogo is not quite the same as highlife; it sounds like a highlife beat that has been turned around.

A minimum of two drums is used, often three. The supporting drummer usually plays a responsive beat, with the leader soloing against it. The drums themselves are short hand-drums like Akan apentima or the slightly larger Sikyi drums. The rest of the ensemble looks like the rhythm section of a dance band – a rattle, bells, woodblock or sticks, and of course an energetic chorus. A Kpanlogo drummer improvises constantly, and the call-and-response pattern of the two main drums is always changing. Many of the best conga drummers in Ghana came up playing the Kpanlogo style. In fact, Ga conga drummers can be found in bands even as far away as Nigeria and Zaire.

The Ga have been an urban people for centuries. In metropolitan Accra, nowadays one can find Kpanlogo drumming in the Ga communities of Labadi, Osu, Mamprobi, Jamestown, and Teshie. Ordinarily, at a Ga funeral or wake, people play Kpanlogo, and amateur musicians who are normally fishermen or earn their living in other walks of life are the drummers. Most wakes are weekend affairs, and Saturday is the night. One might also find Kpanlogo on Sunday afternoons, another typical time for traditional social and recreational drumming in African cities. Kpanlogo musicians may be amateurs, but as at a palm-wine gathering, there is no lack of qualified personnel for an impromptu ensemble. When Kpanlogo drumming gets going, the music becomes a jam, the kind of scene where no one gets offended if another drummer comes around and sits in.

Kpanlogo is performed by just about every Ghanaian folkloric troupe, but although the staged presentation of the dance is a sure crowd-pleaser, it cannot compare to the raw energy of an authentic event. Like the Simpa music of the Dagbamba and the Borborbor music of the Ewe, Kpanlogo is primarily a dance for young people. As such, but unlike most traditional Ghanaian dances and despite the moralistic homilies regarding friendship and love in Kpanlogo song lyrics, Kpanlogo is slightly irreverent. Kpanlogo as it is danced by young men is exceedingly macho, and as danced by young women it is very, very sexy. Originally, the elders of the Ga community tried to ban Kpanlogo, but it survived its critics with support from no less a person than Kwame Nkrumah, who recognised indigenous African qualities perhaps in the improvised artistic expressions of individuality and in the instant community that the vitality of the drumming encouraged among Kpanlogo participants. As danced by Frankie Lane, one of Ghana's best Kpanlogo dancers, Kpanlogo becomes a symbol of manly power and exuberance. Gifty Collins, another well-known dancer in Accra, turns the dance into a metaphor of feminine charm and seductiveness. Dancing together, they convey a more direct and urbanised version of Sikyi dancing's flirtatiousness. Otoo Lincoln, a coffin-maker in the Jamestown section of Accra and one of Kpanlogo's early popularisers, dances with a precision and concentration that speak of

Gifty Collins and Frankie Lane, two of Ghana's best Kpanlogo dancers

masculine control and intensity in a different way. His style of dancing echoes the assertive confidence of the chorus and the drummers, banishing any doubt that these are people who can accomplish anything they set their minds to. In Kpanlogo drumming, singing and dancing, they embody the spirit of the new nation's "believers".

In modern African cities, other types of believers congregate in evangelical Christian churches where the gospel is sung and danced with an enthusiastic enjoyment that is generally out of place in mainstream denominations. Such churches as the Musama Disco Christo Church or the Church of the Cherubim and Seraphim blend elements of orthodox Christianity with African styles of worship. They are known as "spiritual" churches for their orientation to ritualised healing and redemption, and congregations are composed mainly of people who are midstream in the transition from traditional to urban life. Semi-literate women predominate, and if one does not always notice them every night in their white dresses on their way to church, one will at least hear the energetic drumming that accompanies their singing and dancing. Their drummers are often young Kpanlogo or highlife wizards, and their hymns are unmistakeably highlife. Since many of the proverbs that inspire highlife lyrics make reference to God or to the serious issues of life, there is no shortage of songs. These churches are places where the community of members can experience brotherhood and sisterhood in an atmosphere of love, obtain spiritual guidance and support to deal with their problems, and, of course, have a great time dancing and singing. Their music has inspired a genre of highlife that is popular throughout Ghana, and one of the biggest hit records in recent years, "Spiritual Ghana", by the great Sweet Talks Band of Tema, was an extended medley of highlife songs from the spiritual churches.

Jewell Ackah, one of Ghana's leading vocalists, has also had a number of hits in the same vein.

On the same side as Kpanlogo in the contemporary highlife scene is a kind of folk cultural revival. The Christian spiritual type of highlife has informed quite a few hits, but one of the most significant developments in the highlife scene in the past decade has been a direct and commercialised revitalisation of Kpanlogo music. In the same way that the Fuji music of Nigeria looks to the roots of Juju music, this new idiom looks to the roots of highlife. The instrumental ensemble is composed of an acoustic guitar playing in palm-wine style complemented by a battery of traditional drums, bells, rattles and sticks. A chorus sings Kpanlogo songs and older forms. Bands like Wulomei and Maa Amanuah's Suku Troupe shun Western fashions and dress in costumes with traditional flair. Although electrified highlife groups like African Brothers International, Sunsum Band, and Sweet Talks can claim to be leading bands in Ghana, there are very many people among Ghanaians and the international set who respond to the folk revival style of music. It is both charming and heavily rhythmical, and many of the folk revival groups have travelled out of the country to represent Ghana at arts and music festivals. There are dozens of such groups in Accra alone. One reason why there are so many folk groups may be that Western instruments and sound systems are difficult for young musicians to obtain, but the folk revival groups are also in the forefront of the continuing trend towards finding a place for African roots within modern social contexts. Effectively integrating these roots into modern social contexts and maintaining them within national self-consciousness is now viewed by many contemporary Ghanaians as a progressive goal rather than a regressive trend. Authentic art has always been a way of building a sensible foundation for social change by increasing people's historical sympathy and sensitivity.

Highlife music itself has thus been both an agent of and a response to social change. Because highlife is tied so thoroughly to the lifestyle of people, it does not exhibit the same degree of change as Western pop music. Many of the styles of highlife one can hear today resemble highlife one would have heard in the 1960s and 1970s. Much of the development of highlife relates rather to the increasing sophistication of the Ghanaian recording industry and the increasing availability of phonographs and tape-recorders. There has been some modernisation of the music itself, and individual artists have accentuated various aspects of the idiom, but the tradition has grown slowly and organically in a way that has always reflected the situation and the attitudes of Ghanaians. The growth of authentic art cannot be forced. Highlife musicians cannot play soul or Afro-beat music with the same authority they bring to their indigenous music, though they do quite well with reggae because of the cultural connection between Jamaica and Ghana. The relationship between traditional music and modern social contexts is being continuously explored, and highlife is like traditional African music in the way that it helps to establish the relationships that bind together diverse elements into a community.

Since the 1920s one of the most important strands of highlife music has evolved into a unique and complex institution known in Ghana as a "concert-party". The concert-party is a dramatisation, set to highlife music, of the values that tie the rural and urban cultures together. In some ways it resembles a medieval morality play, and in some ways it resembles a vaudeville minstrel show. Those who are involved with the theatre will recognise in a concert-party a number of conventions and structures recalling Western theatrical forms, because like highlife music itself, concert-parties began as a Western-influenced form. English-language comedy sketches at cinemas and dance halls during the period between the wars accompanied musical performances, and gradually this form of entertainment spread to the rural countryside. The parallel development in highlife music was the guitar band, less formal than a dance orchestra but more elaborate than palm-wine music. A major breakthrough came when E.K. Nyame, one of the great highlife guitarists, began performing exclusively in Akan in the period after the Second World War. Today there are several dozen concert troupes continually on tour in Ghana, and their advertisements in the newspapers ("Kakaiku Storming Konongo Tonite", "African Brothers Shaking Koforidua") fill the Amusements section of the classifieds.

Many aspects of Ghanaian life and music are ritualised in a concert-party. Although it is often convenient to discuss conditions in Ghana in terms of a split between rural and urban lifestyles, the people one sees in the city move back and forth to their towns and villages, and even if an individual does not travel, the extended family straddles both realms. A concert-party dramatisation focuses on people and their responses to the different social values with which contemporary life confronts them. As such, the concert-party is an agent of socialisation to new social forms, but it is also an agent of affirmation for traditional values, familiarising audiences with the dangers and foolishness of yielding to the typical temptations of both rural and urban realms, from greed and snobbery to superstition and disrespect.

In a recent production by the African Brothers Band, a villain becomes rich through an evil inheritance scheme accomplished with the assistance of a local medicine man. The villain becomes jealous when a friend goes hunting and encounters dwarfs who reward him for his courtesy with a bag of gold. Despite the fact that the friend shares the gold with him, the villain decides to go to find the dwarfs and get more for himself. When he meets them, he breaks every social convention of proper greeting, but the dwarfs give him a bag anyway, telling him only not to open the bag until he returns home. He thinks that if he takes the bag home, he will have to share it, and he decides to open the bag immediately to remove most of the gold and hide it. Unfortunately, when he puts his hand into the bag, he discovers that he cannot remove it again. Shouting for help, he returns home. The medicine man cannot treat the dwarfs' magic, and in the end the villain must amputate his hand in order to free himself.

The melodramatic quality of the story-line is in sharp contrast to the wild comedy of the presentation. African humour is typically satirical, and the dramatic style of the play owes much to the traditional African love of oral art and oral artifice. Every scene proceeds through layers of dramatic exaggeration, bombastic declaration and hyperbolic oral wit, stereotyped silliness, and ironic twists. A stock character in concert-parties is the Joker, a slapstick figure whose function is total satire and whose characterisation derives from trickster figures in African folktales. The Joker may demonstrate some bumpkinisms like going to meet his future in-laws and consuming all the food himself, or he may do a funny dance that breaks aesthetic norms. We can easily recognise in the play described above a variation of the story of Br'er Rabbit and the Tar-Baby, though the folktale in its original Ghanaian form would feature Ananse the Spider. Many concert-party comedies are adaptations of traditional folktales set in modern contexts, and the trickster figure in the African Brothers play is split with adept artistic liberty into the wicked team of the foolish villain and the outlandish medicine man. Further comedy is provided by the female impersonations of the all-male drama troupe. In addition to moments of high and low comedy, concert-party plays are punctuated by highlife music and songs provided by a guitar band; at any moment, one of the characters may break into a song that relates to the current situation and reflects on the moral of the plot.

When the members of a concert-party troupe arrive in a town, typically some of them hold what they call "the campaign": their bus, painted with a billboard that displays a scene from the current play, cruises through the town with a loudspeaker to announce their arrival and the venue and time of the performance. Meanwhile, the bandleader meets with the local promoter, and troupe members not on the campaign help organise the stage and set up the lighting and sound systems. The show begins at about eight o'clock in the evening with a one-hour musical performance from the band, followed immediately by the play, which can last three hours or more. Audiences always find the affair enormously entertaining. They roar with laughter at the hilarity, sigh at the bathos, shout encouragement to victims, stand up and dance to the music. The participatory nature of an African musical event occasionally inspires a member of the audience to stand up and enter into a debate with one of the characters, advising him or warning him of his impending downfall or even threatening him if he pursues a particular course of action; if the argument becomes entertaining enough either through eloquence or absurdity, another member of the audience may get involved, not to stop the interruption of the play but to join the argument from another side.

Concert-parties are relevant to both rural and urban audiences who share a concern for applying proven traditional values to the contemporary circumstances of universal problems such as friendship, loneliness, money, or separation. Highlife songs, old and new, themselves reflect on these concerns, offering both advice and social criticism. Many songs are based on folktales and proverbs that may also provide the inspiration for a concert-party. Traditional animal stories are a popular metaphoric device. The great bandleader Akwaboah had a hit with "*Se Wo Mame Atu Wo Fo*": the song tells how baby mice were playing with kittens one day, and after they went to their homes, their mothers asked them what they had been doing. When the kittens told their mother, she said, "Ah! Don't you know we eat them? Tomorrow go out and catch them." But the next day when the kittens go to call the mice to come and play, the mice hide themselves and sing, "If your Mama has told you about us, our mother has also told us about you." "*Ebi Te Yie*", one of the many hits by the African Brothers, tells of a meeting which some animals were holding, and the smaller animals started complaining about not having good seats, to which the callous reply from the predatory animals is, "Some are well seated." In another African Brothers song, "*Seantie*" (said and not listened to), the antelope and the tortoise are on their way to a dance, and the antelope begins praising his own gracefulness and abusing the tortoise for his clumsiness, finally challenging the tortoise to dance. The tortoise maintains that his dancing is wonderful but that he is reluctant to demonstrate it, and he asks the antelope not to press the matter. The antelope refuses to listen. After further goading, the tortoise does a dance so marvellous that the drummer breaks his drum, and since an antelope skin is used to make a drumhead, the antelope has to pay the price for his heedlessness.

Of course there are songs that appeal to the spirit of urban youth, like Eddie Donkor's "*Hyia me Nonnum*" (Meet me at five o'clock), K. Frimpong's "*Hwehwe Mu Na Yi Wo Mpena*" (Look well and choose your girlfriend), and Kondu's "*Yere Cu Nsa*" (Let's booze). Many songs compare the human condition to that of a traveller. "*Onantefo*" by Yamoah's Band plaintively expresses the loneliness and suffering of the world and emphasises the temporal quality of life: "If I had known the world were like this, I would not have come. I'm just travelling through it." City Boys Band of Kumasi sing "*Nye Asem Hwe*": the time you get trouble is when you will see who your friends are. Yamoah's "*Sika Mpe Rough*" blends Akan and pidgin English to advise that money should not be treated roughly; it is like a bird, and it will fly away. The Sweet Talks sing "*Nawo To Be Husband*": when you marry, everything becomes worries about money. The Parrots Band sings "*Kae Nea Onyame Aye Ama Wo*" (Remember all the things God has done for you), and Oko's Band sings "*Daben Na Onipa Benya Ahoto*" (When will a human being become free?).

Highlife fans appreciate such songs as much for the sensitivity and wisdom of their advice as for their musical arrangements, and highlife musicians attain loyal followers through the exemplification of their song lyrics and the demonstration of good character. Nana P.S.K. Ampadu, leader of the African Brothers Band, is among Africa's greatest popular musicians. He is certainly among the most successful. For nearly twenty years, he has written hit after hit. Nana also has one of the best concert-parties in Ghana. Unlike many of the successful contemporary musicians who prefer to stay in the cities and play soul, reggae and other types of copyrighted music, Nana continues to spend most of his time on strenuous tours of the rural areas, performing concert-parties with his drama troupe. Although he has international stature as well

Nana Ampadu, leader of the
African Brothers Band

as superstar prominence in Ghana, Nana remains very much a man of the people, a traditional man. His aproach to music can be distinguished as an effort to modernise traditional Ghanaian forms while still maintaining his popular base and his rural appeal. He understands very well that his mission as an African musician entails broader obligations to support traditional values and encourage correct living.

Nana is from a very beautiful area of Ghana, at the top of the mountain near Nkawkaw. The whole area is the centre of the Kwahu group of Akans, and the Kwahus are noted for being among the shrewdest traders in Ghana. There are quite a few very rich people who live in Nana's home town. The mountain itself is a steep scarp, and on top of the mountain is the closest thing to an Alpine landscape one can find in West Africa – lovely, cool villages with large clean houses, set among rolling hills, clouds and mists. The large mansions are maintained by successful Kwahu merchants, many of whom live in major cities like Accra, Kumasi, Koforidua and Takoradi.

Nana's story is the stuff of popular myth. His origins are humble, but as he grew up and went to school, he began to develop his musical skills. In the commercially orientated Kwahu society, Nana's family was not pleased with his choice of music as a career. Nana started out as a schoolboy musician, and he is always pleased to recall some scenes from those days, when he was playing for free on street corners and trying to get recognition. He came to Accra and joined a band, in a typical story of musical dedication outweighing pragmatism. He paid his artistic dues for several years before he was able to organise the African Brothers International Dance Band. Their first album is full of classic songs, and it was one of the first 33 r.p.m. records released in Ghana. One of Nana's earliest backers was D.K. Nyarko, a Kwahu trader who handled Happy Bird Records. Nana now controls all aspects of his business with the assistance of his brother-in-law, Mohammed Malcolm Ben, who is himself a businessman, a musician, and a writer of best-selling popular fiction. Since Nana's start, the African Brothers have recorded hundreds of songs, and their hits are too many to list. African Brothers recordings are available throughout West Africa, Europe and the United States. Nana is now recognised as the leading Ghanaian musician, though no one would want to detract from the other Ghanaian highlife artistes, of whom there are several dozen of international calibre. But Nana has earned much respect in Ghana because everybody knows of his dedication to music in his struggles during his early career.

Within the highlife field, Nana is best known as a singer of stories. Other musicians are more famous for their religious or proverbial focus, and though Nana has sung a number of such songs, he is more noted for folktales. He has also cultivated his reputation as a musical leader by trying to blend highlife with different beats, such as reggae (*"Me Ne Wo Be Tena"*: You and I will stay together) and Afrohili, a mixture of highlife and soul. He has recorded soul rhythms and Afro-beat rhythms (*"Self-Reliance"*), Adowa rhythms (*"Anoma o Woko"*), and he has sung in English. Nonetheless, hits like *"Yaa Amanuah"*, *"Yaa Amponsah"*, *"Nkrabea"*, and many others are all stories.

The stories in Nana's songs usually bear witness to a moral way of living or to a theme near and dear to the hearts of ordinary Ghanaians. *"Yaa Amanuah"* is the charming story of a woman named Yaa Amanuah who has not been able to have children. She prays to God for a child. In heaven, God calls all the souls of the babies who are waiting to come to earth, and God asks them, "Who is willing to go to this woman?" One of the baby boys says, "I'll go, but I won't stay long with her. I'll come back here. The day she scolds me is the day I'm going to leave the world." When Yaa Amanuah gives birth to this boy, she is very happy, but meanwhile the boy is trying his best to annoy her. In a series of incidents, Nana Ampadu tells the story of Yaa Amanuah's patience with her child. In one incident, for example, she tells him not to go by the river, but he goes anyway in order to spite her; a snake comes to kill him, but she arrives at the last minute and kills the snake. As in all the other incidents in the song, the boy thinks that this is the time when Yaa Amanuah will become annoyed, but again she shows her patience with her child. Finally, at the end of the song, the boy gives up, and says, "All right. As she is not going to become annoyed with me, then I have to stay with her." And the boy stays with Yaa Amanuah right up to the time she is old.

Musically, the African Brothers are often at their best when playing for dances. In his recordings, Nana keeps his solos to a minimum, especially in the story-songs where there is so much to say, but when the African brothers play live, they really wind it up. When performing at a dance, they stretch out in the instrumental sections of their songs, laying down a solid groove and taking long solos. Nana is a marvellous guitarist, an authority on highlife guitar styles, and his back-up musicians are uniformly excellent. Nana in particular has always been noted for having a good organist and for pioneering the use of organ to complement the rhythm guitar. Unfortunately, Nana has been plagued throughout his career with frequent bouts of weakness in his singing voice, and he usually carries two additional singers who provide vocal back-up and occasionally take over when Nana feels he should rest his voice for a song or two. Nana is a small man, extremely handsome; the expression on his face when he plays looks simultaneously like that of a wise old man and a playful child. He has especially good rapport with his audiences, and when he plays his guitar, he watches his dancers just as a master drummer would, fulfilling all the interlocutor roles of a traditional African musician. Whenever he says something, the audience roars.

African Brothers dances are not everyday events in Accra. Because Nana is on tour so much, he generally relaxes when in Accra. It is only occasionally, usually on holidays, that African Brothers play an Accra gig. Perhaps half a dozen times a year, Nana and his band will hold a dance, sometimes at a small hotel in a residential section of Accra like Kaneshie or Asylum Down, sometimes at a major nightclub like Apollo Theatre or Tiptoe Gardens. It is always necessary to fight the crowd in order to see him. Once one is past the crush at the door, there is often no place to sit. The dance floor is shoulder to shoulder with fans dancing non-stop. A significant number of people, mostly young men, dance enthusiastically by themselves or with each other, in a mass, facing the stage, always ready to raise their arms and shout encouragement. These are the believers. It seems as if many of the believers consider the event to be a contest between their shoes and the floor, and may the stronger one win.

A bit further back from the stage, where the crowd thins enough for couples to take the floor, one can observe the range and diversity of highlife dancing styles. Highlife dancing is difficult to judge at first because there seem to be as many dancing styles as there are dancers. Most of the people one may see will not look very impressive at first glance, for highlife is a cool dance, a quiet two-step. Most of the dance is in the hips and upper body. Facial expression is important as a means of projecting the dance, and it is often at variance with the body movements. Since the dance is a two-step, the dancers get down with a side-to-side swaying movement. They occasionally take single steps like merengue dancers, usually accompanied by side-to-side shoulder movements. As is true almost everywhere in the world, the women seem to be the better dancers. Among Nana's fans especially one will see a number of young women wearing A-line dresses with puff sleeves, often dancing with a girlfriend as a partner. A young Akan dancer will be straight-backed, perhaps bent slightly forward like an Adowa dancer. If one is at a nightclub like Metropole in a predominantly Ga area of Accra, though the different tribes are all mixed together, someone who is familiar with Kpanlogo dancing may be able to pick out some local residents. When a Ga dances highlife, the body is held in a more open position, hips extended slightly forward and rolling more, occasionally rotating on one foot.

Most people, including the dancers, pay no attention to such differences in dancing styles. Most dancers are simply involved in projecting themselves into the music, and they dance coolly, perhaps singing the songs to themselves and thinking about the lyrics. They do not need a large area, and they rarely collide with other dancers. Their facial expressions are almost inward-looking, though they are always ready to look up, smile and greet each other. Older dancers who may also be experts at Adowa or Sikyi dancing are much more aware of the complementarity of couples dancing, through their experience with supportive dance dialogues, and they relate to each other's steps on the dance floor. Among the younger set, the women who are dancing as partners will be the ones most likely to be watching each other. Highlife is a dance of personal expression, a dance that varies with the feelings and personality of the individual dancer. It is an odd consequence of the social focus of African music and the relationship of African music and dance that one can generally know whether highlife is being danced well by whether the dancer seems to be a nice person. A highlife dance at a nightclub is both exciting musically and civil socially, a place where the relaxed atmosphere of fellowship and enjoyment that one can find among palm-wine drinkers or Kpanlogo dancers is re-created. A nightclub is a thoroughly urban and Western context, but when the music begins, something magical happens. Before the music begins, people will be sitting down around their tables, conversing and drinking, but when the band starts playing, people literally lean out of their seats en masse and take the floor dancing, almost as if they are getting sucked into a vortex at the centre of the floor.

Looking at the way people dance highlife, or better yet, dancing highlife oneself, is the best way to understand the musical inspiration of highlife songs. Westerners who cannot understand the language of the lyrics or who find some of the harmonies unfamiliar can get a handle on the music through dancing. There are many people who would say that dancing is the only way to learn to appreciate African music, including African-American idioms like disco and soul. When one is dancing, one gains a feeling for the essential movement of the beat, the way the rhythms combine on a fundamental level.

The nightclub context is not solely a place for highlife dancing. Ghanaian bands bring to their audiences music from around the world. Just as early Ghanaian dance orchestras played foxtrots and waltzes as well as highlife, modern dance bands play reggae music from Jamaica, soul and disco music from the United States, soukous from Zaire and Congo, and Afro-beat from Nigeria. Ghanaians enjoy dancing to the many important trends in contemporary popular music, and their openness to diverse styles ensures that their own musicians and tastes will continue to be susceptible to new ideas. Young African urbanites respond to the many African musical idioms that are contributing to the current flowering of the African musical heritage. They absorb new influences and transform them, much in the same way that they have transformed the familiar Western nightclub setting into a cosmopolitan place where a sense of national musical genius and national pluralism is expanded to lend credibility to the concept of one world united through music and human fellowship.

Among the many fine Ghanaian bands that play a diverse repertoire of music from all lands is the Sunsum Band, led by Smart Nkansah from Ghana's Western Region. Sunsum, which means "soul" in Akan, is among the top popular bands in Ghana. Smart Nkansah was formerly the leader of the Sweet Talks, another leading Ghanaian band. Smart is a very articulate and intelligent musician who has earned much respect for his efforts to use his awareness of how the music business works to help and encourage younger musicians. He, Ko Nimo and Nana Ampadu currently hold the three top offices in the Musicians Union of Ghana. Like them, Smart is a master musician who has contributed to the advancement of highlife; like them, he has a reputation for sincerity and wholesomeness of character; and like them, he has accepted the responsibilities of leadership to help Ghanaian musicians achieve greater independence from the often disadvantageous management arrangements of the past.

Sunsum is a very versatile and professional band. The bandsmen play different styles of music exceptionally well, handling reggae, soul and soukous with the same authenticity as highlife. Based not far from Accra in Ghana's main port, Tema, the Sunsum band plays frequently in Accra and also tours Ghana staging concert-parties. On stage, Sunsum has a nice look. Smart's own stage presence is very composed: he leads the band with his guitar, and he frequently sings back-up vocals for one of the band's three other vocalists. Although the two female vocalists wear matching clothes, the band members often wear a mix of contemporary fashions, and they manage to project a feeling of individual personalities functioning as a tight group.

When Sunsum is playing at a nightclub, in addition to the danced

communication between sound and movement, there is also a great deal of sensitive communication among the musicians themselves, who move into and out of musical responses to each other's playing. Sunsum's song, *"Gye Wani"* (Be Happy), is an example of a type of highlife rhythm called Kalakala. In some ways Kalakala resembles a soukous rhythm from Zaire and, as such, it is a showcase for the rhythm and lead guitar to interweave complex rhythms that are both dense and open. As if in a traditional drum ensemble, the bandsmen stretch out the beat, providing the grooves into which the melodic line falls with further rhythmic elaboration. The vocalist reminds us: brothers and sisters, a human being's destiny is to live for only a short time before death comes; we have to be good to each other, and we have to be happy. "Be happy, be happy, be happy," responds the chorus. The conga drummer watches the dancers and plays to accent the movements of a dancer he enjoys, occasionally looking back to the band with happy confidence. There is room for the drummer to drive the bass drum, ride his cymbals, and flash syncopated accents on the tomtoms and snares, leading back to the main beat. The vocalists dance their own flashes of inspiration. Each of the bandsmen is playing part of a composite rhythm, tuned in to each other yet making a separate contribution. They are much like traditional musicians, except that in the nightclub setting, the songs they perform are tightly arranged with breaks and changes, polished for a heightened display of professional musicianship at its best. When performing, Sunsum is a model African pop band and to many people in Ghana, the highlife music played by such a band provides a model of their own national situation as a complex unity built out of diverse individuals. It is no wonder that young highlife fans idolise the musicians who are able to provide in a modernised context the same social atmosphere and energy that traditional musicians do in indigenous events.

The young people who are coming up in the Ghanaian musical field stay close to this inspiration through all the struggles any artiste in the world faces. To them, a musician's talent is a gift that revolves on love to become an opportunity for generosity, a chance to give people what they need to live in the world. As Nana Ampadu says, "Music is the food of the soul. You feed your body. You also have to feed your soul." The sons and daughters of Africa who were taken to the West fed their souls by preserving their musical sensibilities through the period of their slavery, and in their liberation they are now feeding the souls of people around the world. In the new nations of Africa, musical vitality is continuing to draw upon traditional roots, and the new music of Africa is beginning to have its impact in Europe and America. Among African villagers, musical participation is still high, and in the cities there is no lack of recruits for new groups. Many aspiring musicians in Ghana learn to play a guitar with people like Ko Nimo or Nana Ampadu or Smart Nkansah as their heroes; young drummers and percussionists continue to cut their teeth in traditional musical contexts.

Young musicians who want to play highlife in the nightclubs, however, face the problem of how to obtain instruments and sound equipment in order

Far left: Smart Nkansah, leader of the Sunsum Band, and Hannah Coffie, one of the vocalists in the band

to get started. Despite the musical and spiritual encouragement the young
musicians continue to receive, they must face the hard reality that, typically,
only a businessman has the resources for the kind of capital investment
required to launch a band. Aspiring highlife musicians often must develop
their skills and consolidate their group before searching for the financial
backing necessary for public performances or recording efforts.

With a smaller investment, young musicians are able to make demonstration tapes which they can use to promote themselves. A facility which
serves this need is the Bokoor Recording Studio operated by John Collins.
John is an Englishman who has spent most of his life in Ghana. He is an
outstanding musicologist, perhaps the leading authority on the history and
development of highlife and other forms of contemporary West African
music. He also has a rightful part in the modern highlife scene himself, for he
has played guitar and harmonica in a number of bands, and he has toured
with a famous concert-party troupe called the Jaguar Jokers. At John's
modest studio, young musicians who cannot afford to hire the expensive and
sophisticated equipment and personnel of Ghana's recording industry can
produce stereo tapes of their songs, and John, relying on his musical
sensitivity and engineering skills, is able to use his four-track mixer to create
master tapes of such quality that many are pressed directly into records.

The bandsmen sit in an open-air shelter facing the peaceful fields of the
farm worked by John and his father, a retired philosophy professor at the
University of Ghana. John runs the wires through a window to his recording
booth. The atmosphere at a recording session establishes in many ways the
links among the various highlife contexts that permeate Ghanaian culture,

Sloopy and Adinkra Band at John Collins' studio

past and present, rural and urban, recreational and professional; one can sense elements of the rustic and slightly formal palm-wine scene, the moralistic and idealistic concert-party, the action-packed nightclub. Musically, the guitars and a jazz drum kit are the essential components of modern highlife, and the musicians replace the rhythm section of a nightclub band with small Ewe or Akan hand drums and percussion instruments, tapping Kpanlogo and other typical rhythms with their fingers to fit the mood of the music. The recording session looks almost like a village get-together. Though the musicians are more professionally orientated than the amateur musicians who enjoy themselves playing and singing palm-wine or Kpanlogo music, there is little noticeable difference in the level of musical skills, a testimony to the overall quality of amateur musicianship in Ghana.

These young musicians are the same type of people one sees at the dances. They have found meaning in the music they play, and they are trying to respond to their need to express themselves as well as answer the country's need for music. They are shy and soft-spoken, but they are able to speak sincerely and directly of their belief in one world of humanity. They will look with appreciation at a stranger who has had the interest to make the long journey to Ghana from a country in Europe or America. With big smiles, both hands raised forward in a Rasta salute, they will greet a representative of the people of the world. They will look around themselves at the musical instruments, the microphones, the wooden stools they sit on, the open fields and the sky, and they will say that this music is what they themselves are trying to do in order to express their love for people and to contribute to understanding in the world. They are the young musicians of Ghana. Inside them is the past, the present, and the future.

BIBLIOGRAPHY

BANE, K.A. "Comic Play in Ghana", *African Arts* 1, no.4 (summer 1968): pp.30–4, 101.

CHERNOFF, John Miller. *African Rhythm and African Sensibility: Aesthetics and Social Action in African Musical Idioms*. Chicago: University of Chicago Press, 1979.

—— "The Artistic Challenge of African Music: Thoughts on the Absence of Drum Orchestras in Black American Music". *Black Music Research Journal* (1985): in press.

COLLINS, E.J. "Comic Opera in Ghana", *African Arts* 9, no.2 (January 1976): pp.50–7.

—— "Ghanaian Highlife", *African Arts* 10, no.1 (October 1976): pp.62–8, 100.

—— "Post-War Popular Band Music in West Africa", *African Arts* 10, no.3 (April 1977): pp.53–60.

DARNTON, John. "Nigeria's Dissident Superstar", *New York Times Magazine*, 24 July 1977: pp.10–12, 22–4, 26, 28.

JAHN, Janheints. *Muntu: An Outline of the New African Culture*, translated by Marjorie Grene. New York: Grove Press, 1968.

NKETIA, J.H. Kwabena. "Traditional Music of the Ga People", *African Music* 2, no.1 (1958): pp.21–7.

RANGER, T.O. *Dance and Society in Eastern Africa: The Beni "Nooma"*. London: Heinemann Educational Books, 1975.

THOMPSON, Robert Faris. "An Aesthetic of the Cool: West African Dance", *African Forum* 2, (autumn 1966): pp.85–102.

WATERMAN, Richard Alan. "African Influence on the Music of the America", in *Acculturation in the Americas*, edited by Sol Tax. Chicago: University of Chicago Press, 1952.

RECORDINGS
GHANA
African Brothers, *Agatha*, LP 7079.
African Brothers, *Ma Poma*, STERN 1004.
Sunsum Band, *Emmaa Bekum Mmarima*, OBL 504.
———, *Susum Odo*, ASA 101.
Sweet Talks, Mewo Road, TKCLP 015.
Various artistes, *The Guitar And The Gun*, 2 vols, (produced by John Collins), A DRY 1.

CAMEROONS
Manu Dibango, *Ah Freak Sans Fric*, 362018.
———, *Deliverance*, AF 1984.

NIGERIA
Ebenezer Obey, *Ambition*, DWAPS 568.
———, *Je Ka Jo*, V2283.
———, *Solution*, STERN 1005.
Fela Kuti, *Expensive Shit*, EM 2315.
———, *Perambulator*, LIR 6.
Prince Nico Mbarga, *Sweet Mother*, RAS 6.
Segun Adewale, *Adewale Play For Me*, STERN 1003.
———, *Endurance*, SARPS 3.
Sunny Ade, *Aura*, ILPS 9746.
———, *Check "E"*, SALPS 26.
———, *Synchro System*, ILPS 9737.

SENEGAMBIA
Youssou N'Dour and Super Etoile, *Immigres*, 6709.

ZAIRE
Franco and Josky, *Choc Choc Choc* (double album), CHOC 003.
Franco and Sam Mangwana, *Co-operation*, POP 017.
Tabu Ley and Mbilia Bel, *Loyenghe*, GEN 107/108.

COMPILATIONS
Sound D'Afrique, vol. 1, ISSP 4003.
———, vol. 2, ISSP 4008.

Afterword

BY DENNIS MARKS

It is three years since Geoff Haydon and I laid out the first tentative plans for a series of films about African-American music. It was provisionally titled *Africa Come Back*: a celebration of the roots of twentieth-century popular music. We steered clear of the word history with its temptations to generalise. We were already nervous about the scale of the subject matter, which could barely be contained in seventy films, let alone seven. The change from the working title to *Repercussions* reflects some of our reservations. *Africa Come Back* was borrowed, perhaps a bit rashly, from one of the African liberation movements. At the time it seemed to mirror one aspect of the subject – the increased assurance with which Afro-Americans were reclaiming and celebrating their African heritage. Now even the term Afro-American must be treated with care. As John Chernoff and Ken Bilby make clear in their chapters on highlife and Caribbean music, we should think of this music as indigenous. However it travelled from the slave ports of the Guinea coast, it has now become a resonant culture in its own right. The rhythm and blues giants who live in the manicured glades of Los Angeles, described by Ian Whitcomb, are above all *Americans*. When Geoff Haydon filmed *Legends of Rhythm and Blues*, he took the working title *Africa Come Back* off the clapper board. If there are links – call-and-response singing, instrumental figuration – with an African heritage, then they are distant and much modified. Repercussions is probably a better word for them.

Nevertheless, no one would undertake such a series without feeling that something, however fragile, bound these seven very different types of music together. There is a hint of what that something might be in the transformations that occurred on that very journey from West Africa to the American plantations. For one of the virtues of the music that developed among the slaves and subjects of the old empire is its propensity for change, its constant power of renewal. In his chapter on Max Roach and the history of bebop, Charles Fox pinpoints one reason for the marvellous ability of the African-American legacy to absorb and modify outside influences. He describes jazz as "very much a matter of listening to what other people do". All these various kinds of music are part of an oral culture, and their history is very much bound up with the same processes as spoken language. In another context (B.B.C. *Arena* 1984), the Nigerian musician, Fela Anikulapo Kuti, talks of Africans as "very virile language makers". Even before the coming of the European-enforced empires, the migration of North Africans to the western savanna, the spread of the ancient kingdoms of Manding, Asante and Dogon encouraged a healthy cross-fertilisation of language. In Africa, language and music are never far apart and this response to change is coded into musical practice. The Jamaican folklorist Louise Bennett gives a good example of this give and take between language and music in the influence on song of Jamaican patois, the language that is spoken when European speech is subject to African grammar and intonation and refreshed by African vocabulary.

Fela Anikulapo Kuti

However, it is wrong to think of this as a one-way process, Europe modifying Africa. There is an old theory that the "blue note" common to most of the music that derived from the blues (the flattened third and sixth) is a result of Africans schooled in a five- or six-tone scale trying to sing diatonic European melodies. Go to Ghana, or Gambia or Senegal or northern Nigeria and you will hear instrumentalists producing the same blue notes they have sung or played for centuries. The whole process is more mysterious than we might imagine. A great deal of the music which Western scholars assumed was produced by Africans in imitation of the West turns out to be rooted in ancient practices. The guitar of palm-wine music is a replacement for the much older, banjo-like seprewa, and its open tuning is very reminiscent of the older instrument. You can still hear the seprewa in modern palm-wine groups, even though guitars are readily available all over Ghana. This co-existence of old and young music is (as Sidia Jatta affirms) a feature of the kooraa music of the Gambia, just as it is a constant phenomenon in Nigeria and Ghana. The Simpa dance mentioned by John Chernoff in his chapter on "The Drums of Dagbon", is a relatively recent import from Togo, and it is very much a part of an indigenous "youth culture". The charming fact is that these youthful innovations are accepted and incorporated into a traditional social structure. As Alhaji Ibrahim says, "music comes to us because of the young people".

This diversity is as characteristic as the buried echoes and similarities. Early in the planning stages of *Repercussions* we discussed how to treat the great river that is the blues. In settling for the tributary that led to California, Geoff Haydon and Ian Whitcomb were not only celebrating an important and neglected strand in blues history. They were also drawing attention to the rich diversity of blues playing and singing. The basic bar structures, harmonic patterns and vocal gestures of blues have been transformed in a dozen different ways according to their context. Ian Whitcomb describes how the blues became tougher and faster as it made the journey from the rural South to the urban North-East, and the differences between the moody lyricism of Delta blues, the driving aggression of Chicago blues and the whooping celebration of West Coast R&B bear witness to just how resilient that tradition can be. Charles Fox also notes how the migration northwards after the First World War in the United States led to a greater individualism and sophistication in jazz. Although much of this music originated in ghettos, none of it became a ghetto in its own right, and just as the barrel-house and boogie piano styles influenced jazz in the 1930s, so the rock 'n' roll of the fifties, itself an offshoot of black R&B, had a crucial effect on the development of jazz in the 1960s.

Away from the specific disciplines of film-making it becomes very easy and very dangerous to speculate. However, one of the rewards of the series was the pleasure of watching unfamiliar music – the music of contemporary West Africa – coming to terms with its own new-found popularity, and wondering whether it would follow Afro-American music – blues, jazz, soul, R&B – into the vernacular of the rest of the world. Western musicians, black

and white, have always been fascinated by the popular music coming out of Africa. Max Roach, in the 1950s, worked with the great Ghanaian drummer Guy Warren (Ghanaba) who started his musical career as a drummer in a highlife band playing both African and American commercial dance music. Ornette Coleman travelled to Morocco to hear and join the pipes of joujouka. In the early 1960s, for a brief period, the South African kwela was popular in Britain. At the beginning of the seventies, Ghanaian highlife musicians found a brief footing in the British popular music world, most noticeably the Ghanaian/Caribbean band Osibisa. In France, the influences were more forcefully felt, possibly because Paris is a more genuinely multi-cultural city than London, with a tradition of playing host to the African diaspora. Interestingly, this stretches beyond the French-speaking countries such as Côte d'Ivoire, Guinea and Cameroun; Nigerian musicians like Sunny Ade and Fela Kuti have rooted the commercial side of their activities in Paris. Two of Africa's most exhilarating musicians – the Camerounian Manu Dibango and the Zairian Franco, prime exponent of the sweetest of all dance music, soukous – are Paris-based. However, it is only in the last three or four years that the music industry seems to have built up the courage to develop African popular music for a wider commercial public.

In popular music it is always difficult to know whether supply creates or follows demand. Notoriety has something to do with it. The music of black America has always generated a certain *frisson* among white audiences, which fuelled its early popularity. Because of its association with juke joints and speakeasies, jazz acquired a reputation for danger bordering on criminality, which undoubtedly accelerated its entry into the commercial

Miles Davis

mainstream. Particular areas like the south side of Chicago, Watts and Harlem, were cultivated and developed by commercial producers anxious to find new trends in popular dance music. A similar process occurred in Lagos fifteen years ago, when that wild psychotic city became a proving ground for the recording giants to experiment in the African market, and Decca, Polygram and E.M.I. all set up studios there. But despite the success of certain individuals, notably the inventor of Afro-beat, Fela Kuti, whose celebrity as a self-styled "black president" and husband to twenty-seven wives has often eclipsed his remarkable creative talent as a musician, the arrival of African popular music in the broad market has been regularly delayed. If a change is happening now (I write in the summer of 1984) then the key may lie in the phrase used above, "popular dance music".

In his chapter on Dagbamba music, John Chernoff describes how in African societies, "music fulfils functions which other societies delegate to different types of institutions". The central thrust of this is the dance. Elsewhere, in his book *African Rhythm and African Sensibility*, Chernoff relates how he asked an African musician whether he knew a certain piece of music, to which he replied, "I know the dance that goes with it." The dance implies and extends the structure of the beat, and in many forms of African and Afro-American music, the one is incomplete without the other. Even the most cerebral of American musical inventions, bebop jazz, incorporated dance in its early stages. The doyen of tap-dancers, Honi Coles, remembers being employed as a dancer by the pioneer bebop sax player Sonny Stit. However, as the individual creative artist explores his own expressive potential, the music becomes detached from its social function. It is difficult to imagine anyone dancing to Cecil Taylor or Anthony Braxton – the music demands that the audience "sit down and listen".

Nevertheless, the need for a music which draws the audience in as participants remains, nowhere more so than among the white Western societies in which the bulk of today's popular music is marketed. There is always a hole waiting to be filled by a new dance music, and it is this need that is currently being served by the joyous polyrhythms of West and Central Africa. Sidia Jatta draws attention to the canard that all Africans are dancers. It is an understandable reaction on the part of an African academic, wearied by Westerners who hear African music as harmonically and melodically naive. However, once we admit the magical poise and grace of such music as the Mandinka kooraa, perhaps we can be allowed to return in a chastened spirit to the kaleidoscopic colour of African dance. Mike Fox, the cameraman who filmed programmes five and seven of *Repercussions*, remarked in northern Ghana, with a mixture of awe and delight, that he had never been anywhere where the people seemed so strongly, at any moment of the day, to be one step away from dancing. This may be a naive comment – in Britain, we bracket dancing off into neat little social pockets like parties and clubs – but it is no less true for all that. It pays tribute to the completeness of the musical act, where a chieftaincy dance in Dagbon derives from a rhythm describing the achievements of a distant ancestor, or where the people of a village, in

dancing to that rhythm, reinforce collectively the values of their society. The urban music of West and Central Africa shares the same characteristics. When dancers take to the floor in a nightclub, they seem to be sucked in by the music. When a singer or a musician executes a verse with particular grace or skill, the spectators will spin up to the platform, press money on the forehead of the performer, and may often embrace or dance with the musicians. A few weeks ago I was filming Fela Kuti at the Glastonbury Festival. As the evening drew on, some enthusiastic kids in the audience leapt up on to the stage and began to gyrate with Fela's gaudily painted dancers. Two sixteen-stone bouncers immediately rushed on from the wings and tossed them unceremoniously back into the crowd. We do things differently in England, and we may be the losers.

At any rate, the men with the money seem to have recognised a need, and are currently using the heavy apparatus of promotion to nurture it. In London in the summer of 1984 you could hear the king of Nigerian juju music Sunny Ade and the crown prince Segun Adewale, the creator of Afro-beat Fela Kuti, the master of soukous Franco, the two supreme South African jazz musicians High Masekela and Abdullah Ibrahim, as well as younger exponents like the Ghanaian highlife band Sunsum, and traditional virtuosi like the palm-wine guitarist Koo Nimo. Professional musicians have been greatly stimulated by the increased availability of African popular music. The British rock composer Peter Gabriel has helped, through the WOMAD festival, to promote artistes like Prince Nico and Kanda Bongo Man; Mick Fleetwood and Brian Eno both made recording trips to Ghana; Stevie Wonder is currently to be heard jamming harmonica on Sunny Ade's latest album; and

Takai dance leader, Alhaji Amidu Jia, Tamale

the prolific New York rock experimentalist David Burn of Talking Heads is continually drawing on the textures of African percussion. It is easy to be cynical about the current love affair with African popular music, ascribing the whole business to the appeal of the exotic, but no more enthralling or absorbing dance music has penetrated Europe and America in the last thirty years. There is also an unselfconscious delight in instrumental virtuosity. Every one of the musicians catalogued above is a superb instrumentalist, and the format of African dances and shows, often lasting six hours or more, gives ample opportunity for soloists to stretch out their instrumental breaks to ecstatic length. Where else can one encounter the combination of several hours of energetic dancing and wave after wave of joyful guitar tone that make up a performance by Nana Ampadu and the African Brothers?

Besides, there is no need to apologise for novelty or exoticism. The development of jazz in the thirties was powerfully modified by the spicy influences of the Latin Caribbean. The incorporation of novel colours and rhythms is another facet of that continual sensitivity to change that is part of the African-American legacy. Thus, the soukous of Zaire is a blend of traditional Ba-Kongo rhythms and the rhythms and melodies of Afro-Cuba. Of course, these same Latin rhythms had their origins in African beats – the rumba and the merengue have affinities with Congolese dances – so it is scarcely surprising that as Africa developed its own contemporary popular dance forms, it drew upon those rhythms that were most familiar. In the same fashion, contemporary Ghanaian highlife bands experiment with reggae, which itself leans heavily on the Asante cult music of Jamaica, while the juju and fuji music of Nigeria has incorporated beats from soul and funk which are themselves reminiscent of Yoruba rhythms. The process is not one of imitation – it is a continuous cycle, in which the patterns and values of African society, as expressed in music and dance, are ever present.

So, in a very crude sense, one can draw a thread from the social music of West and Central Africa to the syncretic music of the Caribbean to the popular dance music of contemporary West Africa. Whether this is a useful exercise is a vexed question. In the past, it was both fashionable and necessary to assert the African-ness of the African-American legacy. It was bound up with the cultural pride that underpinned the independence movements in Africa and the civil rights movement in the States. Kwame Nkrumah's conception of "African personality" had a vital effect on the Black Power movement in America, while Malcolm X and Eldridge Cleaver made an equally strong impact on independent Africa. In the last twenty years there has been another twist to the cycle with the arrival in the United Kingdom of Rastafarianism from Jamaica. A whole new generation of British-born Afro-Caribbeans have forged their own version of "African personality". This process is probably far more important now for the embattled West Indians of Britain's inner cities than it is for the people of Bessemer, Alabama. Above all, music, with its ability to cross boundaries of race, age, class and economic status, will remain the principal avenue through which the African-American legacy infuses the culture of the rest of the world.

In all the changes of title and strategy that occurred during the production of *Repercussions*, one word remained unmodified to the end – the word celebration. If it is dangerous to generalise, it is also sad if the responsibilities of serving the music become so heavy that they distract from its main purpose – the affirmation of joy and brotherhood. When we were filming in Dagbon, the climax of our short stay was the staging of the last two days of the Damba festival. On the penultimate day, all the princes and sub-chiefs dance their own specific dances. The chief himself has no particular dance – he dances Damba. As Alhaji Ibrahim remarked, "Only if he is happy, he will get up to dance; that day we visited Nanton, did you not see how the chief danced . . . he was happy."

The Nanton chief is a serene old man of about ninety, and he danced with an incandescent concentration that hypnotised every member of the film crew. Then, when the filming had finished, the chief sent us the message that, as the Dagamba had danced for us, so we should dance for them. Well, when a chief commands you to dance, you dance, and Mike Fox and I, clumsily and with much amusement on the part of the onlookers, took to the dance floor. When you have taken a film crew, thirty boxes of equipment, several miles of film stock and 300 gallons of petrol to the remote savanna of Ghana, it helps to remember why you went. The Nanton chief reminded us, as did Ko Nimo, Nana Ampadu, Smart Nkansah, the Alhaji, the Maroons of Moore Town, Mamma Zeela, Theophilus Chiverton of San Pedro de Macoris, the Congos of the Holy Spirit, Segun Adewale and all the hundred other wonderful musicians we encountered on our travels. The repercussions remain with us and they will ring in our ears for many years to come.

The Authors

Kenneth Bilby

Kenneth Bilby has a background in anthropology and music performance. He knows Caribbean music from the inside having lived with African communities in Jamaica and Guyana for several years. He has written on the subject of Caribbean music for several journals, but his most widely distributed work has been in recording and annotating Caribbean folk music for the American Folkways record series. All the indigenous Jamaican music in their catalogue has been recorded by Kenneth Bilby and he has also provided liner notes and inserts for the records.

John Miller Chernoff

John Miller Chernoff is an anthropologist and drummer who lives in Pittsburgh. He has studied African drum music for ten years and written a book, *African Rhythm and African Sensibility*, which many people believe to be the best book on the subject ever published – certainly the best book by a non-African. Published by Chicago University Press, it won ecstatic praise when it was published both in the U.K. and the U.S.A.

Charles Fox

Charles Fox is an author and regular broadcaster. He is jazz critic for the *New Statesman* and edits the jazz section of *The Gramophone*. His books include: *Jazz in Perspective* (B.B.C. Publications); *Fats Waller* (Cassells); *The Jazz Scene* (Hamlyn). Geoff Haydon's 1970 B.B.C. T.V. film *The Three Faces of Jazz* grew out of a series of radio broadcasts that Charles Fox had given.

Sidia Jatta

Sidia Jatta has a degree in linguistics and was an Honorary Fellow of the International African Institute in London from 1980 to 1982. He is head of the National Languages department of the Curriculum Development Centre in Banjul, the Gambia. He is preparing a PhD thesis for presentation to the University of Grenoble, France. He speaks fluent French, English, Mandinka, Fula and Wolof, His eminent family is traditionally regarded as a source of patronage by Mandinka musicians.

Doug Seroff

Doug Seroff is a writer, record producer, discographer and field researcher. He pioneered the revival of interest in traditional gospel quartet singing. He was project director for the Jefferson County quartet reunion programme in Birmingham, Alabama, in 1980. This programme was funded by the National Endowment for the Arts. He researched and produced the two-volume L.P. set *Birmingham Anthology* which was nominated for a Grammy Award as best historical album of 1981. He was consultant to the "Programme in Black American Culture" at the Smithsonian Institute in Washington D.C. in February 1982, for which he selected the musical participants, and wrote the published booklet. Articles by him have appeared in numerous specialist and academic journals.

Ian Whitcomb

Ian Whitcomb is an author, musician and record producer. His books include: *After the Ball*, a history of pop from 1892 to 1965 (Allen Lane); *Tin Pan Alley*, a pictorial history (Wildwood House); *Whole Lotta Shakin'*, a rock 'n' roll scrapbook (Hutchinson); *Rock Odyssey*, a chronicle of the sixties (Hutchinson). He was consultant to Geoff Haydon for the 1975 B.B.C. T.V. series *The Friendly Invasion*.